COMMON SENSE AND EXPERT NONSENSE

EVEN THOUGH I DID NOT KNOW WES
FOR THAT LONG WE BECAME VERY
GOOD FRIENDS AND WOULD FREQUENTLY
MEET IN THE BRIDGE PATISSERIE
IN BRIDGE ST WINCHESTER. WE
WOULD ALSO SOMETIMES GO OUT FOR
THE DAY WITH HIS WIFE JANET WHO
KINDLY GAVE ME THIS BOOK.
WE HAD MANY A GOOD LAUGH
TOGETHER AND LIKE TO THINK THAT
WE SHARED MANY THOUGHTS.

GW00371052

Disclaimer

The views expressed in this publication are those of the author Wes White and do not reflect the views of The Memoir Club or his next of kin.

COMMON SENSE AND EXPERT NONSENSE

Some Are Wise, Some Are Otherwise

by

WES WHITE

The Memoir Club

First published in 2010 by
The Memoir Club
Arya House
Langley Park
Durham
DH7 9XE
Tel: 0191 373 5660
Email: memoirclub@msn.com

British Library Cataloguing in
Publication Data.
A catalogue record for this book
is available from the
British Library

ISBN: 978-1-84104-502-3

Typeset by TW Typesetting, Plymouth, Devon
Printed by Papercraft, 5 Phoenix Road, Crowther Industrial Estate,
Washington, Tyne & Wear NE38 0AD

Contents

List of Illustrations

Foreword

Wes was . . .

quite simply, everything to me. He died of cancer in a local Hospice on Friday, 12 February 2010. I was with him for his last 24 hours and, for that, I shall always be grateful.

Wesley White was born in Skegby, Mansfield on 6 November 1934. His upbringing was to a strict moral code yet full of fun and laughter at the same time. Educated at Queen Elizabeth's Grammar School in Mansfield, Wes went on to Carnegie College in Leeds where his first degree equipped him to be a PE teacher. His teaching skills were universally acknowledged to be exemplary and he could (and did) handle the most difficult of pupils/classes. After teaching in schools he returned to Carnegie as one of the staff. The fact that he remained firm friends with many of his students to his dying day is testimony to his popularity and ability to forge lasting relationships. He then went to America and completed 3 further degrees, including a PhD in Behavioural Science. He returned to the UK and worked in further and higher education, returning to the US on several occasions as invited visiting professor.

We started 'walking out together' as he quaintly put it in 1976 when I was 23. I had, however, known him since I was 14 as he and my mother were colleagues. I thought he was a gorgeous chap even then! He took an early retirement from education in 1984 and we moved to Winchester. He helped me grow in confidence and always supported me in my career even to the point of suggesting we move south as promotion prospects were better (how right he was!). He always said I was his soul mate. We got on incredibly well, complementing each other in so many ways.

Wes was an extremely clever man. He was highly principled and loyal but, more than anything, people remember him for his wit and humour which he used to get his point across or diffuse tricky situations. He could (and did!) tell jokes for hours at a time, such was his phenomenal memory. A keen sportsman, he played football well into his 60s then took up tennis which he played daily, walking or cycling to his beloved tennis club situated on the Winchester water meadows. He played until the autumn of

2009 when the chemotherapy/radiotherapy treatments started to take their toll. His last four months essentially were spent in bed yet, although I felt it unfair that a man so fit and full of life should be reduced to such a state, he never complained and never stopped making light of the situation.

He had been writing this book for many years, expressing, in layman's terms, his dissatisfaction with the modern tendency to overlook common sense and what he often referred to as 'common wisdoms'. He continued to make changes to it until November 2009. Over the years he had sent chapters off to publishers who invariably told him whilst it looked interesting, he needed to get an agent – something he steadfastly refused to do saying it went against his principles. I decided that it deserved to be published, so, I hope you enjoy it.

Preface

Governments work in political asylums

Statement by eight year old girl – 2004

Welcome, fellow law-breakers. I know you are because no one could possibly read the prolific number of official laws, rules, regulations, forms, pamphlets and their like let alone obey them. It could not be long before grandmothers require food-gifting, hygiene, catering and business licences to make you a slice of toast. Meeting official demands is becoming a full-time occupation (full-time harassment or imposition – actually). Excess is the modern epidemic in the 'developed' (material) world where the legal rights of one can mean many other people are morally wronged. Expert theories, laws and practices are having such harmful effects on almost everyone. Modern human psyche is increasingly stressed by regular expert pronouncements on what we should think, say and do in our lives. The very structure, purpose and meaning of our institutions and value systems are frequently changed (often on the pet theories of opportunists) and rationalised as progress or modernisation. This essay demonstrates that the vast majority of common, ordinary people have far more sense or wisdom than experts' interference allows us to believe. Evidence is also given to illustrate various myths created by experts who are often not competent or worthy of the power they use and abuse. When leaders misrepresent their followers together with expanding and legalising undemocratic powers, problems in everyday life multiply.

Dealing with questions that have concerned all people the most, throughout history, seems a fruitful method of approach:

What is the meaning or purpose of life?

What do we want or value the most?

How can we get more control and quality in our lives?

How can we make wise decisions or choices?

I have put such questions to various people. In answer to what they want in life a response of our youth-oriented society is, 'I just want to have a good time and party.' To achieve a regular state of euphoria, a consuming ambition is to be famous and rich. We are a culture obsessed with celebrity status which is no cause for celebration. Modern celebrity has become the systematic abuse of power and publicity specifically designed for that purpose. If philosopher Bertrand Russell were alive today, he would turn in his grave. Celebrities are prolific consumers of material resources whilst moralising about the poor. Such values raise other questions:

Does the notion of pleasure have meaning or existence
without its opposite – displeasure or pain?

Can some be rich without others being poor?

We cannot look to leaders such as politicians for inspiration or wisdom. A widely held view is given by Theo Hopkins, 'These days you really can't believe anything any politician tells you – except for Saddam Hussein on Weapons of Mass Destruction.' Much the same applies to lawyers. They are to integrity, truth and justice what Mick Jagger is to fidelity or Pavarotti to trapeze artistry. Church leaders have not exactly covered themselves in wisdom or glory, nor have leaders and experts in other institutions. Scientists proudly proclaim that science is not about what people value most, namely – justice, love and what is right or wrong or good and bad.

Political law-makers and their various expert associates like lawyers, policy advisers and other officials are making people feel isolated, threatened, violated and betrayed. Far too many individual and social problems can be traced back to government 'initiatives', laws, rules, regulations and other bureaucratic demands. So regular and prolific in number is the politicians' output of laws, it is the nearest thing we have to a perpetual motion machine or eternal life here on earth. Taken to a logical conclusion, government administration could swallow up the entire workforce. Constant law-making is unwise; it creates criminals, unworkable legislation and blizzards of unfathomable paperwork. Even Einstein said that income tax was the hardest thing in the world to understand when it was, well, relativity simple.

Wisdom throughout the history of all cultures has always been associated with the pinnacle of good judgement. During the twentieth century traditional wisdom has been 'modernised' almost out of existence with increasing haste. When the issue of wisdom is considered, people ask:

What is wisdom?

Do all people possess some degree of wisdom?

Do animals and plants have wisdom?

How is ancient wisdom the same as, or different from, modern wisdom?

Is wisdom the same as common wisdom or common sense?

Does common wisdom or common sensing imply a collective conscious and unconscious?

If there is a shared conscious and unconscious, do telepathy and other paranormal activities exist more than scientists suggest?

Does wisdom or common sense have laws?

If wisdom has laws do they include moral, legal and scientific laws?

To what extent are any laws of wisdom or common sense reliable, objective and valid or useful?

Experts tell us to modernise: how do you modernise values like truth?

Why has the use of common sense become so uncommon?

This manuscript was started in 1997. I worked at it intermittently and finished the first draft, other than the concluding chapter, by the end of 2000. It is a diary story of folly and wisdom. For several years the script, according to my wife, clogged up precious space and she said, 'So publish it or perish it.' She sometimes quotes common wisdoms to me about it. One is:

'Actions speak louder than words.'

My essay analyses the values we live by along with their consequences and relations to nature at large and humankind in particular. Scores of wisdoms are cited most of which readers will know in one form or another. There are wisdoms on almost every page. One of my aims is to show these wisdoms apply to all aspects of life and can be used to the betterment of individuals, groups, culture and society. Some people believe that wisdom is serious and dull and the opposite of humour or fun. There are numerous wisdoms to refute this notion. One is, 'Many a true word is spoken in jest.' Examples of this wisdom are almost infinite. Here are two to illustrate. The first is, 'If Monica Lewinsky had kept her mouth shut, Bill Clinton's critics would not have had such a down on him.' A second is, 'Politicians do not solve problems, they subsidise them.' Sam Levenson advises on being wise:

> It's so simple to be wise. Just think of something stupid to say and say the opposite.

My criticism of experts must not be unrealistic. Expert theories and explanations can be comforting in the presence of deterioration of our democratic, social, psychological and physical systems. We already have expert explanations for some modern behaviours. The selfish gene and the hyperactivity attention deficiency syndrome are recent expert findings. Can we expect further announcement about the existence of a compensation gene, a celebrity gene, and an anti-social behaviour gene? Possibilities are endless to modern professional experts, but any politically incorrect gene seems resistant to engineering, including surgery. Sometimes the politically correct and the politically incorrect achieve the same outcome but for different reasons. For example, the politically correct can ban talk of Christianity in case it upsets other religions. The politically incorrect can say, 'Forget Christianity and the heavenly father, we do not know who the earthly fathers are.' New gods are on the block and new blocks are on old gods:

> How are wisdom and common sense related to science, religion, truth, beauty and celebrity?

Woody Allen, a celebrity, combines truth and religion with the beauty of humour when he recounts, 'My parents sent me to an inter-faith camp where I was beaten up by boys and girls of all different races and religions.' Science is a modern god which I foolishly worshipped. I am a behavioural scientist and a main target for my criticism is science. I have erred. Perhaps you have heard too, or more likely experienced that science's power is excessive, corrupt and bossy rather like the gangster Al Capone who said, 'If I want your opinion, I will give it to you.' Behavioural science is often associated with psychology and social psychology though many subjects contain various elements of behavioural science. Political sciences, law, criminology, economics, sociology, management, education, medical science and so on and so forth are all examples of subjects that focus numerous aspects of human behaviour. Even physicists, who try to exclude human behavioural contamination from their experiments, cannot avoid the influence of human behaviour. When physicists speak of behaviour it usually refers to the behaviour of things like sub-atomic particles of matter and not human behaviour. Behavioural science does not deal with wisdom because value-judgements are an integral part of wisdom. Put in the modern vernacular, 'scientists, including behavioural scientists, do not do value-judgements'. We shall see, however, science is not all it is cracked up to be. Wisdom, according to some, is the ultimate quality that transcends time and place. Others believe wisdom, like everything else, has to move with the times and, hence, we should have modern wisdoms for modern times. Heraclitus observed:

> No man ever steps in the same river twice, for it's not the same river and he's not the same man.

Today, a dirty unmade bed can be exhibited as art and foul-mouthed, drunken, street-brawling violence by both sexes is becoming a norm. One aim of the modern entertainment industry, to quote some of its gurus, is 'to push back the barriers of violence and bad taste'. Urinating in the street has been taken by the politically correct and used to elevate a common saying to a modern street-wisdom, 'When you've gotta go, you've gotta go.' We know this statement is true, just as we know the statement that some people commit homicide is true, and one characteristic of wisdom is – truth. Will a street-cred, post-modern wisdom become, 'When you gotta kill, you gotta kill?' It is a sentiment increasingly heard and actioned – sometimes for 'a bit of a laugh – a giggle'. Politicians strive for inclusivity and they are producing it in one area, for sure. Violence, involving murder, is becoming more inclusive, an equal-opportunity activity being taken up by more people anywhere and, for some, a modern leisure pursuit or sport:

What are some other modern, post-modern and future wisdoms?

By the very nature of this essay, it has to speak to anyone through common meanings and shared sensings. Hence, I have used non-specialist, non-expert, common everyday language. One characteristic of experts is their specialised language. Chemists, physicists, psychologists and other subjects all have their special words and language. Expert words are only in addition to common everyday language that experts need to do all the many ordinary things in the world such as shopping or socialising. Politicians and other experts give a whole new sense or nuisance of meaning to words like truth, democracy, justice, morality, tax, marriage and playing conkers such that we need a more rapid update of dictionaries. Expert words can be absurd. What you don't understand is often written by 'experts'. People specialising in four-letter words could be classified as experts, in a field sworn to expand. If this field of four letter word usage grows large enough, such expertise would no longer be restricted to a minority; it would become common and the experts would no longer be experts. In respect of language and modern moral activity, 'wannabes' can use language and foul acts to kick-start and maintain them in some celebrity world. Promiscuity and other excesses are enduring practice in show business, but almost everyone is getting in on the act. Society is increasingly dominated by pop icons who, perhaps more than most, embody and boast about modern values or wisdoms. Experts believe modern values, wisdoms and laws enhance the meaning, purpose or quality of life. Many ordinary people plus a few experts have the opposite view and believe modern values or wisdoms diminish us. Because common sense is common while expert sense is not, there are many quotations from ordinary people in this volume. One is:

If you want common sense talk to common people.

I started writing this book in 1997 when T. Blair became Prime Minister. I had planned to have the first draft ready by 2000. Except for being a few pages shy in the last chapter I had met the goal. A few half-hearted attempts were made to get a publisher. I say half-hearted attempts because I was told in this modern age I needed a 'literary agent'. As I am not too fond of the idea of 'agents' (look what soccer and estate ones have done) I didn't seek one. Nonetheless, a relative of mine is a theatrical agent. He seems alright, but I would say that wouldn't I? My view was if my book was good enough someone would publish it without an agent's help. A couple of publishers showed some interest but, in my view, not enough. At least they didn't say, 'Your writings will be famous long after Shakespeare, Mark Twain, Einstein and Mickey Mouse are forgotten – but not until.' Hence, the initial draft has laid around until now – 2008. My wife has prodded me at times to do something about the script. As the expression of common sensing and wisdoms are part of human nature, I have only had to give more modern instances of their uses and abuses. The chapter, 'Further Uses And Abuses Of Your Life' contains the most recent examples. Today, my wife's common wisdom about this script is:

Don't put off until tomorrow what can best be done today.

Introduction

There is no substitute for common sense.

Ancient and Common Wisdom

Two years ago in 1995 I was telling what I thought was an amusing tale to an American professor of psychology. When I was a pupil at a boys' grammar school, I recounted, I saw this graffiti written on the cloakroom wall. The first statement read, 'I love kissing grills.' Just below this in different handwriting it said, 'Surely you mean girls, not grills.' The final sentence in a particularly mechanical form of script was, 'Don't be mean, what's wrong with us grills?' My listener observed me with barely a smile. It wasn't the observing I minded, that is what psychologists do for a living, it was the weakness of the smile. Perhaps he was a government joke inspector or maybe my sense of humour is just poor:

Joke police criminalise politically incorrect humour relating to race or anything experts choose to ban.

The professor still trying to maintain his smile said, 'It could be politically incorrect you know.' I tried not to look blank and asked, 'What-er-how do you mean, politically incorrect?' 'Well,' he replied, 'the way things are going in the U.S. some smart lawyers could argue that saying you like kissing girls is sexual discrimination. It discriminates against boys. Furthermore, these legal eagles could suggest that although the term kissing doesn't necessarily discriminate against oral sex, it could discriminate against penetration of vaginal and anal orifices. In modern culture, people "do their own thing". Modern expert thinking has it that we should not be judgemental and write or say things that might be offensive to people just because they have different values from ourselves or the majority. Basically, as in your country, suing for compensation is often merely a matter of finding a lawyer willing to take on the case.' 'What about justice?' I queried. 'You are behind the times buddy. Most modern lawyers are about winning and money. Believe me, lawyers can make a good case in today's political climate to nail anyone stating they loved kissing girls. In a nutshell,

1

the legal case would be: it is not inclusive: it discriminates against modern sex acts, gender and in other ways I can't even dream of. Therefore, it is politically incorrect.' Trying to make some contribution to this new age or new sense discussion I asked, 'How would the sentiment that a person – er, loved, girls have to be rephrased so that it was inclusive, did not involve sexual, linguistic or other forms of discrimination and would be politically correct?' 'Oh to expert lawyers, that's not a big problem,' he retorted. 'Such a politically correct statement would read: No sexual discrimination, f--k everybody.' Now his smile got broader. He said that a new prayer for new laws is:

> Save us from experts on political correctness, for they aim
> to inherit the earth.

Too much of what goes on in modern society dispenses with common sense or common wisdom. Our institutions and social transactions are in a poor state and seem incapable of halting their downward plunge. There are so many failed policies and laws. Ordinary people are fed up with law-makers' plans and policies as well as other experts who put the policies and laws into practice. What seems clear is that we have a constant and prolific rise in the number of expert legal laws, scientific theories and technologies with a corresponding decrease in common sense laws or wisdoms. Perhaps things are going to change for the better as yesterday, a new leader in Britain was elected. Common sense may be revived and will prevail:

> Hope springs eternal.

Common sense seems to have been banished and we have an increasingly sordid society with poor public services and morale. After yesterday's defeat in the General Election, John Major must have realised, to misquote a common saying: 'Too many crooks spoil the broth.' The new Prime Minister, Tony Blair, has said he will rid politics of sleaze and make his government open and transparent. This is consistent with common sense and is a noble ambition which, if attained, would be a colossal achievement for it will impact positively on many aspects of our lives. There should be no sane person in the country who would not wish that Blair can deliver such a promise. There is certainly a more positive air about in Britain now we have a new broom. Everyone is keeping fingers crossed it will be a cleaner sweeper than that of the soiled Tories. Tony Blair is very popular judging by the size of his parliamentary majority. He appears to be a clean-living family man who loves his wife and children. Also he is a man with religious values which have, at their core, common sense laws or wisdoms. Indeed, one of his major platforms for getting to power was his pledge to head a government that is to be 'whiter than white'. As Mae West inferred snow is white and can drift. Let us hope that this is not the fate of the new Prime Minister. Tony Blair's anti-sleaze campaign recommends a common sense law:

Honesty is the best policy.

Modernity seems to make any government more sleazy and inefficient than its predecessor. As Conservatives have been in power longer since 1950, they have been responsible for more incompetent and immoral acts. If Tony Blair does create a government that is whiter than white, it would be a miracle. Has there ever been a government that has not been corrupt? Also should Blair's national government be free of sleaze, it will be very different from numerous local councils which represent New Labour. Some influential New Labour Party councillors are, to be politically correct, ethically challenged to say the least. Boles Penrose is said to have observed:

Public office is the last refuge of a scoundrel.

On the one hand Tony Blair is associated with traditional values. On the other he identifies with the rock and roll pop generation whose values are modern and are often opposite of common sense or traditional wisdoms. This is one reason why Tony Blair has been described in some quarters as a man who is all things to all people. One mantra of the New Labour Party that is worrying is 'Modernise, modernise, modernise'. How do you modernise common sense wisdoms such as, 'Honesty is the best policy'? Tony Blair, in the run up to the general election, was portrayed like a pop star. Much publicity was given to his image. His looks (cute like Bambi), hair, teeth, his guitar-playing, and rock band associations (as well as other links with show business like his father-in-law being a famous television actor) were all given extensive media coverage. Tony Blair's skill as a political leader has also received consistently high praise. He has overcome many great difficulties and has united the party and gained much success. The message from New Labour is if you cannot trust Tony Blair, who can you trust? Being trust-worthy is associated with common sense laws. John Major was, according to general consensus, a dull and grey man and politician. However, some political commentators have maintained that in the verbal duals in parliament, John Major invariably got the better of Tony Blair. Not only this, but he did it with much wit and charm which was there for all to see when parliamentary debates were televised. Nevertheless, John Major did not generate the same charismatic modern pop-star-like image and appearance as Tony Blair. There are numerous ancient wisdoms or common sense laws that refer to image and appearance and one of them is:

All that glisters is not gold.

The new PM has been in office about a week as I write this. I, along with many others, hope that Tony Blair leads us, indeed, into a golden era of politics and a better society. Anyone who does not wish for this is a fool. I believe Tony Blair genuinely wants to improve the lot of all the citizens. Again, if this were not so, Tony Blair would be an even bigger fool, because his success, that of New Labour and of the whole country depend on it. Let us hope he turns out to be superman. John Major wanted to be superman also, who wouldn't? He half dressed like superman according to some who noted, like the super hero, John Major tucked his shirt into his underpants. Though Tony Blair's motives can be of the highest order, if he is to solve the many problems, as is the task of the leader, he will have to heed common sense laws not the least of which is:

Power corrupts.

I do not really understand the New Labour notion of The Third Way which suggests a new sense of direction in politics and inevitably new laws. Could it be that when New Labour politicians want to drive their message home as in 'Modernise, modernise, modernise,' they say it three times and, hence, the procedure is called The Third Way? Since almost all things, conceivable and inconceivable, have been modernised to be sexy, I thought The Third Way referred to the Karma Sutra. Perhaps it is just as simple as believing that if you say things often enough people will accept what you say. Saying things three times is also tantric. A tantra is a Buddhist or Hindu mystical or magic text. The principles of the tantras involve mantras, meditation and yoga. New Labour could do far worse than to examine religions of the East to guide their government. The morals contained in Eastern religions are virtually the same as those of Christianity. It is sad that though the core values of all religions are shared common sense laws, they have had a bloody history, though not all the time or everywhere. Leaders of the Christian Church have too often abandoned its core common sense laws to accommodate modern culture, its excesses and lack of morality. Consequently, Christianity has gone into decline. Muslims, for example, describe the modern Western World as immoral, degenerate or worse. Islam is one of the growing religions including converts from Christianity who agree the West is intolerably decadent. The vast majority of ordinary Muslims and other Eastern codes observe common sense laws or wisdoms far more diligently than Christians. Hence, Eastern religions provide a refuge to people dissatisfied with moral standards in the West. One of the many common sense laws that followers of Buddhism, Hinduism and Islam obey more than Christians is:

Practise what you preach.

If Tony Blair practises what he preaches in respect of doing away with sleaze in public life, he is on a winner. If he preaches what he seems to practise in his own moral, private or family life and religious life, he will score another goal for they exhibit common sense laws. Blair's history reflects major elements and conflicts that I wish to talk about in this book. Being a politician he is a law-maker of new laws as opposed to common sense laws that go back a long way in man's evolution. Previously, he was an expert lawyer and lawyers interpret and administer the laws. He identifies strongly with the rock and roll generation. Rock or pop is associated with glorifying foul language, violence, promiscuity, drug abuse and deliberately breaking common sense laws in very excessive ways. Tony Blair also recommends some common sense laws, some of which are destroyed by the modern laws made by politicians and used by expert lawyers. He is a politician with a pop star ethos. Tony Blair's election to office coincided with the start of my book and provides factors and principles that I wanted to examine and discuss. Just as Princess Diana has become a pop princess and world icon, I think Tony Blair looks ready to become a pop prime minister also with international appeal. His pop star status was on the rise before he became Prime Minister:

There are many ways to fame and infamy.

This book looks at ancient wisdoms or laws and common sense laws or wisdoms in which the evolution of all types of law is embedded. It examines the interaction of these older laws or wisdoms with modern scientific laws and the perpetual flow of new legislation, theories and initiatives from our 'experts' political or otherwise. The interaction of old wisdoms and new pop laws is done in relation to the behaviour of individuals and institutions. To achieve this the book deals with: the will of the people, science, technology, personality, intelligence, justice, health, the family, education, work, politics, popular culture including sport, paranormal sensings and so forth. The makers of modern laws seem fixated on the warren model:

Modern laws breed faster than rabbits.

As in this introduction to the book, in the subsequent chapters I mention some people by name to illustrate certain issues. This does not mean they are the best or worst examples of particular behaviours. For instance, I could say John Lennon was not only a musician but also a moral philosopher and reportedly a man of violence at times. Being abusive whilst advising peace can be used to illustrate oppositional modes of good and bad in all personalities. John Lennon was not the best or worst man in respect of music, moral philosophy or violence. It is just that I know something about him. This applies to other people I cite. The names of people I use were probably mentioned in the media around the time I was writing the section in which the names appear. To quote an old wisdom:

Nothing is so good it can't be better and nothing so bad it can't be worse.

In any case for this celebrity-obsessed culture, some pop stars deliberately cultivate an image of an immoral bad boy or girl to get publicity. To a large extent in modern society a new sense pop law is: the more notorious or immoral a person can become, the greater the celebrity and icon status.

Thus, some people I refer to might thank me for the publicity, good or bad. Who said, 'In modern times, there is no such thing as bad publicity?' Also, was it Madonna who described herself as always having been a little tart? Less of the 'little' some politically incorrect person might say or is it what a politically correct person should say in our inverted new sense society? Once again, on a good to bad scale of singing ability or being a tart, Madonna is not best or worst in the world, just someone who came to my mind. Perhaps an extreme of promiscuity is defined by one actress about another, 'She is the party who gives everyone a good time.' Madonna doesn't. Is immorality the new morality? Pop law or new sense says, orgasmically, 'Yeeees! Yeees! Yeeees!' An old sense or common wisdom warns:

> Serving one's own passions is the greatest slavery.

Pop began as an abbreviation of the word popular but evolved into a whole modern philosophy. It has come to mean anything that gets attention no matter how lewd in its self seeking expression. Reversing old common sense meanings is its main strategy. Hence the name – new sense. Some examples are: black is the new white; having it all now is the new spirituality; nymphomania is the new virginity and so forth. So fashionable and widespread are these mantras, they have become modern laws:

> Old common sense meanings and laws are opposed by new sense pop laws.

Experts have misled the majority such that we no longer recognise the extensive knowledge and wisdom that exist within us all. We face deterioration of virtually all systems in our natural, social and built environments, so what use is it to be told by politicians that the economy is booming? Most people we know have debts that frighten my wife and me and all of us are constantly encouraged to acquire even more debt. Perhaps Dolly Parton should run the world's economy. She makes astute observation about modern money matters. One of her sayings is something like, 'It takes a lot of money to look this cheap.' Also, as a nation we still have not paid off our debts incurred by the Second World War. The traditional wisdom advising not to buy something until you can afford it has been modernised by our consumer or materialistic society to:

Have it all now – pay later.

In all sections of this book, common sense laws are used liberally throughout the text. This is of course deliberate, nay unavoidable, as the essence of what I write is to validate common sense as the main source of our knowledge, wisdom and evolution. Some common sense laws are repeated in the text at times as they are relevant to a variety of contexts. Common sense laws apply to far more situations than modern scientific theories and legal laws constructed by so-called experts. Unlike the regular production of ever-changing expert laws with their incomprehensible technicalities, common sense laws are simple, well-known and understood by all:

Common sensing is nature's gift to all, but experts have debased it.

What is written is to give voice to the inherent, instinctive values that are woven into the fabric of humanity and our genes. Common sense laws have been tried and tested by millions of people over millions of years. It is the common sense of the masses of ordinary people that can bring about a better state of affairs in society including politics. The monarchy can help or hinder in improving the quality of society. Over the years, whenever the monarchy has been criticised, invariably it has been when its members have broken common sense laws. Expert legal laws cannot bring about a better state of affairs in Britain or anywhere. Science and technology cannot do it. Celebrity worship and fame cannot do it. Economic focus and material gain cannot do it. Common sense can do it for it contains wisdom. Its use can make for a better world. It is our greatest resource. It is our least used asset. It has become increasingly outlawed. Its revival is our best hope for the future. Without it:

The future just ain't what it used to be.

CHAPTER 1

Against Our Will

> The will of the people is the only legitimate foundation of any government, and to protect its free expression should be our first object.
>
> Thomas Jefferson

The essential function of politicians and government is to represent the will of the people. This is the foundation of a wise and just democracy. Politicians increasingly do not represent the people even when the will of the citizenry is very obvious. Many political theories and practices run counter to the better aspects of human nature. Expert ideologies, policies, theories and laws force most of us into doing and witnessing what we thought belonged only in nightmares, horror movies and states such as those of Hitler, Stalin, Mao Zedung and in the likes of George Orwell's novel – *Nineteen Eighty-Four*.

Expert laws and policies are so bad they have to be continually changed.

Astronomical financial costs to the tax payer of these unrepresentative judgements and vast unworkable bureaucracies are not the main concern. What is more important is the abuse of peace of mind, justice, quality of life and the suppression of the human spirit and freedom. Minorities, especially political elites, business power-brokers, expert lawyers, behavioural theorists, other academics and celebrities have forced their views on the 'silent majority'. An old wisdom and common sense saying is:

The tail should not wag the dog.

Cicero stated, 'The good of the people is the first law' and 'The laws should place the safety of all before the safety of the individual'. When the majority does voice its views, a not uncommon expert reaction is given by the American politician Dick Tuck, 'The people have spoken – the bastards.' What follows are examples of situations that I believe, from talking to people, personal experience and researching, run counter to the desires or

9

will of the majority. You will, no doubt, be able to compile a more meaningful personal list of examples of your own. Such incidents are everyday, or should it be every minute happenings? They fly in the face of common sense. It is against the will of the majority of people that:

1. Morality is being dispensed with by many modern experts who claim that different values and lifestyles are equal. If all values are equal then right and wrong become relatively meaningless and so do the purposes and quality of life. Some experts insist we should not make value judgements at all. That is, we should imitate science which scientists claim cannot say what is good or bad or right or wrong. Who other than expert power-brokers with an axe to grind would deny the centrality of right and wrong to humanity? Of right and wrong, Warren Buffett said, 'It is better to be approximately right than precisely wrong.' Noam Chomsky speaks of the issue of will and science. He says, 'As soon as questions of will or decision or reason or choice of action arise, human science is at a loss.' Science has been responsible for the explosion in technology. We wonder if it will destroy or save us or do a bit of both. When my local pub's philosopher heard the technology was now available to produce a virgin birth he exclaimed, 'For Christ's sake; what will these experts do next, play Dog?' He is dyslexic according to many experts. I like the view of Lewis Thomas on science, 'The cloning of humans is on most of the lists of things to worry about from Science, along with behaviour control, genetic engineering, transplanted heads, computer poetry and the unrestrained growth of plastic flowers.'

2. Rewards and punishment in modern society have become confused and unjust. Increasingly evil is rewarded and goodness punished. When political correctness decrees values and life styles are equal then reward and punishment predictably become haphazard and lack justice. Frail old people in poor health can be jailed for refusing to obey unjust expert laws whilst some individuals can literally get away with murder on some legal technicality. The Tory Police and Criminal Evidence Act of 1984 has made the police virtually impotent to act against crime. Modern trials are not about trying a suspect, they are about trying the way the evidence was collected and how the prisoner was treated.

3. Mass killers, like politicians, hardly ever go to jail. Inmates must feel the injustice of such treatment of elites.

4. Brutal killers, raping and torturing their victims to death, should be given appropriate custodial sentences. Some of their victims have been as young as five whilst others have been old ladies of eighty.

5. Children who commit violent murders and a whole range of other crimes have been defined by experts as being unable to tell the difference between right and wrong until they are of an age when they can produce babies of their own. Ordinary people think this is expert nonsense. E. Burke says, 'Bad laws are the worst tyranny.'

6. Teenagers committing awful crimes remain unnamed and are given inadequate sentences. Often, they see their 'punishment' as a huge joke. They leave the court laughing, making obscene gestures and snarling. However, the antics of these criminals do reflect the views of the majority on many expert laws. They are laughable, obscene and give rise to anger. Expert legal wisdom is a contradiction in terms.

7. Prisoners in jail are allowed to have alcohol, drugs, sex, cosmetic surgery, the use of prison staff to act as shoppers and errand boys and other similar services. People thought such activities were illegal or forbidden to inmates. We now learn that some experts on behaviour actually recommend some of these activities as useful for rehabilitation purposes to transpose the bad into the good. Perhaps the experts subscribe to Mae West's school of rehabilitation? She said, 'When I'm good I'm very good, but when I'm bad I'm better.'

8. Expert judges hand out life sentences knowing full well the law does not mean what it says. Pretend long sentences or even real long sentences are not effective answers. What criminals do when they are jailed has to be concerned with hard useful work, rigorous study of ancient and modern wisdoms, vocational training and the acquisition of practical living skills.

9. Young criminals have been allowed to go on expensive holidays because experts' theories tell us it will steer them away from crime. The majority feel this is rewarding the bad behaviour of those who have already had a holiday – too much freedom with little or no responsibility.

10. An old man in his eighties was prosecuted for defending himself against constant bullying by young men. He had complained on more than a score of occasions to the police who, due to existing laws and practices, could do nothing effective. In desperation, he decided to fire a gun over his attackers' heads to scare them off. He nicked one of the young

bullies. There was talk of the old man being charged with all kinds of dire consequences, such as attempted murder or manslaughter. He was ordered to pay his tormentor several thousand pounds compensation.

11. A young policeman was in danger of losing his job and being prosecuted for punching a youth who threatened to throw the officer's baby out of a train window. The policeman would have been more politically correct if he had arrested the man after he had chucked the baby out of the window. No longer is a policeman in a business where the customer is always wrong – quite the reverse. Expert laws have made it difficult for policemen in modern society to be in the right.

12. Another policeman risked losing his job or being suspended for restraining a young teenager from constantly making an old lady's life a misery.

13. A soldier doing his duty was sentenced to life imprisonment for murder. He was in a life-threatening situation at a vehicle checkpoint in a terrorist area. A car came careering through the check point. He shot at the vehicle which he thought contained terrorists. Instead, they were 'joy riders' and one was killed. Some would say the joy riders should know they could be shot at trying to drive through a guarded and armed vehicle check point. Also, others could claim joy riders are terrorists. They do terrorise people. They have run people down some of whom have been killed or reduced to a life-long vegetable state. This soldier was a political or legal pawn and illustrates the point that politicians will lay down your life to enhance their cause. A German proverb is also apt here, 'A lawyer and a wagon wheel must be well greased.'

14. A man was treated worse than most criminals for discovering an armed intruder in his home and killing him during a life and death struggle.

15. Known dangerous stalkers have been allowed to prowl the streets until some young children are raped, maimed and brutally killed. There are too many rights and not enough wrongs.

16. Governments and politicians spend our money on projects that are against our welfare and interests. The London Dome, supporting evil foreign dictators, having infinite, interminable, useless inquiries, hiring consultants and 'creating jobs for the boys and girls' who are political sycophants are a few of the many incompetent and corrupt strategies that come to mind. Those who say we can get rid of corrupt politicians (these soothsayers are usually corrupt politicians themselves or their supporters) by the ballot box are not in touch with the real world.

Political ideologists, their followers, or paymasters select the new political candidates who are likely to be at least as unrepresentative of our views as the ones we got rid of. Those of us who get modern politicians to represent us and the majority with common sense views are exceptions to the rule. We are told that, since we are a democracy, anyone can get to the top in politics. After seeing our politicians we know that it is indeed true – anyone can get to the top in politics. Will Rogers reflects many views when he points out, 'I don't make jokes, I just watch government and report the facts.'

17. People cannot walk the streets, even in daylight, without being verbally and sometimes physically abused or even murdered by aggressive beggars, vagrants, drunks and other anti-social individuals and groups. Experts argue these acts are not new. This misses the pertinent point. It is the *scale* of violence and its continual expansion that is frightening. Politicians' main characteristic is misrepresentation.

18. Children, nine years old and younger, can be seen on the street at midnight, smoking, drunk or drugged and being very abusive and threatening or attacking passers-by. The chances of seeing police foot patrols on the street get less and less. They are too busy filling in forms, promoting political correctness and going on ethnic and homosexual awareness and other diversity courses.

19. Expert ideas of care in the community result in highly disturbed persons being seen in pathetic and dangerous states in public and private locations. Closing local specialist facilities for disturbed individuals along with local amenities such as shops, hospitals, post offices, local services and so forth have all contributed to the destruction of the pillars of meaning, purpose and quality of life – namely sense of community or belonging.

20. Foul and abusive language can be heard at any time of the day or night in almost any place you could mention. It comes from the mouths of an increasing number of people, some as young as four years old. It is becoming normal speech.

21. Many expert theorists, including politicians, deny a relationship between violence on television and destructive behaviour in the wider society. Politicians promise to reduce violence and the causes of violence. However, after all is said and done, more is said than done.

22. Politicians and other experts force the majority to take responsibility for the welfare of children of irresponsible parents. Many of these

parents are young, single and know full well they are unable to look after themselves let alone children. They expect the majority of us to provide for them. The law, not justice, has made this a part of these people's rights. As Henry David Thoreau pointed out, 'Any fool can make a rule.' It is a politician's main function.

23. A woman with eight children by four different fathers can expect, by law, to have her children and herself supported by the state. Perhaps she has taken political advice to heart and is celebrating diversity.

24. Some welfare benefits are paid to rich claimants, a vast array of fraudsters and other people who choose to be anti-social. Welfare has become a way of life for too many people. It does far more harm than good to many who receive it. There are better ways of helping people. Expert theories and practices enshrined in law are destroying traditional families which are central to, and the building blocks of, good societies.

25. Public money can be paid almost indefinitely in one way or another to people who do not choose work. A cursory glance at any city or town indicates there is much work to be done in the community and the environment if our quality of life is to have meaning.

26. Technologies which the experts promised would free us have, in fact, enslaved us. As more information has become easier to push around, experts have thrust great wads of it at people down the line such that they cannot do their jobs properly.

27. Expert theories and laws force the majority to pay for policies that encourage an increase in population. We are overcrowded and overcrowding results in crime and violence.

28. Political and other expert theories have been used to legalise the influx of too many immigrants into this country over the last fifty years. The 'population bomb' has been with us for some time now and it has been exploding with increasing violence over a period of years. Excessive immigration is a powerful detonator.

29. Legal aid can be given to rich criminals and other undeserving cases on the whim of expert theorists and practitioners and greedy lawyers. Lawyers have always had an unenviable reputation for hundreds of years but modern lawyers have never been disliked so much as they are in the early part of the third millennium. As well as being ambulance chasers and advertising their wares in toilets, as long ago as the early seventeen hundreds John Gay had this to say of the legal profession, 'A

fox may steal your hens sir,/If a lawyer's hand is fee'd sir,/He steals your whole estate.'

30. Compensation can be paid for anything or nothing. The whole of society could grind to a halt. Everyone will soon have to be escorted by a lawyer because it will be difficult to find any activity or object that cannot be seen as a potential compensation claim. Even Goldilocks could be viewed as a racist term. Rape could be defined as an assault with a friendly weapon. Paradoxically, the more expert laws the politicians make to try to get the population more accountable, the less the politicians become accountable themselves. They claim anyone's success as their own policies at work but with mistakes, the buck stops anywhere but with the politicians.

31. Justice is hard to come by in modern times and on the rare occasions justice seems to be done it can take a very long time. For example, some people suffer numerous forms of abuse from neighbours not for a few hours, weeks or months but for years and years. Some have died waiting for justice. This benefits criminals and lawyers – not the victims.

32. Experts have created a gigantic imbalance between freedom and discipline and this is manifest in the field of teaching and learning. Education and other child rearing practices have been in far too many cases spectacular failures. Elementary meanings of language, number and social values are lacking even in many university graduates. Wrong principles have been used. Expert theories have denied the true nature of learning. H.G. Wells (in *Outline of History* Chapter 15) said, 'Human history becomes more and more a race between education and catastrophe.' Guess where the big money is in respect of modern education in England at the turn of the second millennium?

33. Experts come up with all kinds of reasons to put the blame for anti-social behaviour on anyone or anything except on the will of the wrongdoer. Expert theories and practices too often give great support to vicious criminals, but little to their victims or their relatives. When government can't catch criminals, it criminalises those it can catch, namely ordinary, law-abiding citizens.

34. Expert scientists viewed man as a machine, a biological one, but nevertheless a machine. Science was applied to work and management and operations were split into smaller and smaller parts. This gave rise to mindless repetitive labour. Man is treated as a machine programmed and

controlled by experts. Power-brokers have virtually destroyed the noble aspects of work as the centrepiece to the evolution of our language, culture, values and our life's purposes and meaningfulness. Seeking cheap labour at home or abroad has always demeaned societies and reduced their wisdom, spirit and quality of life. Even an immediate material gain by such strategies results in future financial and social disasters.

35. Directors of big organisations in public and private sectors are given huge benefits via golden handshakes, lucrative pensions and the like even when they have been so incompetent and/or corrupt that they have ruined the organisation for which they worked. Politicians awarded themselves such generous packages also whilst the workers in the enterprises they have destroyed get little or nothing. It is politicians who do most damage to society so I agree with Edward Langley's sentiment when he said, 'What this country needs is more unemployed politicians.' They would do less damage on the dole.

36. Violent, vulgar and stop-at-nothing commercialism that exploits the worst side of human nature has been legalised and richly rewarded. Getting money and publicity no matter how unjust, offensive or harmful the behaviour to achieve these ends, is becoming a cultural norm. Everything has been sexualised, even tiny children. Greed, image-creation and opportunism can be seen almost anywhere you look. Government, business, advertising, television, music and sport are a few examples. Traditionally, fame was associated with high honour-able achievement and infamy with the opposite – dishonour and foul acts. Now, in modern society, fame and infamy are being given equivalence. Modern celebrity status is inclusive; it includes the cream of society and the dregs and some vile behaviour can be rewarded more than the truly great and the good. Grotesque behaviour in the pop world including sport is not just accepted from celebrities, it is becoming expected and glamorised. Vile behaviours are rationalised as being necessary characteristics to those who have 'made it' or are 'winners'.

37. Some government ministers have the arrogance to say in 1996 that any suggestion that there is a crime wave in this country is a myth. Actually, the politicians may be technically correct. To call criminal behaviour that has been accelerating with increasing rapidity over forty or fifty years a 'crime wave' is not a realistic description. It is not a

wave of crime. It is a sea of crime and violence, a tidal flood drowning all of us. To err is human; to lie is politics divine.

38. Confidence in the National Health Service has been diminished by expert theories including management theories. If hospital matrons and nurses are not good managers, who is? It was the common sense management by nurses of people in life-threatening situations that gave the National Health Service any good reputation it had. Expert specialist managers, like others who specialise, often cannot see the wood for the trees. Government's increasing interference is counter-productive whether in the National Health Service, Education or elsewhere.

39. European politicians, lawyers and other expert bureaucrats are adding to the number and complexity of our own failed, expert laws in Great Britain. Everything we do is becoming subject to expert European law and this means we lose our freedom and nationhood. The claim by British politicians that we should be at the centre of Europe guiding it to success is a rationalisation of politicians' incompetence. We cannot put our own house in order. Signing up to Europe lessens our autonomy, justice, identity and freedom. The majority has little enough of these already. Does joining Europe mean Britain is going to be totally incontinent? The European Union looks like the United Nations, incompetent and corrupt – rather like national and local government but on a larger scale. By comparison the British Empire was honourable.

40. Many politicians and scientific experts have led us to believe that nuclear waste and the nuclear industry can be handled in a safe manner. This is one of the most dangerous expert myths.

41. Expert theories and practices have led to the continuous destruction of the natural and built environment. Animal species are disappearing at an alarming rate as are essential rain forests and other crucial resources of nature. It is becoming increasingly difficult to breathe clean air, drink unpolluted water or eat uncontaminated food.

42. More and more houses and roads are being built when we have too much of our natural habitat submerged beneath excesses of concrete, tarmac, cars and people. After creating ugly environments experts use an old saying that was given more credence when an expert philosopher David Hume popularised in the 1700s the saying, 'Beauty is in the eye of the beholder'. This is emphasising that beauty is mainly

subjective thus excusing experts' foul creations. Science, as well as experience and common sense, has demonstrated that beauty has a high degree of objectivity; that is, lots of people agree on what is beautiful and ugly.

43. Politicians in 1996 award themselves a twenty six per cent pay rise when the majority have to make do with a small fraction of this. Some ordinary people are having wage cuts and are being made redundant. Since most politicians do not represent the will of the majority of the population, any money they do receive is literally immoral earnings.

44. Etcetera, etcetera; forty three and it could be many more.

All these incidents have happened as a result of experts scorning some principles of nature. One used by Cicero is stated earlier in this section, namely, 'The law should place the safety of all before the safety of the individual.' However, Cicero did not invent the principle. The wisdom was around long before Ancient Rome and Ancient Greece came on the scene. You already know it is a common everyday saying which can be expressed in numerous ways. One is:

The whole is more important than the part.

This is a law of nature and like all laws of nature, it is very powerful. We ignore it at our peril. Modern science has yet to fully appreciate the meaningfulness of this law. Cicero just applied this law of nature to the safety of people. Put in a political, cultural or social framework, it would read:

The majority is more important than the minority.

Because the law is that the majority is more important than the minority, does not mean that the minority is unimportant. The views of the minorities must gain representation, but they must not dominate. Our cultural values no longer coincide with our common sense values. The modern emphasis is on individual rights rather than being a member of a team or group and larger whole. Margaret Thatcher said that there was no such thing as society, only individuals. This is a mistaken view as people gain meaning and purpose of life as well as self-concept from their interactions with society. Thatcher's view can encourage the expression of the selfish aspects of our nature. However, Margaret Thatcher was representing common sensing or feeling of the masses when she stressed that individuals should take more responsibility for their own actions rather than blaming society.

Thus, the lady Prime Minister was wrong about there being no such thing as society. We know that everyone makes mistakes, but experts, particularly politicians, give the impression that they do not. How often do we hear a politician admit to error? D. Bonheoffer points out:

> If you board the wrong train, it is no use running along the corridor in the opposite direction.

Politicians, lawyers, financial experts, big businesses, entertainment 'stars' and any other individual or institution that has power (and celebrity status does have power) are increasingly a law unto themselves. Ordinary people feel surrounded by, and at the mercy of, incompetent and corrupt officials and you feel helpless to challenge the wrongs, particularly in court. Marty Vail expresses a common sentiment crude, rude but true when he states, 'You want justice, go to a whorehouse. You wanna get fucked, go to court.' In a nutshell, it is against the will of the majority that:

> Common sense is being replaced by expert nonsense.

Chapter 2

Your Common Sense Versus Expert Theories

Expert theory is often the opposite of common sense.
It is uncommon nonsense.

Anon.

What you already know but may not think you do

Politicians are self-promoted experts who, in association with other experts, make policies and laws. Central to their expertise are rationality or reason and scientific findings or theories. Experts in reason and modern science have made us ridicule our own common sense. They have replaced common wisdoms with theories that are inaccurate and dangerous. Common sense has been badly misjudged and classified as cliché or platitude. How often do we hear comments which pour scorn on common sense. Some examples are as follows:

That's obvious, it's only common sense.

Everyone knows that. It is common knowledge.

That's far too simple. It's just common sense.

Common sense is no substitute for science.

That is an old wives' tale. Be objective.

Let's not let feelings interfere with the facts.

The gentleman opposite over-simplifies what is an
extremely complex issue.

That's a gut-feeling.

We need cold, reliable, scientific data.

Subjective judgements or vague, instinctive feelings of
what is right have no place here. We want logic, reason and
objectivity.

Intuition is for women. We are men of science, surely (praise
for women or what?)

That's old news. It is common-place.

Business is business. What's justice, morality or fairness got
to do with it?

We are talking economics here. Feelings don't enter the
equation. Be rational.

We can't measure common sense, let's stick with numbers.

The twentieth century has been associated with The Age of Reason, The Age of Science, The Age of Technology – The Modern Age. Modern means a departure from traditional styles and values, so most periods could be called 'modern' in their time. Post-modernist is a term which really means 'We are the clever-dicks ahead of the present game.' Often post-modern actions boil down to breaking traditional taboos in ugly, vulgar ways. Post-modernists do suffer for their art; it is called PMT (post modern tension). Political correctness is the current generator of taboos such as freedom of speech. We would be ill-advised to describe our present era as The Age of Common Sense or Wisdom. Other labels for our decade spring readily to mind. Greed, violence, blame, consumerism, technology, drugs and pollution are but a few:

Experts named us homo sapiens or wise man, but now we
hear much of the homo but little of the sapiens.

In one way or another, reason has been around for a very long time. Experts took original reasoning ability and separated it from intuitive and 'feeling' aspects of common sense. Common sense in its wholeness prevented true knowledge seekers getting at the real facts, the experts reasoned. They made what was initially simple, integrated and harmonious wisdom into specialised, divisive, academic fields or intellectual theories. Queen Victoria was not amused by the growing experts of reason or rationality and warned against its outcome. She said:

To try and find out reason for everything Is very dangerous
. . . making you very miserable.

Modern science maintains that observation, experiment and measurement are more accurate than reasoning alone. However, rationality is still an essential ingredient to all the stages of the scientific method. Experts in science complicated, corrupted and diminished common sense still further. They made the separation of scientific knowledge from common sense and morality into a complete divorce. As Winston Churchill said, 'Science should be on tap, not on top.' To give them their due, most scientists would not have corruption consciously in mind. Perhaps the line from a poem by Milton is relevant here:

> The road to hell is paved with good intentions.

Politicians, lawyers and scientists are amongst society's greatest rationalisers to justify policies, laws and experiments. They are also responsible for the masses of complicated information and interminably complex bureaucracy that grind people down. Today one report says it has taken twelve years to prosecute continually violent neighbours. Experts in reason and science have reversed many age-old common wisdoms including:

> Keep it simple.

Many forces in society, such as politics and education, have conspired to make people worship new gods – reason, modern science and technology. Deep down we feel uneasy about these gods and outrage at how experts use them. On the surface, it is logical to believe experts know more. It stands to reason. Superior knowledge is what defines experts. Their knowledge is the best money can buy. However, look at your own everyday world. After what you see, is it not wise to examine so-called expert knowledge? Is expert knowledge really as reliable, objective and valid as knowledge contained in common sense? I am saying categorically, it is not. Mark Twain lampoons scientists, their theories and their instruments of measurement:

> Scientists have odious manners, except when you prop up their theory; then you can borrow money from them.

> If thermometers had been an inch longer we would have all frozen to death.

Let us compare reason, modern science and common sense. The majority of people are not recognised experts in reason and science. Experts are a minority who have great power over the majority. Not being an expert may make us rely more on common sense. If this is so, and common sense does contain more accurate knowledge than modern theories as I claim, the majority should exhibit more accurate and meaningful knowledge than experts. We have become conditioned by experts, particularly scientists, that they know best and we must be told what to do. Before science specialists came on the scene self-educated generalists had to rely on common sensing which made for greater understanding of the world. Even though their factual information or knowledge was less, they understood more. They realised mankind was the best model for studying the universe. This is why ancient philosophers from such cultures as China and Greece were more in touch with meaningful realities of the world. So were and are most philosophers including modern ones for they seek meanings. Einstein's thinking reflected more Taoism than scientism:

> Knowledge is not the same as understanding which requires identifying causes and consequences.

Wisdom is the use of effective understanding for the betterment of things. You have the whole wisdom and history of the universe enfolded within you. Some scientists agree this is so. What scientists have failed to recognise is your wisdom is superior to and contains vast knowledges. They see wisdom and knowledge as *separate*. In their more modest moments, scientists admit they have only the tiniest fraction of all possible knowledge. A common wisdom that puts scientific knowledge into perspective in relation to your own common sense or wisdom is:

> A little knowledge is dangerous, wisdom or common sense is not.

Before reason and science dominated, man had to depend on common sense. It has served him well for his thousands of years of history. Only for a speck of time in man's long existence have reason and science so governed our lives. Common sense was essential to man's evolution. It is nature's wisdom or instinctive valuing of things. It is a sensing, common to all, of what is good and what is bad for us. Its purpose is to guide our participation in life as a whole, not just in smaller and smaller bits as expert scientific and legal laws replaced it. Inner sensings or feelings were present long before they gained spoken and written expression. Common sense or wisdom was passed down from generation to generation. Without these inborn sensings to choose good over bad, how could we have developed or evolved? Common sense sayings are the accumulated wisdoms of man's interactions with his environment and himself. Reasoning and intellectual abilities are not separate bits of inheritance. What permeates and joins everything together is nature's wisdom inside and surrounding us all. It is everywhere. It is common. To have meaning, intellect and reason have to operate as integrated parts of common wisdom as a whole. Separated from common sense, they are about as meaningful, in terms of seeing, as a pair of eyes torn from our bodies and put in a display jar:

> Common sense is integrated energy of the whole of bodies, minds and spirits.

Common sense sayings that originated in early history, we now call ancient wisdoms. Most of our present day common sense sayings are old or ancient wisdoms passed down to us. Common sense is old. It is ancient wisdom that has been tried, tested and modified over thousands of years by countless numbers of people. Similar wisdoms or sentiments exist in different languages, cultures and periods of time. Common wisdoms are to be found in all modes of expression such as poetry and song, but especially in ordinary everyday sayings and conversations. A particular wisdom is stated differently according to the situation or period in history but still keeps the same basic meaning. For example, since words could be spoken people have said things like:

> There are advantages and disadvantages to everything.

> Life has its ups and downs.

Children of the present 'cool' or 'disco' generation might express the same feelings by announcing:

> There is a flip side to everything.

One rather amusing example of the law that there are advantages and disadvantages to everything is given by R.N. Westcott:

They say that a reasonable amount o' fleas is good fer a dog
... keeps him from broodin' over bein' a dog mebbe.

One wisdom has a tremendous range of situations to which it applies. To test this claim, take the common sense saying, 'There are advantages and disadvantages to everything.' Now, try to find an aspect of life to which it does not apply. If it applies to many situations, it is not just a saying, it is a *law*. The more situations to which it applies, the more powerful is the law. Common sense laws come from nature; science theories are man-made or synthetic by comparison. O.W. Holmes compares science and nature:

Go on fair science; soon to thee
Shall nature yield her idle boast;
Her vulgar fingers formed a tree,
But thou hast trained it to a post.

Robert Browning speaks of nature's laws:

I trust in nature for the stable laws of beauty and utility.

Common sense has come to mean the opposite of rationality or reason and science. A main criticism of common sense is that it is irrational and unscientific. Expert rationalists say that the procedures of reasoning, like logic, give true knowledge and certainty. True knowledge, they claim, cannot be found in feelings or in sense experience. Experts maintain reason alone gives knowledge of nature and what exists. It is deductive in character and everything is explainable. Some rationalists state true knowledge already exists within us in the form of innate ideas. However, reason, as experts see it, is in the realm of the intellect, not feeling. Common sense laws or wisdoms do not accept intellect or reason as separate from other aspects of man's whole nature. Two ancient common sense sayings illustrate the point:

All things are related.

The whole is greater than the sum of the parts.

In spite of their endless theories, Edward Tyron sums them up in a common sense way, 'The Universe is simply one of those things that happen from time to time.' The main activity of rationalists and modern science has been chasing causes or reasons for events. Problems have now arisen which common sense sayings clearly predict. The consequence of splitting or separating things into smaller and smaller parts in pursuit of reasons or causes can be readily demonstrated. Stick your nose on to the page of this book and you will illustrate a common universal law which is, 'The closer you get to something the less you see of it.' This is not just true of physical bodies, it also applies to situations of mind and spirit. You all know this common sense law, but perhaps do not readily appreciate what highly meaningful and extremely important knowledge it is. Once more, no rationalist, scientist or any other expert has discovered a more significant law than this or other common sense laws. Again this taken-for-granted, too obvious law may be expressed in different ways depending on circumstances and culture. One well-known way of stating this is:

Not being able to see the wood for the trees.

This is exactly what happened to modern science. Now, some scientists at least are admitting that this common sense saying turned out to be true knowledge with wide implications. Separating things excessively and focusing on small parts blinded the experts to the reality of nature, its wholeness and its true laws. The experts' difficulty with explanations, cause or reason might well be illustrated by looking at any common scene. This is an example of a parent and child in conversation:

Child: May I have an ice-cream?
Parent: No.
Child: Why not?
Parent: I can't afford it.
Child: Why can't you afford it?
Parent: Because your daddy is out of work.
Child: Why is daddy out of work?
Parent: Oh stop it. We all know everyone can go on asking 'why' questions for ever.

In the last statement, the parent identifies a persistent problem of experts. However, if ordinary people were asked what the 'Infinite Regression

Problem' was in science, the majority of us would probably say, 'What's that?' Yet its meaning is in the very common observation of the parent's final comment that 'why' questions can go on being asked for ever. The expert term for this is 'The Infinite Regression Problem'. It also illustrates another common wisdom:

Expert terminology does not mean better problem identification or better knowledge.

What does happen if 'why' questions are asked *ad infitum*? Such a process would get back to the beginning of time, if there was a beginning. It would also show that all things in the universe are related, including causes, explanations or reasons. In addition, if enough 'why' questions were asked, one conclusion reached is that everything causes everything else. This is reflected in very old common sense sayings such as:

All things are connected.

Nature is its own cause.

Furthermore, one cause can be an effect also. In the parent-child example, 'not being able to afford it' caused the 'no ice-cream' for the child. However, if we ask what was the effect of daddy being out of work, the answer is 'not being able to afford it'. Thus, 'not being able to afford it' is both a cause and an effect:

One cause is the effect of another cause.

After observing sub-atomic particles, scientists found that causality lost much of its meaning. Particles only had existence and meaning in their relations or connections to the whole situation. To ask what caused what was rather like asking, 'Which caused which, the chicken or the egg?' This shattered the scientists' world. Causality was the foundation stone of all science. Scientists found the notion of non-causality difficult to grasp. To them it did not exist. It was the opposite of the reason for science existing at all. Matthew Prior does not believe science can find causes or explanations with certainty for anything. He points out that:

Science is uncertain guesses.

In the real world, everyday conversations show ordinary people accept non-causality as meaningful. Two examples of such statements are:

Everything doesn't have to have a cause, you know.

Some things don't have a reason.

We all appreciate the existence of both causality and non-causality. If we ask, 'Why did you put on your raincoat?' and the response is, 'Because it's raining', the situation has meaning and contains causality. Conversely, when observing someone dressing and the question asked is, 'Why did you put on your left shoe first rather than the right?' and the answer is, 'No reason', the situation has meaning. Causality here is not significant. Things happen to us without meaningful reason – by chance, accident or luck. Many times, causes and effects or consequences are crucial. Unlike all science, common sense does not place excess emphasis on pursuing causality or reasoning to the extent of senselessness:

Common sense laws reflect both opposites: non-causality or chance and causality or reason.

Scientists, of course, like the rest of us have common sense and can be known to express it. For example, Wernher von Brown, the successful rocket scientist points out, 'Man is the best computer we can put aboard a spacecraft and the only one that can be mass produced with unskilled labour.' During recent decades, modern science has been supplanted by 'The New Science'. At the cutting edge of the new science is quantum theory which is associated with the study of sub–atomic particles. Quanta is the name given to the packets of energy discharged by electrons in radiation. Quantum physics appears almost the opposite of modern physics. A law of modern science was, 'Matter cannot be treated or destroyed.' At the sub–atomic level, some scientists now say, 'Matter can be created and destroyed.' To their credit, nudged by necessity, some scientists are putting up their hands to recognising the past mistakes and inadequacies of science. Harry Weinberger says:

The greatest right in the world is the right to be wrong.

Sub–atomic physics is more simple than we might think. A building brick for example looks solid and static. Observed at sub–atomic level, it resembles a railway station in the rush hour or thoughts rushing around in your mind. The dynamic energy of matter enfolded in solid objects was well-known to even the most 'primitive' of tribes. They called it 'spirit' as well as energy and worshipped it. To them it was universal essence that gave existence and meaning to everything, themselves included. Just because you cannot readily see the dynamic motion inside a solid, do not think your common sensing does not apply to sub-atomic levels. Your own body looks solid, but you cannot normally see the blood cells and other tiny things moving. You cannot see time, weight or length either, only solid representations of them. We do not see energy really, just the consequences of it. Electricity is an example. Nearly everything we value the most cannot be observed or touched directly. Love and justice are illustrative. We sense or feel energies even though we might not see them. Scientists have a self-imposed restricted view of the material world. This is narrowed further by trying to strip morality out of their observations. Thus, the following common saying hinders the scientist more than the rest of us. Scientists have convinced themselves that they do not see what they *believe*, only what they see, but common sense says that:

We believe what we see and see what we believe.

Expert theories in modern science separated mind from matter. Matter was split further into living and non-living matter. Scientists believed in evolution and that living matter developed from non-living matter from which humans evolved with mind. It is surprising then, that modern scientists treated matter as if it were separate from mind. They believed their own observations and minds did not influence the results of their experiments. Scientists called it being objective. It impressed and fooled us and the scientists too. Modern science has made us think our unscientific knowings are unreliable. They are not. Arthur Eddington, an important person in the history of science, speaks in common sense terms when he says, 'Every body continues in a state of rest or uniform motion, except insofar as it doesn't.' People who claim science produces better and more objective knowledges and laws than common sense have created a myth. Thoreau stressed:

All science is makeshift, a means to an end that
is never reached.

Modern science is being replaced by the new science which is reflecting some relatively common sense views:

MODERN SCIENCE	NEW SCIENCE
Universe is a great machine.	Universe is more like a great mind.
Causality is basic to all science.	Non-causal relations being considered.
Focus on how world began.	Focus on how world ends.
Stresses orderliness of universe.	Discovering opposite of orderliness – chaos.
Separating or splitting things.	Recognising the wholeness of things.
Influence of part on part and on whole.	Influence of whole on parts considered more.
Mind and matter separate and different.	Mind and matter seen as interacting whole.
Tries to resolve paradoxes or opposites.	A little more acceptance of paradoxes defining reality.
Rejects common sense laws as inadequate.	Forced to accept common sense laws more.
Aims to control nature, sees no disadvantages.	Aims to control nature, but beginning to see problems and disadvantages.
Claims no morality, so facts, too often, lack real meaning.	Claims no morality, so facts lack meaning, but more aware of problems of amorality.
Focuses on one end of opposites like gravity and light or bright matter etc.	More acceptance of opposites such as anti-gravity and dark matter etc.
Belief in Darwinian slow, gradual change evolution and competitiveness for survival.	Questions rate and cause of changes. Focuses co-operation more and problems of missing links.

It can be seen that modern science has almost been reversed by quantum physics or the new science. There seems to be movement from one side of things to their opposites. If there is a speed of light, is there a speed of dark? Such a reversal in the beliefs of scientists makes their claim of the reliability, objectivity and validity of science more than a little suspicious:

> Quantum theory is a new expert name for a bit of old common sense or wisdom.

Whenever quantum science has made a worthwhile 'discovery' it has, in essence, been a *rediscovery* of common sense laws. We all know the main findings in quantum theory. They have existed in everyday common sense sayings for thousands of years. It is difficult to find any primitive culture that did not possess these knowledges in one form or another. Most experts do not admit this in spite of the evidence. Perhaps it is far too common or obvious for the experts. The following related common wisdoms are similar to some of the major 'discoveries' in quantum theory:

Common Sense Sayings or Laws and Quantum Theory

> Nature is its own cause.
>
> All things are related or connected.
>
> Few things in this world are certain.
>
> The whole is more important than the part.
>
> The whole affects the part.
>
> The whole is more than the sum of the parts.
>
> The part affects the whole.
>
> The whole is reflected in the part.

This last common wisdom is echoed in a line from a poem by William Blake:

> To see a world in a grain of sand.

Numerous other common sense sayings demonstrate our knowledge of the fundamental laws of quantum theory:

No man is an island.

In the context of sub-atomic physics, this would be translated to:

No particle is an island.

You may have better common sayings of your own to illustrate aspects of quantum physics. My contamination by experts may be greater than yours. Because I speak of common sense to you does not mean I'm as common sensical as you. Please add, subtract, multiply or divide to use some scientific operations. Better still, use any process from anywhere to link common sense sayings to quantum theory because all things are interconnected. Man is only given existence and meaning by his relations with other people and other things. This applies equally to a sub-atomic particle. The universe is more like a great common sensing mind than a big machine. The trouble is that experts have conditioned us to believe their knowledge is vastly superior to that of our own. To them, quantum theory is only for experts. Do not be fooled by complicated words or mathematics. They are only tools to get at the laws. They are not the laws themselves. You know the most important things – the laws:

Sub-atomic particles, like humans and galaxies, depend on relationships for existence and meaning.

All these common sense laws, some being rediscovered by quantum scientists, might be applied to non-living matter, to mind and to social organisation. An interesting little exercise is to see how common sense laws apply to different things and to different situations. Cicero, cited in the last chapter, applied the law, 'The whole is more important than the part', to the safety of people, to justice and to the social order. It does apply, of course, to sub-atomic particles as well. We tend to accept science as inevitable, but we are getting tired of scientists. So was Mrs Patrick Campbell:

An elderly scientist bored her for hours about ants.
He told her that ants had their own police force and army.
She replied: 'No navy I suppose.'

Science has retained one belief contained in common sense. Facts are far less important than laws. To the extent that quantum science has re-discovered some common sense laws, it is more like common sense than is modern science. Nevertheless, quantum science, like modern science, still uses facts in attempts to join them up to build new laws. Common sense already contains the laws. Common sense laws can be applied to new situations, observations and facts. For example, one observation or fact is that roads are jammed with cars. There are many common sense laws that apply to this modern situation, observation or fact. Car jams is one of the many examples of one common sense law that contains both action and consequence:

Too many cooks spoil the broth.

This is a law that predicts the consequence of having too many cooks. In the context of cars and roads, jams spoil many things in the human broth. Travel, the environment and health in body, mind and spirit are examples. Some people assume because there is a common sense law which is the opposite of 'Too many cooks spoil the broth' that the law is negated. The law, 'Many hands make light work' is true until there are too many hands and then its opposite – too many cooks – comes into existence. Keeping a balance rather than having too many or too few is the key to wise actions:

Common sense is universal feelings for relationships and their consequences – good or bad.

Contrary to science, common sense has always recognised the essential wholeness or relationship of all things, but at the same time, has due regard for the part. Indeed, common sense maintains that opposites give meaning to things. Without the notion of the whole, the part would not be particularly meaningful. However, the whole has more importance and value than the part. One example is a law in science (a greater whole) is more important than a fact (a part). Another example is that the human body (a greater whole) is more important than, say, the foot (a part). Some surgical operations do in fact have to sacrifice a body part deliberately to save the whole. In the larger theatre of war:

Sometimes individuals have to be sacrificed when there is danger to the survival of the group.

One of the errors of physicists in modern science is that they did not appreciate the great influence the whole has on the part. Ordinary people can readily give many examples of how the whole affects the part. The effect of the family (whole) on a child (part) is one instance. Scientists can rationalise some issue that non-scientists can't. For example a scientist could tell his wife that his mistress was a necessary control in his experiment to improve his marital sex. Modern science has removed its expert systems from the common, the obvious or real life situations into the realm of the abstract. One common wisdom specifically states:

> Look to the common, the obvious and to the ordinary for
> reality and truth.

Quantum science is having to return to good old-fashioned common sense laws to get to grips with any objective reality. The most significant event then, in the whole history of science, is its forced move back to the future, to common wisdom. Sadly, most experts have not yet admitted the simplicity of how to make science respectable. Since the best reality science has come up with is common sense laws, why do scientists not use more of them? One thing is likely if they did, their power over us would fade to the benefit of us all. Isaac Newton himself admitted that his 'discoveries' already existed in ancient myths and he just unwrapped them:

> Scientists have not been able to see for looking.

The greatest condemnation of common sense sayings by rationalism and modern science is that they are full of paradoxes. They contain opposites that appear to conflict. One example is, 'Better safe than sorry' and 'Nothing ventured, nothing gained.' Another example is, 'Fools rush in where angels fear to tread' and 'He who hesitates is lost.' Also we have;

> More haste, less speed.

They contradict themselves said experts. According to these academics, it did not stand to reason, nor was it open to scientific testing. Both opposites could not possibly be true. However, our own everyday experience of the world tells us quite clearly that, 'More haste, less speed' is true. How many times have we rushed into doing things and made a mess of them? The mistakes we made by hurrying too much did, in fact, slow us down or even stop us. This is an example of a wider common sense law which is that:

Excess in one thing leads to its opposite.

The essence of common sense or wisdom is that opposites, or paradoxes, actually define much of our reality. Opposites exist together. We only know what 'big' is by knowing what 'small' is. 'Success' gains existence and meaning by its relation with 'failure'. Life and death are opposites, but inseparable. An old wisdom is:

In the midst of life we are halfway to death.

Physicists struggled long and hard to resolve the 'wave-particle' paradox. Sub-atomic bits sometimes appeared as waves and sometimes as particles. A wave occupies a big space, a particle occupies a small space. They are opposites – a paradox. Such a finding defied logic or reason. It flew in the face of scientific theories. Eventually, experts were forced to accept the 'wave-particle' paradox. Opposites could exist together, some experts told us. For almost all its history, modern science focused only one side of opposites. They still do it far too much in spite of their own experience saying they should not. As common sense laws would predict, they would, sooner or later, have to deal with the other side of opposites. Scientists built theories around gravity and matter and were subsequently confronted by their opposites, anti-gravity and anti-matter:

Opposites characterise our physical, psychological and social world.

How do opposites contained in common sense laws relate to 'Big Bang Theory' as an explanation for the beginning of the universe? If there is anything at all to the theory, scientists will bump into its opposite at some period. There are several possibilities. One is 'Small Silence Theory'; another is, 'Many Bangs Theory', others are, 'Small Bang Theory' and 'Big Silence Theory'. If explosion and great heat of 'Big Bang Theory' are focused, then implosion and cold will have to enter the equation some-where. By pursuing 'Big Bang Theory', scientists continue their obsession with causality or reason. Even if there was a 'Big Bang' to begin with, what of the end? And, scientists would still be left with the question:

What happened before the Big Bang?

John Irwin makes a relevant point when he observes, 'The Big Bang theory – in the beginning there was nothing, which exploded.' Science has problems with the opposites of something and nothing. Science has been responsible for one undeniable 'Big Bang Theory'. It has produced an explosions technology. In doing this, scientists have not been very successful in their real mission, to *discover new laws* that did not already exist in some form in the history of wisdoms. Technology also has been separated from common sense. Hence there is an imbalance between its advantages and disadvantages. It is destroying nature including human kind. Max Frisch has a wry, but telling comment to make on technology:

> Technology . . . the knack of arranging the world so that we need not experience it.

Modern society believes basing decisions on reason or rationality and scientific findings produces good results. Conversely, lack of reason or being irrational is associated with poor outcomes. As a well-known comment would suggest, 'It ain't necessarily so.' Hitler saw the Jews as creating problems for Germany. His solution was, if you got rid of the Jews, you got rid of the problems created by them. To Hitler and many others, this was logical and rational. He took the advice of scientific experts on how best to kill and dispose of the bodies. Almost all politicians, lawyers and other experts use reason and science to justify their actions. So do the majority of us when we get the chance. Ray Santoro highlights another problem in the world of experts when he computes, 'If A = B and B = C, then A = C except where void and prohibited by law.' Experts depend on numbers to illustrate and maintain their expertness. Gregg Easterbrook puts this into realistic perspective when he maintains, 'Torture numbers and they'll confess anything.' We have been thoroughly conditioned by experts against the real knowledge and wisdom of our own common sense. This is very unfortunate as the laws of nature are those reflected in common sense laws. Another paradox is:

> We have opposite feelings about science, we admire and dislike it at the same time.

We were all born into the culture of reason and science. It can be difficult to push against a powerful tide of beliefs that are backed by government, laws and experts in all walks of our lives. Over the years, there have been some critics of reason and science. Oscar Wilde had this to say:

> I can stand brute force, but brute reason is quite unbearable.
> There is something unfair about its use.

George Bernard Shaw also put reason into realistic perspective when he observed:

> The man who listens to reason is lost. Reason enslaves all
> whose minds are not strong enough to master her – all
> progress depends on the unreasonable man.

Since common sense is regarded by experts as unreasonable and we are slaves to reason, it is difficult to disagree with Shaw. Of science, Miguel De Unamuno said:

> Science is a cemetery of dead ideas.

Einstein himself warned that science without wisdom or morality would be disastrous. This prediction of his turned out to be more accurate than scientific predictions. However, although he gave common sense great importance, he saw it as outside of science itself, like almost every modern scientist who has ever lived:

> Scientists regard morality as essential to survival, but see it
> not as a part of science.

Reason is an element of man's whole being. If separated from the whole it becomes not only meaningless, but dangerous. When instinctive feelings and reason coincide, all well and good. If reason and science conflict with inner sensings of what is right, they become corrupting influences. In a nutshell, it would be ill-advised to let reason or science over-rule your common sense. There are a few, a very few, expert physicists who do believe in common sense knowledge as more accurate and extensive than scientific knowledge. Nonetheless, our present state of society is run by rationalists and modern science:

If we are a scientific society and scientists claim science has
no morality, what does this mean for society now and in the
future?

Some scientists say space is infinite. Not here it ain't. Modern life is
crowded, we move from one queue to another. Could it be the population
is a big bang more infinite than space? As I have indicated earlier, the main
mission and prize of science is to discover the laws of nature. Lots of
scientists refuse to accept that many laws of nature already exist in common
wisdoms or common sense sayings. Science observes facts and tries to find
relationships amongst them to establish laws. Common sense can do the
opposite also. Some of its laws can be used to explore varied situations,
consciously or unconsciously, to discover new facts and, more importantly,
their meanings and their relation to other facts, meanings and laws. Wisdom
facilitates existence in a free and just world:

Science has observed many facts but produced few real
meanings.

Scientists, not unsurprisingly, may know more facts about things they have
concentrated on than those who have not spent so much time looking at
them. Similarly, you know more facts about what you have seen and
focused than scientists who have not looked at the same things. For
example, astro-physicists know a lot of facts about planets. They spend their
lives examining them through sophisticated technologies. On the other
hand, if you are a cat lover, you will know more facts about cats than
scientists who are not interested in them. Facts, alone, do not mean much.
I saw a film, is a fact. It is not very meaningful, is it? We give far too much
credit to scientific facts, particularly when we do not know much about
them. Montaigne points to this common failing:

Nothing is so firmly believed as that we least know.

Science and common sense are in complete agreement that laws contain by
far vastly superior and extensive knowledges than facts alone. Therefore, if
you are willing, unlike scientists, to recognise the laws of nature contained
in common sense, you have much more meaningful and powerful

knowledge than science has produced. Common sense laws enable us to explore and find limitless numbers of new facts with their meanings or consequences. Common sense laws apply to everything. Because the interests of scientists have enabled them to develop technologies, it does not mean they have discovered any new laws of nature or better knowledges. At best, modern technology helps us to see more examples of nature's wonders. It did not create or increase nature's wisdoms. At worst, technology is a tool which man may choose for his own destruction and the planet's too. A quotation that is indicative of some people's sentiments about technology is being used more frequently:

> To err is human, but to fully foul things up requires modern technology.

One of the problems for ordinary people is that scientists have conditioned us to dismiss the obvious. It is non-expert. Common sense is obvious, too much so for experts. Scientists wish us to respect and admire science. We do this, even if we know little about it. Experts are conditioned themselves. One generation of experts trains the next. Admiring what is mysterious and unknown is a common characteristic as is dislike and fear of the unknown. These different feelings can exist in a person all at the same time. Some of these feelings are opposites or paradoxical. To experts they are irrational feelings. To us they are normal, everyday experiences. Funnily enough, experts experience these paradoxical feelings as much as we do. Science has trained them not to accept these common sensings of reality in their professional roles particularly in public. Sub-atomic particles also behaved in an irrational, illogical or paradoxical manner according to expert scientific theory. Professionally, sciences are also caught between what is considered two mutually exclusive contradictions, opposites or in a paradox: a universe governed by chance or determinacy. Chance, according to common sense law, that in certain conditions *one thing can turn to its opposite*, may well result in chance being determined in the long run. However, individual humans are here relatively for the short run, even if they live to be a hundred, so chance is *meaningful*. When James Bridie says, 'Eve and the apple was the first great step in experimental science' was Adam weighing up his chances or was a nibble predetermined? Bertrand Russell describes science in a paradoxical way. He says, 'All exact science is dominated by the idea of approximation.'

Our life is paradoxical and paradox is reflected in the whole and in the particles.

Common sense law or knowledge is nature's wisdom embedded in bodies, minds and spirits. Reason and science have been deliberately separated from wisdom. They are intellectual exercises. Scientists say that science is value-free. That is, they readily admit science cannot tell the difference between good and bad or right and wrong. Have we become like science itself – unable to tell the difference between good and bad or right and wrong? How have reason and science affected our institutions? What about justice, which is basic to them all if we are to have wise and true democracy? As one Spanish proverb puts it:

Science is madness, if good sense does not cure it.

Einstein was usually a big supporter of common sense and wisdom as well as being a man of science. He said, 'The whole of science is nothing more than a refinement of everyday thinking'. In a throw-away comment about common sense and the young he was less complimentary, 'Common sense is the collection of prejudices acquired by the age of eighteen.' Common sense is the world of everyone. It is what links people from all different countries in shared thoughts, feelings and actions. Common sense statements and actions are universally accepted as the truth. Sayings such as, 'I have a body' or 'I bumped into a door' are accepted as true without the need to produce scientific or rational proof. It presents a world view of realities. Human nature seeks truth; it is a common sensing which gives purpose and meaning to life. When we discover some truth we seek more, for truth has infinite expressions and relations as does beauty. As you know, there is much agreement (a high degree of objectivity) about what is beautiful.

This widespread feeling about beauty is also a common sensing and its pursuit gives meaning and purpose to life – just like truth. Indeed, sometimes beauty and truth are interchangeable or even the same thing. Common sense is the essential shared currency for solving world problems. When it is absent from situations they become unpredictable and dangerous:

Common sense is far more likely to promote a peaceful world than expert theories, science and technology.

Of course not all experts are suppressing common sense and making it illegal. Many guilty ones are to be found in the physical and behavioural science as in physics, political science, law, economics, psychology, sociology, education and so forth. What these experts have in common is they deal with theories and laws. Such experts exert considerable influence over our lives according to the current fashions in their theories and laws. Some experts in poetry, plays, novels, music, art and humour demonstrate far more accurate and meaningful knowledge of nature's laws including human behaviour with their universal common sensings than expert scientists. Douglas Adams, author of *The Hitch Hiker's Guide To The Galaxy* (1979) makes a relevant observation that could apply to all professional politicians; 'Anyone who is capable of getting themselves made President should on no account be allowed to do the job.' So embedded in our nature is common sense that even expert scientists have it, but their expertise can make them suppress it. Nevertheless it cannot be contained completely and some delight in expressing their common sense. I think it was Richard Feynman, the world renowned scientist, who emphasised that, 'Nobody has ever figured out the cause of government stupidity and until they do (and find the cure) all ideal plans will fall into quicksand.' On the other hand, it may not have been Feynman who said this. It could have been the street-cleaner or cafe waitresses I discuss things with; so many people say similar things. My own recommendation is:

> The way to cure governmental stupidity is to dispense with career or professional politicians and lawyers.

CHAPTER 3

More Laws, Less Justice

The more corrupt the state the more numerous the laws

Tacitus

Britain, perhaps more than any western country, demonstrates vast corruption by its prodigious number of expert laws. Politicians, lawyers, other experts and the majority of people agree that the purpose of laws is to get justice. The powers that be mean that to combat rising crime, you create more laws based on expert theories. As Cicero pointed out long ago, 'Law is founded not on theory but upon nature.' In the last few years, new laws have appeared with increasing frequency and they are bad laws for they defy common sense and the will of the people. Since the crime rate is expanding so rapidly, politicians find they are unable to produce new laws fast enough. Law makers may be better advised not to ignore such common wisdoms as:

Bad laws are the worst form of tyranny.

More haste, less speed.

Let us take two of many examples to illustrate the inadequacy of existing expert laws. A teenager can be out on the street committing a crime only hours after being caught, prosecuted and sentenced for another crime. Not only this, the same teenager had committed over three hundred crimes previously. He had been caught and charged for some of these offences. A stalker, about forty years old, can harass and abuse a young girl, not far into her teenage years, for month after month without effective prosecution. The authorities knew about the stalker's activities. Do expert laws have to wait until a stalker rapes and kills? Many common sense laws are relevant to these cases. Two examples are:

There are none so blind as those who will not see.

A stitch in time saves nine.

Politicians and lawyers furnish us with 'expert' rational and logical explanations for these obvious injustices. The reason, they tell us, the stalker was allowed to get away with it was because, out of the galaxy of laws, there was none specifically to cover stalking. As Richard Littlejohn would say, 'You couldn't make it up.' To cater for the quiz-master character in us all, the saying by Littlejohn is a variation of a common sense law – which one? If you want a clue, here it is. A cross-word puzzle compiler said that when he died he wanted to be buried in a grave two across and six down – is it true? Experts say we can rest assured though, politicians in consultation with lawyers and other experts on behaviour, are in the process of producing more laws to deal with stalking. If politicians had to read, never mind understand, all the laws they voted in, there would be about five of them – laws or politicians that is. Producing more and more laws and professional politicians runs counter to common sense laws:

> Quality is more important than quantity. One common sense law is worth thousands of expert laws.

Common sense laws have far more quality than any legal laws created by experts. What is more, there is a sufficient number of common sense laws to cover all situations more effectively. Following the experts' line of reasoning along the way to its logical conclusion makes for a highly depressing outlook. What experts are doing shows their reasoning is, that the more crime situations you get, the more laws you need to deal with them. Hence, experts believe, in theory, the non-criminal majority cannot feel totally safe until there are enough effective laws and punishments to cover all possible criminal eventualities. For example, carrying knives in the street is dangerous, the experts tell us. Knives in the street could be banned by law, if they have not been already. Will more laws have to be designed to deal with a housewife buying a carving knife for her kitchen? Will it become law that she has to hire a policeman to escort her from the place of purchase to her home? Further, will her husband, because of new safety laws, have to rent a security guard to protect him at home as his wife is known to get upset when he comes home late? After all, she does possess a dangerous weapon. Will laws have to be developed to cover frozen chickens as they can be used as murder weapons? Expert laws can make criminals out of innocent housewives. Carrying a kitchen knife in their shopping bag on the street could do it. Modern expert law is moving to criminalising your thoughts, words and deeds. Martin Luther King reminded us about the effects of expert laws when he said, 'Never forget that everything Hitler did in Germany was legal.' We would do well to heed a common wisdom which predicts expert laws make criminals out of innocent people:

> **When you create a new law, you immediately create new outlaws.**

Almost all objects in the world can be used as lethal weapons. Combine all these objects with the total number of human situations in which crimes can occur and we are looking at an infinite number of potential expert laws. At the rate politicians are bringing in new laws, we are heading in that direction. A common feeling about the continuous production of expert laws is expressed by John Arbuthnot's observation:

> **Law is a bottomless pit.**

More and more laws have not resulted in less crime; the opposite is the case. Expert theory and reason alone have not worked. Crime continues to soar. Laws to prevent the carrying of lethal weapons do not stop criminals doing so:

> **There are always ways and means to cheat the law.**

All the injustices listed in the earlier chapter 'Against Our Will' are consequences of the number of laws created by experts and their theories. Old men being prosecuted for protecting themselves from violent young persons, rapists and killers released from jail to commit further atrocities and endless other injustices you can think of are related to expert theories and laws. These laws have achieved the very opposite of what they were intended to do. They have given greater freedom to criminals and seriously limited the freedom of the innocent, law-abiding majority. One common sense and universal law is:

> **One man's freedom is another man's bondage.**

By far the most dangerous aspects of putting expert laws into practice falls upon the ordinary policeman. The policeman's lot is not a happy one – and no wonder. Police can receive the brunt of public anger. They are the most visible and easy targets. Real culprits are less accessible. They are tucked away in guarded government buildings or in cloistered law chambers and ivory towered academic institutions. With such obvious failure of expert laws, some negative views of the police are understandable. People feel frustrated, helpless, frightened and outraged. Blaming the police is rather like berating the postman for delivering letters you dislike. Advice from a common sense saying is:

Do not blame the messenger for the news he brings.

Police are called pigs, filth and numerous other abusive names. Each day or night, they can be exposed to violent threats, physical abuse and their lives are constantly at risk. Most ordinary people have criticised the police at one time or another. Negative attitudes towards the police are growing. Many people regard them as the enemy and can sadly furnish evidence for doing so. Police have become increasingly politicised and invisible when you need them. Jeff Mander points out, 'We live in an age where pizza gets to your house before the police do.' Today's police are vastly different from what they used to be. James Joyce's observation gets the point over here:

There's no police like Holmes.

The policeman is being *ordered* to target certain behaviours rather than allowing him to use his own discretion and common sense. To make crime figures look decent, the police can be directed to prosecute easy targets as catching real villains is getting harder and harder with the endless production and constant changes in expert laws along with the growing rejection of common sense evidence and witnesses. Let's hope it is not the policeman's own choice to operate as he does. Every aspect of police duty is becoming governed by expert laws, rules and regulations perhaps more than other jobs – well, maybe not; we are all gagged and bound. How police talk to offenders, what they say, how they make the arrest, how they take them to the police station, how they make the charge, how they collect, record and present evidence and so on and so forth, are all subject to strict directives of political correctness. Expert theories are used to try to programme his every action. To create a perfect robotic policeman is an ideal for experts. Scientists are working on it. In the meantime, the human policeman is being treated like a mechanical being. With modern police dress he looks like one. This is, of course, a consequence of the long held view of modern science that the universe, including man, operates like a great machine, more recently, like an electric one – the computer. Such a view reflects the main aim of science – and many of the power elite – which is to control behaviour of objects, events and people. One wisdom is:

> Co-operating with nature is the act of a wise man; trying to be her master is the act of a fool.

To do the duty prescribed by experts, the policeman would have to know their laws inside out. Being aware of all the expert laws, let alone memorising, interpreting and applying them is mind boggling and impossible. To keep up with the persistent production and changes of laws, sees the policeman attending courses of increasing diversity. Like science, law experts split 'justice' into more and more parts in which to specialise and develop new laws. Human rights, welfare rights, ethnic rights, parents' rights, women's rights, gay rights and prisoners' rights are a small sample. Excess rights leads to wrongs. There is a common definition of experts:

> Experts are those who specialise in knowing more and more about less and less.

A policeman's work gets more prolific. For a slight misdemeanour, he may have to fill in almost as many forms as for arresting a serial-rapist killer. At the present count, thirteen pages seems a minimum, while at maximum, the sky is the limit. The number of expert laws a policeman is supposed to know to do his job, is impossible – like the rest of us really. It is not the policeman's fault that most criminals escape justice on technicalities or otherwise. Even when he arrests a criminal time and time again, the wrong-doer can be out on the street in less than a day to carry on offending. The teenager who had done 300 crimes, mentioned earlier, is a case in point. It is not the will of the police, common sense, justice or the better judgement or the will of the majority that allow such incidents. It is the self-defeating laws created by never-ending impractical expert theories:

> Nothing is as practical as common sense.

There are almost as many interpretations of expert laws as there are lawyers. R. Waldo Emerson reminds us, 'An appeal court is when you ask one court to show contempt for another court.' The public image that expert legal justice is more reliable, objective and valid than common sense justice is a myth. Interpretation of technicalities and complexities permeating expert laws are specialities of expert lawyers. In this way, they create a need for their own existence, harmful though it is. Prosecutors try to interpret a particular law or technicality in one way and defence lawyers in another way to suit their purpose, not to serve justice. Recently, a report gave an example of different interpretations of technicalities in law. The result of one interpretation is likely to allow 500 prisoners to have their sentences slashed. Eventually, it could turn out that thousands of criminals are set free early rather than just 500. Some of them are highly violent and include brutal sex offenders. Large groups of criminals could be circulating amongst us sooner than anyone expected. As a consequence of other expert technicalities and interpretations of the law, these early release prisoners could claim compensation that could cost the tax payer one hundred and forty million pounds sterling and much, much more in the final analysis, especially social costs. If someone says their compensation is a stigma and stressful could they get compensation for being compensated?

Costs can never be counted in money alone.

Policemen must despair as much as the rest of us. They were the ones who spent much time and effort pursuing, arresting and processing the criminals in the first place. Probably, they may have to do so again and again in many cases. Linked to the pressures put upon the policeman by experts is that applied to the majority of us. We expect a policeman to have the wisdom of Solomon, the patience of Job and the capabilities of Superman. His political and legal masters seem to demand that he arrest a highly violent criminal who is possibly trying to beat him to a pulp or kill him, without leaving a bruise on the assailant. If the criminal is marked, there are often screams of 'police brutality' or cries for an 'independent enquiry'. Police have been made to feel they cannot do right for doing wrong. To say how much pressure the policeman has to endure daily, he deserves much praise for struggling on, often with good grace. Like the majority of us, the policeman is not a superman. He is human and, like all of us, he makes errors. Common sense laws apply to the policeman like anybody else. Three interrelated laws are illustrative:

No one is perfect.

Everybody makes mistakes.

There is good and bad in all of us.

The British 'bobby' has been known the world over for the application of common sense in the performance of his duty. He did not earn his reputation by exhibiting great knowledge of expert theories of law. Now his rating has gone down. Expert laws have severely restricted his use of common sense. The policeman is probably more frustrated and angry than anyone. He is at the forefront and at the receiving end of injustices created by expert theories. Any success at preventing crime and catching offenders is in spite of expert laws, not because of them. It is no longer realistic to expect police to protect us. Ordinary police have been rendered impotent by their political masters and their politically correct superior–inferior officers who rise in the ranks to direct immoral acts. Joe Orton in his 1966 play *Loot* uses the lines, 'The British police force used to be run by men of integrity. That is a mistake and has been rectified.'

Experts have literally ruled out the use of common sense by police and others.

How many times do we read headlines that say: 'Police hands are tied' or 'Police unable to act' or other similar statements? Who is largely responsible for making the police and law so impotent? It is not the ordinary police themselves. Though society tolerates gross injustices via political correctness, it goes against the grain of our inner nature. It is not the traditional criminals this time who are the main offenders. There are no prizes for identifying those who have the power to impose destructive theories and laws on us. Prizes can be earned by the majority of people if they do something about this unwise state of affairs. Rewards of greater justice would come from appropriate action. Yes, we have to have a revolution. It could improve most aspects of people's lives. Justice is a necessary thread that is woven throughout the fabric of a life and determines its quality. It is essential for balance or harmony which is a basic characteristic of nature. One common wisdom that experts seem immune to is:

We should learn from our mistakes.

Experts have immunised themselves and us against common sense with regular injections of science and reason that are separated from their moral origins. They promote imbalance and disharmony. Unfortunately, too many of us have been passive patients. In this respect, we are as much to blame as the experts who have doctored us. We must have due regard for the majority's lack of effective influence on minorities and expert lawyers are a minority, but like criminals, a growing minority:

The whole affects the part; in respect of justice the majority of us have been complicit in its destruction.

We have paid dearly for law-makers to destroy our common sense police, freedoms and morality. One Welsh proverb is, 'The houses of lawyers are roofed with the skins of litigants.' It is hard to imagine that ordinary policemen who put their lives at risk on a regular basis for the benefit of others are complicit in lawyers' motives of money. At times, we and the police seem to see some justice done. This happens when expert law interpretation coincides with a common sense law. It can also occur when juries ignore expert laws and use common sense. Sensible acts like this have become increasingly rare, particularly over the past twenty years or so, though expert law has always been problematic; Voltaire says, 'I was never ruined but twice: once when I lost a law suit and once when I won one.' With the passage of time, expert theories and laws have made common sense illegal. Several decades ago, when common sense was used more, Rabbie Burns, the poet from Scotland, rightly mocked expert law in relation to common sense:

But what his common sense came short,
He eked out wi' law, man.

Today, now that common sense has been banned in almost all our institutions and replaced by expert theories and laws, Burns' lines would have to change to properly reflect modern society to read:

But what his expert law came short,
He eked out wi' common sense, man.

Expert theories and laws have become common. Everyone is beginning to talk like expert lawyers and behavioural scientists, even in pubs and nursery schools. One tiny tot, having watched a television programme on children's rights, telephoned the police to put his mother in jail because he had to pack his toys away and go to bed at bedtime. This child was imitating the philosophy that science and other power elites have bestowed upon us, 'If it is possible to do it, do it' – sounds like Mick Jagger's sexual technique. Sadly, science, lawyers and an increasing number of us have little regard for consequences of self-centred actions. Can't help it – culture or genes innit?

> **Often what is legally right is morally wrong.**

We know our individual rights. Teenagers leaving school can have much knowledge of their rights even when they can hardly read or write or show any social responsibility. We can produce endless reasons to justify our rights. Common sense or wisdom needs no justification in a balanced society. If a man strokes and feeds his pet cat, he does not have to justify the act to anyone. It is a natural and common sense thing to do. To let the cat starve through the man's laziness or to kick the cat due to a bad day at the office, requires justification. It needs to be rationalised or explained away. Lawyers recognised that the pen or mouth is mightier than the sword for making money. They are financial winners even when they lose. Lawyers are exceptions to the old saying that words are cheap. The more lawyers specialised, the more laws became separated from wisdom or common sense as a whole. In turn, law gave rise to more and more expert laws which favoured the parts (minorities) at the expense of the larger whole (majority of people). For the majority, silence is out of balance and is no longer golden, it's yellow. We have become cowards. Demonax points to the futility of expert laws in relation to the well-behaved majority and a criminal minority. There are no reasons for them:

> **All laws are useless, for good men do not need them and bad men are made no better by them.**

Like scientists in modern physics, lawyers have been obsessed with parts to the neglect of the whole. One of the common sense sayings that points to the folly of both expert scientists and lawyers is:

> **Not being able to see the wood for the trees.**

Put in a legal frame of reference the wisdom would be:

Lawyers cannot see justice for the laws.

Enough injustices occur by foolishness, mistake, accident or chance without expert laws adding to them. Throughout history, whenever experts have torn reasoning from its roots in wisdom, injustices have resulted. Ancient Chinese, Egyptians, Greeks, Romans and all other cultures have complained about expert laws and lawyers. All cultures continued to do so down the centuries. Lord Halifax, in his era, noted the concerns of the English:

If the laws could speak for themselves, they would complain
of lawyers in the first place.

People's anger is not new, just greater. Today, the cumulative effects of past laws and injustices together with the present rapid rate of production of new laws are destroying us. Common sense is an endangered species, close to extinction. In 1996, two people sold a house in which they were squatting for £100,000 and were allowed to keep the money by an expert law from the earlier part of the 1800s. The majority, who have worked hard all their lives with no hope of buying such an expensive house at one fell swoop, were not amused. Now, there is more to be anxious about than in the time of Lord Halifax. Today we have many more expert laws and lawyers. Experts rationalise that what they are doing is good for us. Even if this were true, as one common saying indicates:

You can have too much of a good thing.

I love strawberries, but being forced to eat several bucketfuls would probably kill me. However, expert laws were not a good thing in the first place. In spite of the great number of injustices, like majorities in past histories, we have permitted experts to continue separating reason from wisdom. Experts give the impression that the more we perfect rationality or reason, the more we perfect justice. This obsession of experts with reasoning and logic is inherent in the claims of Sir Edward Coke and Sir Jake Powell:

The law which is the perfection of reason.

For nothing is law that is not reason.

Such views run counter to common sense laws or the laws of nature. For example:

Few things in the world are perfect.

Reason alone is a dangerous substitute for wisdom.

A common sense saying is, 'Nothing is perfect' but, compared with expert laws, common sense laws give more justice more of the time. Even common sense laws cannot satisfy everyone constantly, all of the time, particularly anti-social or unwise people:

Nothing can suit all of the people all of the time.

With increasing specialisation and professionalism in the legal system, the more expert justice has become materialistic and devious. The spiralling number of expert laws are of greatest benefit to lawyers themselves. Expert laws need experts to interpret their technicalities and meanings of the convoluted language seen in legal documents. Without experts, who would possibly be able to understand the language of law? This suits experts down to the ground. It is what makes them charge the fees that they do. Using common sense laws, known by everyone, would make lawyers' expertise unsaleable and they know it. They are unlikely to lobby for the restoration of common sense laws. Experts have blinded us to our own common sense and thus increased their own power:

In the world of the blind, the one-eyed man is king.

Justice deals with good and bad behaviour, that is, with morality. There is no evidence, scientific, religious or any other kind, to show that political law-makers, judges and other lawyers know any more about good and bad, or right and wrong than the man in the street or even criminals. If anything, the reverse is true. Experts are the ones responsible for creation, interpretation and administration of laws that negate morality, justice, wisdom and nature itself. Lawyers' dishonour is added to further by their demands for huge fees to maintain a lucrative life-style and increase the power of an ever-expanding empire. The consequences of the actions of these dictators of law are, violence out of control and general degrading of society. Amazingly, lawyers make us pay them money for prohibiting us using common sense. George Herbert got it right in his conclusion about experts:

Lawyers' houses are built on the heads of fools.

The wife of a shadow cabinet minister in the House of Parliament is said to earn £200,000 a year as a lawyer. Compared to some other lawyers, this is considered 'modest' by some legal eagles and is, by no means, the best of salaries. It could take many ordinary people a dozen years or more to earn such a figure. A case can occur where a multi-millionaire has swindled ordinary people out of their life's savings and pleads poverty whilst he and his family continue to live like millionaires. If such a person is declared legally bankrupt, lawyers still get their lucrative fees. It is called giving 'legal aid' from the public purse. Legal bankruptcy means, in too many cases, that rich criminals get to keep the proceeds of their crime and, at the same time, get the tax payer to foot the bill for an expensive trial. Legal aid costs the British public millions of pounds annually. No wonder this is so, for it is basically lawyers who decide on the distribution of legal aid. Who do the offenders have to pay with their legal aid? It is the lawyers. Legal experts are world renowned for their deviousness. We have all been legalised. Kay Ingram gives an example when she says, 'Women prefer men to have something tender about them – especially the legal kind.'

Lawyers detach reason from wisdom to 'prove' black is white.

As well as lawyers receiving high fees for their services, they, like politicians, get additional expenses and perks, many out of the public purse. One judge's accommodation alone for just one week has been as much as £10,000 sterling. Another famous legal 'big-wig' rationalised this expense saying judges had to be apart from the public to be more objective in the performance of their duties. Again, put in perspective, £10,000 sterling is more than many people can earn in a year. Judges are transported in chauffeur driven limousines. Roads are cleared so as not to inconvenience their cars. They are given a team of support personnel who cater for their every need. What is ironical is that judges get protection from the violent society they have helped create. Like all powerful experts, they are accorded very high status in national and local communities. To say there is a growing lack of confidence in the justice system is a gross misjudgment of public outrage. There is great objectivity or agreement about this feeling:

Ignoring public sentiment is experts' greatest skill.

In our modern materialistic society, people can use expert laws to sue for financial damages for almost anything and everything. This includes criminals in jail. One story tells of a prisoner who was going to sue the warden because the inmate's breakfast was late. Perhaps the prisoner suffered stress, or painful unfulfilled expectancy syndrome. An important point about compensation cases is that expert laws and lawyers create them. Without the backing of lawyers, many compensation cases would not be thought of, let alone get to court. Who amongst us could not sue for scores of grievances? Long ago Petronius was aware, like most people before and after him, of the self-serving interests of expert law:

Law has bread and butter on it.

Another example beggars belief – well not really, it is getting to be normal. A grossly over-weight lady gave an interview to the media. In it she said that she wanted to sue the government for not warning her that eating mountains of hamburgers and ice-cream made you fat. I never did catch up with whether she pressed her case through the courts. What we do know is that expert laws and lawyers have encouraged and made possible such compensation claims. It is a boom area for lawyers' personal economies. If the people don't bust them, who will? I have stressed the dangers of using reason separated from common sense. Some of the growing number of compensation claims are good examples of this separation:

You can find all kinds of reasons for anything if you try.

Groucho Marx, for example, when caught kissing a chorus girl by his wife, is reputed to have said he was not kissing her at all, he was merely whispering in her mouth. Any number of common sense sayings or wisdoms apply to the hamburger lady, to many other claimants and greedy lawyers. I am sure you can readily supply many which are very fitting. After seeing the type of compensation cases that have succeeded, there is not a single person in the country who could not sue for a whole host of things that have happened to them. The laws are such that claiming compensation could become a full-time occupation for us all. Perhaps this is the politicians' secret weapon for rationalising unemployment problems:

If experts reversed all their theories and laws, they would be closer to reality, justice and wisdom.

Number, complexity and technicalities of expert laws have made for longer and longer legal processes including trials. The case of O.J. Simpson in the United States of America went on month after month. Is there any common sense person anywhere who believes the length of the trial was in the interests of justice? The length of this trial was certainly in the financial interests of the lawyers. Their more than substantial fees are not unrelated to the length of the trial unless my primary school mathematics are failing me. The O.J. Simpson affair was an image to show starring expert lawyers parading their interminable rationalisation skills. It had little to do with justice, common sense or wisdom. Expert justice, as opposed to common sense justice, seems to depend more on the ability to afford slick, fashionable lawyers than on what is right and wrong. Expert laws have fashions; they can be seen on the pratwalk:

Expert law is the goose that lays the golden egg for lawyers.

If the O.J. Simpson trial had been limited to a day or two, it could have cut down the experts' lengthy rationalisations and focused minds on relevant or more common sense matters. An unwritten rule for experts seems to be that the longer a trial lasts, the more justice you get. In practice, so general is its use by expert lawyers, it is becoming a pervasive practice, fallacious though it is. Its power is growing as trials are getting more and more drawn out. Some people have waited ten years or more for expert justice to take its course. Many have given up because they cannot afford to go on any longer. Even Queen Victoria said, 'The law is not a moral profession.' Lawyers can drag out even ordinary, everyday transaction to their benefit. Buying or selling a house in England is an example:

Time and tide wait for no man, except, it seems, expert lawyers.

Often, it takes several months for lawyers to deal with a house transaction. Sometimes it is an underpaid clerk who does the real work and completes all that is necessary for the deal to go ahead in a few short hours. However, lawyers charge hundreds or thousands of pounds for their expert services in this everyday matter. Hence, the transaction is delayed for months. To admit to customers that the work took just a few short hours and then charge such huge fees would look like what it is – unethical practice. Dragging out the transaction for months makes the lawyers and the prices they charge appear respectable. In our society, image has become more important than truth, wisdom or substance. Our outrage with expert laws and lawyers has been festering and growing for centuries. In 1793, Bishop Gilbert Burnet wrote:

> The law of England is the greatest grievance of the nation,
> very expensive and dilatory.

House purchase and sale and many other transactions should be what they are: when stripped of expert legal trappings, very simple. An uncomplicated bill of sale, rather like a car log book, would do. Expert laws encourage a person to go back on their word for financial gain. In the property and housing market, this legalised cheating is called 'gazumping'. We must apply common sense laws. In the case of property transaction, the following is one of the many that are relevant:

> A man's word is his bond.

Indeed, it is difficult to think of any situation that involves transactions to which this law is not highly pertinent. It certainly has meaning, relevance, and applicability to relationships in the family, in schools, in business and everywhere else, though it is increasingly ignored. Expert laws encourage dishonesty. You can be involved in a car accident and know full well it was your fault. What does your insurance company advise you to do? They often advise you to say nothing. Saying something could damage their greedy legal position. Such an attitude is to the benefit of the guilty and to the suffering of the innocent. Of lawyers, Mark Twain reminds us, 'To succeed in other trades capacity must be shown; in the law concealment of it will do.' The guilty, in particular, chant the experts' rule, which sadly does not apply to all men:

A man is innocent until proven guilty.

This gives criminals further opportunity to cheat. Innocents do not need the rule. You will notice the reflection of the legal rule in the widespread view of scientific experts, even though they have made many mistakes:

Nothing can be accepted as true fact until science says so.

Another experts' rule for lawyers and criminals, which would be unnecessary if common sense laws were applied, follows but, again, it does not apply to everyone:

A man has a legal right to silence.

What a pity lawyers do not take this legal right to keep their mouths shut. Lawyers themselves recite these with righteous indignation if their views about their clients' rights are questioned or, in a trial, when non-scientific evidence like common sense is used against them. When we know we are guilty, for instance in a car accident, we are definitely not innocent until some expert lawyer or scientist proves us guilty. Expert laws promote dishonesty. Common sense laws have been reversed:

Traditional value: Honesty is the best policy.

Modern value: Honesty is not the best policy.

The practice of common sense law has been sunk in a swamp of expert laws, lies and rights. We must revive the traditional honesty in all our institutions and endeavours. Lawyers specialise in interpreting facts so that their meanings are slanted to benefit their clients and their own lines of reasoning. The majority of us are getting pretty good at these kinds of rationalisations. Experts should be models to be copied but they are not. P.C. Knox, The Attorney General, was asked by President Theodore Roosevelt for a legal justification for the acquisition of the Panama Canal. Knox replied, 'Oh, Mr President do not let so great an achievement suffer from any taint of legality.' Criminals are as good as experts. They get the same amount of practice as them. We are amateurs, though, compared to the real professionals. Lawyers train their clients to give answers to questions to put themselves in a good light irrespective of truth or justice. Winning is the aim:

Professional criminals, political law-makers and lawyers
share a common trait, they have little regard for truth and
justice.

To discredit witnesses, lawyers will get them to admit they have told a lie or two in the past. Then later, if the witness produces evidence that does not fit the lawyer's line of reasoning, the lawyer will say something like, 'We have already established that this man lies. How can we believe anything he says now?' Common sense tells us that because a person has told a few lies in the past, does not mean he is generally a liar. If this were the case, we would all be branded as liars – judges and lawyers as well. Are there any people who have never told lies at any time? Most of us have told lies at some time and admitting it is being honest:

Finding a man who has never told a lie is difficult; finding
law-makers and lawyers who don't lie on a regular basis is
almost impossible.

There is a cultural shift in modern times away from simple, open, honesty to political and legal, jargonised deceit. Will Rogers points to the modernisation of truth when he says that nowadays people are letting their lawyers be their guides rather than their consciences. Lawyers also use scientific or forensic evidence to suit their own purposes rather than truth or justice. They give scientific facts meanings they do not have, as do scientific experts. In court, one scientific expert will say a set of facts has a particular meaning. Another scientific specialist will say the same set of facts has a very different, or even opposite, meaning. There is not much objectivity in such situations. Indeed, it is too often less than zero. Scientific experts demonstrate the very opposite of objectivity – perfect disagreements on the meaning of a set of scientific facts. Thus, scientific evidence is highly questionable. A main claim to fame for science is its so–called objectivity. One upside is:

Legal trials have shown the objectivity of science and legal
laws leave much to be desired.

Common sense and science agree that facts are relatively meaningless in themselves. It is their meanings and relationships that are crucial. Science has concentrated too much on processes and producing facts without coming up with much in the way of real causes, consequences or meanings. Common sense laws are highly meaningful to everyone including criminals. Meaning is a necessary ingredient of wisdom. We can train a parrot, witnesses and public officials to recite scientific facts and legalese where meaning is minimal. Sterne said of science, which contains rationality:

Science may be learned by rote but wisdom is not.

A judge can make nonsense of real meanings and justice in his 'summing up'. His interpretation and insistence on expert legal technicalities can force a jury to give the opposite decision, of innocence or guilt, to what their common sense tells them is right and just. The essence of law-makers and lawyers seems to be 'Let's identify what the people including juries want and then stop them doing it.' Laws are so bad, expert reforms are always coming forth. Mr Justice Astbury puts reforms into context when he exclaimed, 'Reform! Reform! Aren't things bad enough already?' One aspect of the legal system that still retains an element of common sense is using juries. A jury is supposed to be made up of ordinary people chosen at random. This means they are not experts in law and, according to what I have said before, are more likely to rely on common sense than expert lawyers. Common sense has been devalued in proportion to the rise in experts down the ages, but never so rapidly as in recent years. There have always been some experts who have retained their recognition of the importance of the man in the street. Caecilius Statius reminded experts that:

There is often wisdom under a shabby cloak.

Even the process of selecting the jury at random has been corrupted by lawyers. The O.J. Simpson trial showed that jurors themselves are tried before the real trial begins. If biased lawyers do not like the jurors' responses to their heavily loaded questions when interrogating jurors before the real trial gets underway, some of these ordinary people can end up as non-starters. We have to increase the real involvement and freedom of jurors to use their common sense. H.L. Mencken highlights our feelings about expert courtroom practices:

Courtroom: A place where Jesus Christ and Judas Iscariot would be equals with the betting odds in favour of Judas.

To regain true justice, juries have to be selected completely at random. If the random selection included ex-criminals who had served their time, they should serve on the jury. Criminals know as much about right and wrong as any one of us. Jurors would do the questioning of anyone they wished including defendants. Often in trials, jurors are keen to ask common sense questions as the trial goes along. Expert laws prevent this action. Jurors would use common sense laws, which we all know, and would replace expert lawyers and laws. Common sense laws are based on millions of years of evolution and experience. By comparison, expert laws are new. Francis Bacon highlighted a difference between expert and common sense laws:

> To be wise by rule and by experience are utterly
> opposite principles.

Not only would juries decide on innocence and guilt, they would decide on punishments also. These types of juries would represent the people far more accurately than experts. Punishments by juries would be of their own choice and not chosen from a list laid down by experts. Jurors would allow offenders and their victims or relatives to say what they think would be a fitting punishment at the end of a trial. Criminals, lawyers and other experts want to reap what they have not sown which is the opposite of a common wisdom:

> You should only reap what you have sown.

These new juries with real powers would be called Justices of The Peace and would serve for about, say, a month at a time. Then they would be replaced by another group chosen at random and so on and so forth. Justices of The Peace would be in session at local level every day. Cases ranging from misdemeanour to murder would be dealt with by them. Since these groups of Justices of The Peace would be widespread throughout the country and in constant use, a single individual may be called to serve on numerous occasions in his lifetime. This gives true meaning to ordinary people having a stake in society:

> The man who has a true stake in justice, has a real stake
> in everything.

When politicians talk of ordinary people being stake-holders or share-holders, they are referring to material or economic gains or inducements. Politicians, in this way, are appealing to the worse side of human nature – to greed and consumerism. Being regular, active participants in the justice system gives true meaning to people's lives, to their peace of mind and quality of being. Justice has to be taken back into your own hands. Amongst other things, it is noticeable that the power elite like politicians, lawyers and people from other various realms of the world of celebrities, are treated differently by the law. Many from the power elite have some things in common, one of which is how they approach situations and problems with an open mouth. This new state of affairs, returning to common sense that is, can be achieved by ordinary people exerting their will and better judgment:

United we stand, divided we fall.

What we all appreciate is that, if something is not done soon, our predicament is going to get irretrievably worse, if it is not there already. By putting justice back into the hands of the people, great financial saving will be made. More importantly, huge savings are possible in social costs. An additional benefit would be that some of the literally unjust monies given to lawyers would be paid to the new Justices of The Peace. There would be, for them, a good day's pay for a good day's justice. Amongst the many conflicting characteristics of human nature is the desire to serve our fellow man in a really meaningful and valued manner. The involvement of being a Justice of The Peace achieves this. It gives people control over their lives rather than being at the mercy of experts and their unnatural or synthetic theories. Enfolded in true justice is as much freedom and peace of mind as there is to be had. Down the ages, justice has always been recognised as the foundation stone of the better society. First from Agesilaus and then from D.D. Field we have:

Justice is the first virtue.

Above all things is justice.

Stanislaw J. Lee observes, 'The dispensing of injustice is always in the right hands.' One of the arguments put forward by politicians and lawyers for the necessity of having all these expert laws, judges and other professional lawyers is to make the application of justice fairer – more standardised or objective. Their strategy does not seem to be working. Judges and magistrates give widely differing interpretations to expert laws and punishments. Increasing criticism is being aimed at judges and magistrates for their inconsistent application of laws. With a prolific growth in number and complexity of unfathomable and unwise expert laws, the chance of getting much consistency or justice gets more remote. The French playwright Jean Giraudoux suggests, 'No poet ever interpreted nature as freely as lawyers interpret truth.' There is much agreement about common sense. It is more standardised. Experts' rationalisations to promote their own existence have to be viewed with common sense:

Self-praise or interest is not the best recommendation.

Expert laws have made police and other instruments of justice impotent in protecting us. It is inevitable that people would take the law into their own hands. When people have tried to protect themselves, experts have treated them worse than the criminals who attacked them. People are becoming more organised in doing what expert laws are failing to do – protecting the innocent majority. For example, in one small community near where I grew up, people are using strong men to deal with the local criminals. Like police of old, they believe there is much justice in a truncheon:

There is more than one way to crack an egg.

Quite often local people and police know who is committing crimes in their area. Criminals cannot be taken to task as evidence complicated enough to satisfy experts' laws gets harder and harder to obtain. Thus, these strong men go to known wrongdoers, question them and find out who is responsible for particular crimes. They then approach the thieves, retrieve the stolen goods and return them to their rightful owners. If the guilty hide their offences from the questioners, they get punished in one way or another. For a violent crime committed on an old lady they will be given a good hiding. The victims do have a say in how their assailants are punished. A common wisdom from Dryden fits the need of people:

Self-defence is nature's oldest law.

As in the film *The Godfather* local criminals are made an offer they can't refuse. Perhaps a worst punishment could be if these local vigilantes decided to sing, say from *The Mikado*, to their anti-social brethren, 'Awaiting the sensation of a short, sharp shock from a cheap and chippy chopper on a big black block.' Using local strong men is not seen by the majority as ideal, but they see it as having more justice than expert laws which they have tried time and again without success. Ordinary people did take to heart the slogan of experts: 'Don't take the law into your own hands.' This has been a potent part of our cultural conditioning since birth. Now we are beginning to think laws are not safe in the hands of experts and that:

Justice belongs in the hands of the people.

Politicians and lawyers give the impression that the more laws they make the closer to perfect justice they get. A parallel of this view exists in science. The belief is that more science will produce progress toward certainty and perfect explanations, prediction and control of things. These positions of experts defy wisdom and common experience. Our judgments are not always perfect by any manner or means. We make mistakes, though we try not to do so. Actually this is not quite true. Traditional crimes are being defined out of existence. You'll soon be able to get away with murder, rape, stealing and so on so long as you say politically correct things and do not commit politically incorrecticide. Even using common sense laws, there will always be injustices. Many common sense laws point this out themselves. Here are three old wisdoms to illustrate. The first two are from Ovid while the third is from Pliny The Elder:

The judgment of men is fallible.

Chance dispenses life with unequal justice.

No one is wise all the time.

Binnie Barnes' observation fits many politicians and lawyers. Barnes says, 'He's the kind of bore who is here today and here tomorrow.' In some ways ordinary people are doing what high profile politicians, lawyers and other expert celebrities are doing. They are having bodyguards or 'minders' to look after their welfare. When officials of the expert laws of the land won't protect you – who will? Organised opposition to their so-called expert laws and justice is going to grow further. Private protection armies and militant groups are going to use increasingly violent methods and more destructive technologies to achieve their ends. Self-protection individuals and groups are striking back on a small scale. This is going to change and more expert law-makers and administrators are going to be targets along with other power elites like pop and sport stars. Ordinary people are getting to trust local hard men more than they trust experts who are remote, destructive and will not hear their pleas:

> Better the devil you know than the one you don't.

Experts have destroyed common sense laws. They believe that you have to devise more and more laws to reduce crime. In other words their rule is, 'More laws, more lawfulness and justice.' This is the exact opposite of the common sense law, 'Excess in one thing leads to its opposite.' We have shown one example of it, 'More haste, less speed.' In the legal framework the common sense law is:

> More laws, less justice.

Common sense laws are not perfect. Indeed, there are several common sense laws themselves that emphasise this point. Also, real justice will not suit everyone, especially criminals. Livy said:

> No law can possibly meet the convenience of everyone:
> We must be satisfied if it be beneficial on the whole and to
> the majority.

We do not need expert laws. They create injustice. The application of common sense laws to all the instances of injustices cited in this book so far and any others you know of would have secured better justice. Two related laws alone cover many situations and would have achieved far more justice than any number of expert laws:

> Do unto others . . .

> Do not disturb the peace of others.

I notice in today's newspaper that the Home Secretary (our top law man) has given special powers to the police to deal with drunken, offensive youths roaming the streets. Since when have the police to be given special power to do their job? If special powers have to be given for this common behaviour, are we to believe that in the galaxy of expert laws there is not a single one that applies to this situation? This speaks volumes for expert laws and lawyers. The reputation of lawyers is illustrated when a judge asked a man who was defending himself if he was guilty or innocent. The man replied, 'Of course I'm innocent. If I was guilty, I'd have got myself a lawyer.'

Common sense sayings are nature's laws put into words.

Fortunately, there are few, but an increasing few, law-makers and administrators of laws beginning to speak out against the unjust nature and number of laws. We are even importing laws. What proportion of our laws is thrust upon us from Brussels? There are other experts who feel the same, but do not speak, due to political correctness and the fact that greed has overcome their conscience or better judgement. Some experts also agree that modern expert laws have focused almost exclusively on individual rights and freedoms at the expense of the welfare of the majority. Experts have fostered opportunism, great selfishness and the cult of personality and image. More than this, political law-makers and their acolytes, lawyers, have created myths that we have been conditioned to, or even forced to, accept. By creating unfathomable legal language or esoteric jargon that only specialist lawyers can interpret, these vain, legal-babble merchants, with regular law changes, are constantly reinforcing the notion they are indispensable or necessary to our existence and justice. Who was it who suggested that we could develop an attachment for lawyers – preferably one that fits over their mouths?

Laws that the people do not understand are immoral and destroy justice.

If, as Bertrand Russell suggested, few people can be happy unless they hate some other person, nation or creed, then law-makers and lawyers must be a main source of happiness for most people. Plato said that whatever deceives seems to produce a magical enchantment. Bad boys are rarely short of girlfriends. Perhaps politicians and lawyers are just trying to entertain us with their cheating and lying. Most people like to entertain rather than bore. Well, Plato may have a point; we tend to admire people who can do things better than us and this could include cheating and lying. One fact, however, is that many young people want to study politics and law. It is logical that politicians and lawyers prefer their expert laws to common sense laws and justice. With a return to common wisdom or morality and truth, many politicians and lawyers would be unemployable or in jail:

> **Law-makers and lawyers defining who are criminals, liars and cheats is ironic.**

In summary then, we have to dispense with the services of professional lawyers such as judges, barristers and solicitors. We have to replace them with local teams of randomly selected Justices of The Peace who will be replaced by other people from the community at regular, short intervals. These Justices of The Peace will do all the questioning as well as deciding on innocence or guilt and on punishments for the guilty. True justice must be taken back into the hand of the people. Any just legal system mirrors common sense and its laws with real, day to day involvement of the citizenry at large. Wisdoms that have been tried and successfully tested for many thousands of years that are to be found in the common sense sayings must be revived. There is an increasing number of instances where sanctions do not fit the misdeeds and where some people are over-acclaimed and some are not valued highly enough. Such is the reversal of common sense values that failure is rewarded and it is enshrined in contracts by lawyers especially for the power-broking, celebrity elite. It is common sense that:

> **Punishments must fit the crimes.**

> **Rewards must fit the achievements.**

CHAPTER 4

Your Personality and Behaviour, My Pet Cat and other Experts

Experts try to blind us with science, legalese and psychobabble.

Common sensing

The over-emphasis of physical science and expert legal systems on separating things and focusing on smaller and smaller parts is reflected in the science of human behaviour. Personality theory is part of behavioural or social science. Behavioural science is separated into such areas as psychology, social psychology, sociology, political science, economics and so forth. Like physical science, these areas were split into smaller and smaller parts. For example, psychology, which is the study of an individual's behaviour, was divided into further parts. Personality, motivation, learning, intelligence, perception and attitude are illustrative. In one way or another there is a science of anything and everything. Is there anything that we do not have a *psychology of* nowadays? We even have a psychology of psychology and a science of science not to mention a psychology and a sociology of science. There is, of course, psychology of sex. Some research showed men fantasise of being in bed with two women. Women quite like the idea too; it gives them someone to talk to when the man falls asleep. Specialisms get narrower:

> Observation of smaller and smaller things can make for a small mind.

All the common wisdoms I used earlier to put physical science into perspective apply to behavioural science and all that could be repeated here. This comes as no surprise as behavioural science tried to ape the physical science. Physics, in particular, was ideal to be imitated as it was regarded as the queen of science. Physics was seen to have great control over its experimental procedures. It had accurate measuring instruments and could use mathematical calculations in its methods. Some hard-nosed physicists and other physical scientists said that behavioural science was not really a science at all. With human behaviour, factors being studied could not be controlled or measured easily as temperature, weight, length, volume, speed, density and so forth. Physical scientists also pointed out that things behavioural science wanted to measure could not be seen or observed and observation was crucial to real science. When it was pointed out that the main concept in physics, time, could not be seen either, physicists replied that this was different. They had clocks of great accuracy didn't they? 'When does Zurich stop at this train?' asked Albert Einstein. Expert time measurement is a copy of parts of nature's rhythms:

> Science's attitude is, until experts measure something, it has no real existence or meaning.

The major mission of behavioural science is the same as all other science, to establish laws. Behavioural science developed measuring instruments such as intelligence tests, personality inventories, attitude scales and so on and used the scientific method of the physical scientists. Numbers or quantities were given to behaviours like intelligence so that mathematics and statistics could be used as in the highly respected physical science. Like the physical science, behavioural science aimed to describe, explain, predict and control behaviour. A key aim of science is to make all events predictable. If they achieved this central aim, imagine what life would be like. Who would want to go and see sports matches where the results were entirely predictable? Certainty could make us into efficient machines or computers that, with technological advances, never broke down and were totally predictable. Establishing accurate predictions, or certainty, which is a major aim of science, can neglect the effective exploration including opposites that common sense or wisdom insists is the reality of nature. People seek uncertainty, chance or risk as well as their opposites, certainty, predictability and security. If science achieved its aim of making all things predictable, life would become relatively meaningless.

Here is a fact that some of you may not know. Painful though it is to them, most scientists will admit the truth. It is no fairy tale:

> Children's comics and science fiction writers have made far more accurate predictions than 'real' science.

As mentioned previously, physical science purports to be amoral. Scientists say science has no morality, it cannot say what is right or wrong or good or bad. This is seen as a necessary condition to get pure knowledge, scientists maintain. The fact that metal expands when it is heated is neither good nor bad, it just is a fact. Wonder if this applies to sexual expansors or hot things used for torture? Similarly, this principle of not being able to tell good from bad applies to behavioural science, say scientists. That personality measurements, for example, show that someone is an extrovert or an introvert does not say it is either good or bad. It is purely a fact of the matter, though not to people who regard these characteristics, who may view them as a pain or pleasure. Such a state of affairs is very fortunate for all, as the main concern of people the world over is good and bad behaviour. How we behave determines our quality of life. It reflects our morality:

> Social science like, physical science, claims it cannot contribute to wisdom which contains morality.

Although science says it cannot make any contribution to morality or wisdom, it does, in fact, have a tremendous impact on what is good or bad. It has replaced common sense which is laced with morality or wisdom. Though experts have separated knowledge into smaller and smaller parts, the separation of knowledge from morality has been far more destructive. Whereas science claims to produce amoral facts, common wisdom contains laws that integrate knowledge and morality and is concerned with meanings:

> To the extent that we are a scientific society, it seems we are, like science, dispensing with morality.

Intelligence is a central area of investigation in behavioural science. To study and purify knowledge about it, uncontaminated by human feelings or morality, intelligence was divided off from common sense and became a specialised field of study for some expert psychologists. Intelligence was seen mainly as abstract reasoning ability in language and mathematics. Tests were constructed to reflect and measure this abstract reasoning ability. By being divorced from common sense, the diversity, wholeness and concrete aspects of wisdom were lost:

> Intelligence testing detached from wisdom is misleading, unreliable and harmful.

Psychologists composed tests of what they considered was intelligence. Basically, they believed that the best example of intelligent behaviour was in academic performance – in verbal and numerical reasoning. Thus, their tests were made up of a sample of questions that were used in education institutions to train abstract reasoning in verbal and mathematical perform- ance. Their own expert reasoning or logic told them that, from scores on these academic abstract reasoning tests, they would be able to predict future academic performance. By using expert reason to predict expert reasoning, behavioural scientists expected good results. Rejecting wisdom, as experts have, by separating reasoning or logic from common sense, it was predictable experts would produce poor outcomes. One study of Cam- bridge University students showed that the predictive ability of intelligence tests was low, very low. Intelligence as measured by expert tests accounted for only about ten per cent of academic performance. That is, around ninety per cent of academic performance was due to something else – not intelligence:

> Psychologists can't see common sense for looking at their own false creation, expert intelligence.

We should be thankful that expert IQ tests are not 100 per cent predictive of academic performance. If they were, it could mean the whole education system and academic performance were like intelligence tests, devoid of wisdom. A few experts recognised that IQ tests measured narrow, abstract reasoning which was linear and convergent and did not tap creativity. Hence, some creativity or divergent thinking tests were devised. They used the opposite of convergent or rational thinking test items, namely, divergent thinking problems. However, keeping to the traditions of science, this approach still lacked wisdom and was detached too much from the greater whole. One question to ask experts about their studies of intelligence is:

> What new insights have the study and testing of intelligence achieved?

Who said that measuring an individual's intelligence was rather like measuring the temperature of an individual molecule of gas? Whatever the reply experts give, you can be sure that any of their so-called discoveries which might contain meaning relationships are more extensively and better expressed in common sense sayings. In reality, IQ tests and their disciples have obscured and corrupted the true knowledge, meaning and nature of human abilities. In spite of the powerful conditioning we have endured from experts and their followers to accept IQ testing as valid, we are still instinctively suspicious of them. Their widespread use has not stopped us regularly expressing our awareness of the tremendous limitations of expert ideas on intelligence and its measurement or testing. Everyday sayings make this obvious:

He seems very intelligent but lacks common sense.

She has tons of academic qualifications and not an ounce of common sense.

Intelligence is no substitute for common sense.

Dolly Parton was asked what she felt about the dumb blonde jokes and stereotype. She replied, 'It doesn't bother me, I know I'm not dumb and I know that I'm not blonde.' Would you say that Dolly's reply was intelligent or wise? Intelligence, like most expert creations, has been overrated in modern society due, in the main, to experts' claim to be able to measure it. Its logical abstract reasoning power is supposed to be the basis for effective decision making. Any meaningful knowledges of intelligence are grounded in wisdom. We speak of intelligent parenting, but we do not mean that mother and father have high scores on expert intelligence tests. The good parenting decisions are laced with emotion or feelings, as are all important decisions. What we are really talking about here is common sense. A few experts have begun to see a little light and are looking into the idea of emotional intelligence. In their struggle to maintain expert status, they have to tell us something we do not know or they could not be called experts. The notion of emotional intelligence is a little nearer to common sense than intelligence as measured by IQ tests. In a few cases, experts are catching up a little on the common sense of the ordinary man in the street. There are many instances when common sense is incorrectly called intelligence. So conditioned are we that many prefer to have our personalities described as intelligent, as defined by expert IQ tests, rather than being referred to as a common sense person:

We think with our feelings and feel with our thoughts.

Rejecting common wisdom as intelligence tests do is not, in reality, a very intelligent thing to do. Some experts have realised that by separating things excessively, many obvious, natural relationships are thrown away. Knowledge areas which were falsely separated by experts are being re-combined. We had physics, biology, chemistry, physiology, sociology and cybernetics for instance. Now, in addition, we have such areas as biophysics, biochemistry, physiological psychology, psycho-cybernetics and even quantum personality theories. In nature, opposites like division or separation and integration or combination go hand-in-hand. A fertilised egg in the womb is an example as are your family interactions and many processes at work, play or anywhere else:

Nature or common sense strives for balance between division and integration, experts do not.

Areas of behavioural science do make use of opposites. Personality inventories or tests contain some opposites like selfish and unselfish and competitive and co-operative and so forth. Attitude scales also use opposites. Nevertheless, in keeping with science's attempted purification of knowledge, scientists maintain these areas are separated from wisdom or value judgments. Often again the individual or part is focused to the detriment of common sense and the more important group or whole:

Like physical science, behavioural science cannot see the wood for the trees either.

Behavioural science is a little more realistic than physical science in one respect. Scientists studying human behaviour appreciate their observations might affect what they are observing, namely, people. However, there is not a great deal they can do about this, so they have to carry on bearing this source of influence to mind. When behavioural scientists do use opposites, some seem to regard the opposites merely as incidental to their theories or as unavoidable evils. They appear not to appreciate the true significance or power of opposites in coming to grips with reality of things. This is logical to scientists, including experts on human behaviour, as their main criticism of common sense is that it contains opposites together, or paradoxes to be resolved. Paradoxes make up nature, reality and our own existence. We know far better than experts when it comes right down to wisdom, which contains reality and everything in one way or another does come down to wisdom or common sense sooner or later. Let us hope it is sooner:

What behavioural science says about the nature of man is reflected in all our institutions.

For many years, the expert view was that some personalities contain characteristics or traits and others did not. This is not quite the case. All of us, with very few exceptions, have the same characteristics, but different degrees of them. Where we differ is in the extent to which we express these characteristics. For example, I have never met a person who was totally unaggressive or submissive all of the time. When we say someone has an aggressive personality, we mean he is that way too much of the time. He is out of balance between aggression and its opposite. We speak of a balanced personality. What follows is a list of characteristics common to everyone. It is a sample and other opposites would be included to get a fuller picture. Please add any others you think are important:

Your Personality Is Made Up Of Opposites

Good	Bad	Curious	Indifferent
Material	Spiritual	Lead	Follow
Determined	Weak	Share	Keep
Irresponsible	Responsible	Compete	Co-operate
Belong	Solitary	Accept	Reject
Rational	Irrational	Independent	Dependent
Reality	Illusion	Discriminating	Undiscriminating
Reward	Punish	Forgiving	Unforgiving
Divide	Integrate	Humorous	Serious
Work	Play	Mysterious	Open
Modest	Boast	Learn	Teach
Creative	Destructive	Sexual	Platonic
Relaxed	Tense	Quantitative	Qualitative
Subjective	Objective	Honest	Dishonest
Public	Private	Love	Hate
Sociable	Unsociable	Selfish	Selfless
Aggressive	Submissive	Introvert	Extrovert

You will notice, in one way or another, all these opposites are related or interconnected. We oscillate between a particular pair of opposites. For instance, in the pair competitive and co-operative we move back and forth between the two. These opposites exist together, though one may seem to predominate in our mind at a particular moment. If we play in a football match we compete against the other team. Nevertheless, co-operation is built in the situation. We co-operate with our own team members and with the rules of the game as well as with the other agreed traditions rituals of the contest. As well as oscillation between pairs of opposites in personal characteristics, we also fluctuate amongst the various pairs of opposites. Sometimes we feel curious, kind, love, hate, humorous, serious and so on and so forth in a short space of time or even at the same time. A common saying is that we can love and hate someone at the same time. Another common, homely example is that we can watch a TV film that terrifies us knowing full well we can leave the room. While watching the film, we can eat chocolate, stroke and smell the dog, cuddle a loved one, admire the actors, have memory flashes of our work place or holidays, fantasise, hear a noisy neighbour and feel cold. The five senses which science acknowledges and other sensings that science has not yet recognised exist, work together as a whole. We may focus one of our sensings consciously, but the whole including the unconscious is necessary for the part to have existence, never mind function:

We can exist in different spheres of reality and illusion all in an instant.

The oscillating rhythm between opposites in our personal characteristics is reflected in Einstein's equations about the nature of the universe. Some experts consider a great discovery of modern science is that the universe is expanding. Einstein's calculations produced alternative predictions. One was that the universe would go on expanding. Another was concerned with oscillation between opposites, namely, that of an alternate expanding and contracting of the universe. Common sense laws insist that opposites define reality and that there is oscillation between them. Therefore, the Einstein equation that represents oscillation between expansion and contraction reflects common sense laws. His formulation that predicts the continuous expansion of the universe is not in keeping with common sense laws:

Einstein's oscillation prediction reflected nature and ancient and common wisdom about oscillation and opposites.

The idea of an oscillating, rhythmic, organic, expanding and contracting universe has existed in mythology for thousands of years. In other words, the best of what Einstein's equations produced was common and ancient knowledge long before he or modern science was conceived. In addition, the ancients believed that humans and the larger universe behaved in the same way and were as one. The observations of some scientists are compelling them to believe that the ancients had a better view of reality than anything science has produced:

Scientists did not use the obvious part of nature that could speak for itself about reality – man.

Most early cultures viewed nature, the universe and themselves as reflections of each other. Their behaviour and that of nature at large were basically seen as interchangeable and were characterised by rhythmic oscillations, fluctuations and cycles. These beliefs were common for generation after generation, long enough perhaps to have genetic coding. They are still much in evidence in our own culture today. They are to be found in all manner of expressions, in song, music, literature, dance and common sayings. Indeed, the essence of song, poetry, music and dance is rhythm, oscillations and fluctuations that are connected to opposites in some way or another. Some examples of the present-day existence of these ancient and common wisdoms are in the following everyday expressions:

The rhythm of life is a powerful beat.

I kept going from one idea to the other and back again and so on.

What goes around comes around.

Life always has its ups and downs.

My mind was here, there and everywhere.

For a time, I felt at peace and at one with everything.

There are many examples of common sayings which show our personality and behaviour share much in common with the characteristics of nature and the universe generally. Could it be otherwise? We are literally offsprings of the universe and speak instinctively of Mother Nature. Science has conditioned us to believe the opposite of what common sensings make obvious. Science has a very long way to go to catch up with the mysticism, mythologies or folklore it so often dismisses as just so much nonsense. Is there any area of our lives that does not have its rhythms, cycles and oscillations reflected from, and to, other aspects of the world and universe?

> The rhythms of nature and the universe affect our own
> rhythms and behaviours which, in turn, affect nature
> and so on.

Common sense and experience tells us that our own characters and those of others oscillate between and amongst opposites. We have a dark or evil side to our nature or personality as well as a good or bright side. Some of the evils that criminals perpetuate do cross our minds and imaginations at times. Our feelings are such that, on occasion, we feel we could kill someone. With society going the way it is, these feelings are becoming more common. Rage is spreading and it will continue to grow. More ordinary people are going to defend themselves with violent retaliation when violently abused themselves, when they cannot get justice from expert legal systems. This is not really a prediction, it is happening now:

> We all have the killer instinct.

Let us look at our killer instinct with a specific example. In the Second World War, the Japanese treated their prisoners of war horrifically. Who amongst us would not have executed these brutal sadists if the killing could have been done at the pressing of a button? Without some suppression of the darker aspects of our nature, we could all be destructively violent. Criminals do not have different emotions from the rest of us. They act upon them more. Conversely, we are all capable of great acts of goodness and even huge sacrifice. We are a mixture of opposing characteristics:

> There is good and bad in all of us.

Opposites also exist in our biological system. The sympathetic and parasympathetic systems relate to aggression and its opposite, self-transcendence. These two opposites work together to balance aggression and self-transcendence. Balance of course is the key. A balanced personality is what brings harmony. In essence, this means, if in all our thoughts and actions, we have a balance between good and bad, we are doing alright. If we examine all our thoughts and actions honestly, most of us would admit that half of them fall into the good category and half into the bad. Of course, this does not mean that if we feel like killing someone ten times in our lifetime, balance is achieved by killing five of them. Balance is steering away from extremes or excesses by choice and by the application of will. Do unto others is one example and another is:

Moderation in all things.

Personality is related to how we see ourselves and how others view us. One source of unreliability of expert measures of personality is we have several different selves. We have a father or mother self, a son or daughter self, a leisure self, a work self and various other selves. A person can be aggressive or bossy at work and very submissive at home. Each of these different roles has several dimensions. Alphonse Karr illustrates some of them:

Every man has three characters: that which he exhibits, that which he has and that which he thinks he has.

Now let us turn to a close relative of personality theory, the science of motivation. One influential theory amongst experts is Drive Reduction Theory. Experts reasoned there were basic or primary drives like hunger, sex and thirst. They also proposed the existence of less important urges or drives such as curiosity or exploration and need for companionship or affiliation. These, the experts called secondary drives. Basically, the theory says that these basic urges create tensions and people are driven to reduce these urges:

Expert Drive Reduction Theory means when you are hungry you eat and so reduce your hunger.

We all know this. My cat is an expert in this behaviour. Every cell in every plant knows it: cells act upon this inborn wisdom or knowing. If plants and animals did not reduce their intake after having a certain amount of food, there would not just be a lot of overweight plants and animals, there would be exploding vegetation and bodies everywhere. Come to think of it, more and more people are exploding; heart attacks and violent attacks on others. So, there are some plants and animals that do destroy themselves and others with excesses. This applies to many behaviours, apart from the intake of food. If cells and plants have the ability to reduce drive, do they have purposes of their own? Survival, taking in nutrients and reproduction are examples of purpose. Having purpose is the same as having goals and being motivated. According to ancient wisdom and common sayings, they do have purposes. One ancient saying is:

> Everything has its own purpose.

Scientists have to accept plants and cells have purpose, but argue they do not possess awareness of purpose like us. It is true they do not speak or write about purpose like humans. However, they do choose some nutrients and places of habitation over others. That is, they show preferences and the ability to discriminate and make selections. They know what is good and bad for them. We seem to be losing this ability. When apes see the destructive behaviour of humans, they must be very worried to be described as our closest relatives:

> Animals and plants seem to have adapted more wisely to their environment than modern man who destroys.

Apart from being separated from the whole, Drive Reduction Theory has the other usual draw-backs of expert scientific thinking. Experts ignored the opposite of drive reduction. Common sense and experience tells us that we seek excitement. You can all testify to that. Cells, plants and animals seek *drive excitation* as well as drive reduction. Here is another example of expert theory containing far less real knowledge than the common sense of ordinary people. My pet cat spends about half his life seeking excitation. He dashes about chasing things, real or imagined and links up all kinds of plants, leaves, twigs, toys and any objects that cross his mind or path, in his search for stimulation. The odd somersault, shadow-boxing and other acrobatics are sometimes thrown in to add to his excitement. After a time, he reduces all this exciting activity and flops down to catnap or snore. His experience of drive reduction and its opposite, drive excitation, is extensive and common. It is a shame that my cat did not communicate his feeling to expert theorists. He could have corrected some of their inaccurate knowledge:

> Getting hold of the wrong end of the stick is bad enough, but experts do not even recognise a stick. A stick has two opposite ends to it.

After considerable time, effort and expense, experts had to deal with the opposite of drive reduction. They discovered what has been common knowledge for thousands of years; humans seek to raise their excitement levels. Now expert psychologists say they reject Drive Reduction Theory in favour of arousal level. Today's brand of expert theory is to believe people seek *optimal* drive or arousal. We all know about drive reduction and its opposite, drive excitation, and much more. There are many common sayings which illustrate our knowledge. Two are as follows. The first reflects drive reduction and the second, its opposite:

> When you get what you want, you don't want it.

> The more you get the more you want.

Common experience and observation forced experts to alter their rationalisations about curiosity and its place as a less important or *secondary* drive. They found that in experiments starving rats, even in the presence of food, would explore a new situation before they would eat. They discovered also, that animals found exploration and novelty rewarding for their own sake, that is, without other rewards like food. Unless we have been conditioned by expert theories too much, common experience tells us that curiosity or the need to explore is basic to behaviour. One common sense saying refers to cats, but it applies to people also:

> Curiosity killed the cat.

This saying means that curiosity is so powerful that cats are prepared to die for it. This also applies to humans. How many people have died by being curious about drugs and many other things? In one way or another, drives such as sex and hunger can be accounted for by curiosity or the urge to explore. We are curious about sex and we explore or experiment.

Curiosity has advantages and disadvantages. One saying that relates to a disadvantage is:

> If you play with fire you can get burned.

Curiosity and exploration do not just apply to self. Finding out what others experience is an imperative of human curiosity. To focus too much on one's own selfish curiosity is imbalanced and moves you into the danger zone. Sometimes it can be wiser to learn from the outcomes of the curiosity of others. We do not have to walk in front of a moving bus to find out if it hurts. A common wisdom that applies to drug-taking and various other activities is:

> You can learn from the mistakes of others as well as your own.

The assessment of the need for affiliation as a secondary drive, by experts, did not do it justice. Having friends or companions and other associations gives meaning and existence to an individual. As indicated previously, man is defined by his relationships with other people and other things. We saw, too, that the sub-atomic particle was also defined by its interconnectedness or affiliation with other things. The same common wisdom used earlier also reflects man's need for affiliation with others:

> No man is an island.

We know in addition, from common sense and experience that the opposite of this is real or true:

> We need to be alone at times.

Expert behavioural sciences, out of necessity, have had to soften their positions somewhat in respect of common sense. Initially, many dismissed common sense with the attitude that science was the only way to establish real knowledge and laws. Now some experts say one of their tasks is to test the reliability of any common sense sayings. In respect of motivation, experts drew attention to the conflict of two common sense laws that are paradoxical. They say opposite things:

Absence makes the heart grow fonder.

Out of sight, out of mind.

As common sense insists, they contain opposites which define reality. We all know that with the passage of time, 'absence makes the heart grow fonder' usually changes to 'out of sight out of mind'. In the last fifty years or so these old sayings have been put to the test by behavioural science researchers. They discovered what experts call a *curvilinear relationship* between the two. This translates to what we already know, namely, with the passage of time, 'absence makes the heart grow fonder' changes to 'out of sight out of mind'. Modern science experts still regard such common sense opposites lightheartedly or as a problem or paradox to be resolved rather than being at the nub of the real world:

Common sense and opposites define the reality of nature
and the nature of reality.

We all know a great deal more about absence and fondness. Common sense and experience tell us that 'absence makes the heart grow fonder' and 'out of sight out of mind' do not apply in every single instance. There is a common sense law that states so specifically:

There are exceptions to every rule.

This law is much more powerful and objective than either 'absence makes the heart grow fonder' or 'out of sight out of mind'. It applies to far more situations. Ironically or paradoxically, there are few exceptions to this rule. Even if we say, all men die, it is not strictly true. We gain immortality by passing on our genes to future generations. Also our bodies are recycled into all other living things. In death, we truly become part of a greater whole. All of us know far more about human motivation than all the expert theories and laws.

Now let's look at something inseparable from motivation. We will deal with learning, in relation to expert theories and common sense. The theory that has received the most publicity in the world of scientific experimentation is *behaviourism*. At the core of this expert theory is operant conditioning. Operant conditioning means that if you perform an act and get rewarded for it, you will repeat the act. If you get punished you are less likely to do so. Operant conditioning is a common sense law put into more scientific language. The ancient and common wisdom is:

Reward encourages, punishment deters.

How many people can there be in the world who do not know this? My cat certainly does and he did not need experts to give him this knowledge. This knowledge is as old as the hills and has existed in every known culture including animal groups. The theory is well-known as the *stick and carrot* system. In the time of the caveman it was probably known as the *club and berries* strategy. Our conditioning by experts is done by operant conditioning:

Operant conditioning is expert language for using a carrot and stick technique to shape behaviour.

Of course, experts will claim they have refined this caveman theory. Instead of the terms carrot and stick or reward and punishment, expert language speaks of positive and negative reinforcement. Experts will tell you they have discovered that if you reward a behaviour only some of the time rather than every time, the behaviour does not fade so easily. They label this partial reinforcement as opposed to constant reinforcement. Partial reinforcement is sometimes called variable or intermittent reinforcement. Lots of grandmothers used to advise any young ladies in their family who were getting married:

Don't let your new husband have sex every time he wants or he will take you for granted.

If this is not recommending intermittent reinforcement, what is? There are many such common sayings which bear testimony to our knowledge of variable or intermittent reinforcement:

Expert language or theory does not mean better knowledge or laws.

Out of all the theories in psychology, operant conditioning lent itself to the scientific method most readily. It was easy to measure things like the number of times a rat pressed a bar, time intervals and weight of food as reward. Teaching machines and programmed learning are based on operant conditioning. In the true tradition of science, programmed learning books split knowledge into tinier and tinier parts. Such small steps in learning or 'shaping behaviours' were seen as ensuring that everyone could be successful with no mistakes almost all of the time. Experts reasoned that learners would be positively reinforced every tiny step of the way. Negative reinforcement was considered counterproductive to learning. In other words it was all carrot or reward and little or no stick or punishment. No matter how much you like carrots, having them as a constant diet can make you thoroughly bored and finally sick. This is what happens with operant conditioning and is reflected in society. Expert operant conditioning defies many common sense laws. Three examples are:

We can learn at least as much from our mistakes as we can from our successes.

You cannot appreciate reward without knowing punishment.

You can get too much of a good thing.

Operant conditioning has its place in supporting the development or training of some closed skills and habits. It has little to do with the excitement of true exploration and creative learning. Goals of operant conditioning are mainly set by others. Inner motivation and wisdom to select quality goals are characteristics of us all and result in better forms of learning. If we are anything, we are by nature learning beings and we do not have to be conditioned to do it. Operant conditioning changes or shapes behaviour or learning in tiny steps. Nature's learning process enfolds the opposite of this also such as deconditioning and large steps or leaps in learning or imagination. Deconditioning can be useful when you get stuck holding the wrong end of the stick:

Just as nature is its own cause, the motivation for learning is to learn.

In the early days of expert operant conditioning, a psychology professor was explaining it to a neighbour who was a coal miner. The professor said that he had conditioned his own pet cat. He told the miner he would demonstrate when the cat came in from the garden. As soon as the cat walked in, it went up to the professor, mewed, walked to the refrigerator door and tapped it three times with its paw. The professor immediately opened the refrigerator door and gave the cat a piece of roast chicken. 'There you are', he said to the neighbour, 'I've apparently conditioned my cat to tap on the refrigerator door.' The coal miner replied, 'I reckon it is the cat who has conditioned you. He has just got you to give him a lovely bit of chicken every time he taps the refrigerator door.' Expert psychologists specialising in perception have rediscovered bits of knowledge that have been around for thousands of years and they apply here:

We see what we believe and believe what we see.

We see not only with our brains but also with our feelings.

Cat-watchers will tell you that cats change the behaviour of their owners more than vice-versa. Cats are clever trainers of people:

Cats condition humans as much as humans condition cats.

Another professor of psychology came out of his office at the university and saw a blind old man with his guide dog some hundred yards away. The old man was about to cross a very busy road. Suddenly the dog led the blind man into the thick of the traffic. There was a screeching of brakes and several cars collided to avoid the blind man. When he got to the other side of the road, the blind man pulled out a biscuit from his pocket and was about to give it to his dog. The professor dashed up to the blind man and snatched the biscuit from his hand and said, 'Stop, the dog nearly got you killed. I'm a psychologist, and I know that if you'd given him the biscuit, it would have reinforced his dangerous behaviour and the dog would be encouraged to do it again.' The blind man replied, 'Well, I'm no psychologist and I'm not deaf. I was giving him the biscuit to find where his head was so that I could wallop his back-side.' A common wisdom relates to this situation:

Things are not always as they seem.

Thorndike has been one of the most influential psychologists since the early 1900s. He rationalised that animals acted mainly in a reflex manner and were not flexible problem solvers. To test his theory, a cat was put into a cage and to escape, it had to manipulate a series of devices like bolts, pedals, loops and rings. The cat did not operate the devices, let alone in the required order. Thorndike concluded that 'animals are incapable of higher mental processes such as reasoning and insight'. A common saying that refers to horses, but which also applies to humans, is relevant to the cat in this experimental situation as well:

You can lead a horse to water, but you can't make him drink.

The problem situation did not have the same meaning for the cat as for the experimenters. It was about as meaningful to the cat as locking Thorndike in a barn and expecting him to lick the backs of his hands and catch and eat three mice before he could be let out. Like the problem for the cat, an additional requirement would be that Thorndike would not be given the slightest clue as to what he was supposed to do in the first place. When my cat sees me bring out his cage with its door, bolts and leather loops, he hides. It means a visit to the cat doctor and he remembers he does not like that. This shows insight and anticipation of future consequence:

Animals make predictions.

Other experimenters have shown cats and other animals can figure things out and solve problems when the situations have real meaning for them. Furthermore, cats are well known for their independence of mind, even when highly domesticated. We can all tell of incidents where animals have come up with very clever solutions to problems without being trained, by working things out for themselves:

Animals are smarter than experts think.

When my grandmother's cat was twitching and making noises in his sleep she, along with the rest of the family, would say, 'He is dreaming.' Scientists could not accept this. It smacked too much of higher mental processes involving abstract thought and mind. Another word for mind is *psyche*. Cat dreaming did not sit well with the description that expert theories had conditioned the majority to accept, 'dumb animals'. It was not until recently that expert scientists had to admit that cats do, indeed, dream. When brain waves could be observed by attaching electrodes to the head, experts discovered that cats could have dream experiences. It took modern science, yet again, almost the entire length of its history to establish what most people have known since dreaming was dreaming and cats were cats. For those who are great believers in science, this finding by experts must be quite reassuring. On second thoughts, perhaps not. My grandmother would not have been impressed at all. What she would have said of this scientific discovery would be, 'Well it's common sense. Haven't they got something better to do with their time?' What can we expect from experts next? Soon scientists will be telling us that cats have feelings, emotions and individual character traits or even wills and minds of their own:

> Making animals inferior makes man superior, especially experts.

In the early 1960s Rosenthal did an experiment on experimenters themselves. To one half of his research team he gave what he described as 'genius rats' bred specially for fast learning of mazes. To the other half of the experimenters, he gave 'stupid rats'. They were to compare scores on maze learning of the two groups of rats. Indeed, genius rats scored much better than the stupid rats. However, Rosenthal had tricked them. In reality, all the rats were the same. This experiment shatters the claim for the reliability, objectivity and validity of science. Two of the numerous common wisdoms that are relevant here are:

> We see what we believe.

> Give a dog a bad name ...

We have already seen that sub–atomic bits can express themselves as a reduced particle or as an expanded wave. We know too, that cells, plants, animals and humans can express reduced or expanded excitation. In similar fashion, we have noted that the universe can express itself in reduced (contracted) or expanded form. Thus, reduction or expansion is another pair of opposites which are contained in all levels of nature from tiny particles to galaxies and the universe itself. This gives another example of two common sense laws mentioned previously:

> The whole reflects the part.

> The part reflects the whole.

Expert theorists are increasingly stumbling and faltering over some ancient and common sayings or wisdoms, but still struggle to resist them.

Let us put together what it takes to become an expert psychologist or any other kind of specialist in modern scientific society. Some basic requirements are that you would have to split off a part from the whole, separate it from wisdom or morality, focus it excessively and ignore its opposite. To enhance your fame and fortune, you would, of course, write papers, hold conferences and broadcast your detached bit of rationalised knowledge in which you had specialised and so achieve celebrity status, in spite of your theory being devoid of common sense. Indeed, unless your specialism contained absolutely no morality, you would not be taken seriously by true scientists. The more extreme and narrow you can make your focus on a very small part, the greater is your degree of specialism and expertise:

> **Expert theorists seem to believe nothing succeeds like excess.**

All the specialist areas in behavioural science share similar drawbacks. The main result of them all is they have discovered no laws that have meaningful reality which do not already exist in common sense sayings. One example in social psychology is that one group of subjects was made anxious or fearful, another similar group was not. The finding of this experiment was that people who were anxious or fearful sought to be with other people more. This is well covered by common wisdoms such as:

> **Pain or adversity seeks company.**

Common sense and experience also informs us there is an opposite law that is true and there can be oscillation between these opposites:

> **Pain or adversity seeks being alone.**

Some sociologists have described themselves, jestingly, as follows:

> **Sociologists are experts who spend millions of dollars to find a house of ill-repute.**

What this means is that sociologists have spent a great deal of time, effort and money discovering the obvious or what everyone already knows.

Though sociologists treat this description of themselves as a joke, it is one of the most accurate pieces of knowledge they have ever produced:

Many a true word is spoken in jest.

There are, of course, some experts who use more common sense than others. In psychology, perhaps Carl Rogers' work has more contact with common sense than most theories. His actualisation theory is in essence that:

The organism has one basic tendency, to actualise, maintain and enhance the experiencing organism.

This view, coupled with his belief that the best way to understand behaviour was from the internal frame of reference of people, is not at odds with some of common sense. However, Rogers did not fully recognise the extent, accuracy and widespread power or usefulness of common sense laws of behaviour.

H.J. Eysenck, Britain's most celebrated personality theorist, acknowledges the importance of the 'obvious' which common sense is. He is a very strong supporter of science but that:

Science should be used to illustrate the obvious.

Such a view is much to Eysenck's credit and wisdom. Had he used the opposite of this he could have gained greater insights:

The obvious or common sense should be used to illustrate – anything.

As pointed out earlier, Einstein was a great believer in the importance of common sense. Nevertheless, he saw science as separate from common sense in the pursuit of reliable, objective knowledge. Einstein did not discover or invent The Theory of Relativity. It has existed in common wisdoms and sayings for thousands of years and is still much in evidence today. There are many common sayings which make this abundantly clear. One says:

All things are relative.

Einstein's esteem for common sense was such that when explaining The Theory of Relativity of Time, he used simple, meaningful common everyday terms:

> The Theory of Relativity of Time is if you sat on a red-hot stove for a second, it would feel like an hour. If you are with the one you love, an hour feels like a second.

From our own feelings and everyday experience, we can all give many examples of relativity of a variety of things including the relativity of time. For instance, we can be in one job interview for ten minutes and it can feel an hour. In another interview, we can be in for an hour and it feels like ten minutes. The Theory of The Relativity of Time is stated categorically by common sense sayings. One is:

> Time is relative.

What Einstein did was to get a mathematical handle on an example of the common sense law concerning relativity. My cat is very aware of The Theory of Relativity. He prefers some kinds of food to others, some places to sleep rather than others and so forth. The relativity of food, place and many other things are well known to my cat. Perhaps I should have named him Einstein-Plus. He might appreciate a double-barrelled name:

> Animals, along with cells and plants, feel and know the relativity of many things, like quality of food.

There is a law in science which is named after a physicist. It is called Heisenberg's Uncertainty Principle. Again, Heisenberg did not discover or invent this principle. He merely observed an example of common sense law at sub-atomic level in the behaviour of particles. There is a variety of sayings used by the layman that refer to common sense laws on uncertainty:

> Little in the world is certain.

> The only certain thing in this world is uncertainty.

> You can't take anything for granted.

Furthermore, common experience will tell you that, not only does uncertainty exist, we seek it at times and if there is not enough of it around, we create it. Sub-atomic particles certainly created uncertainty for Heisenberg and other physicists. Part of the games I play with my cat is creating uncertainty. It is an element of play, games, humour and teasing, not to mention most other aspects of life and the universe.

A small number of expert scientists see common sense or wisdom as the true keeper of reality. F. Capra, an expert physicist, provides the most compelling case for common wisdoms. He demonstrates how common wisdom contains more true knowledge of physics, including quantum theory than any modern scientific theories. He examined in great detail the common sayings and beliefs in Eastern Mysticism. If you read his book, first published in 1975, you will find he produces overwhelming evidence to support the superiority of knowledge and laws expressed in common wisdoms and sayings. Another expert physicist, F. Pleat came up with similar findings to those of Capra when he studied the common wisdoms and sayings of Native American Indians in his recent book, *Blackfoot Physics*. He, too, found awareness of quantum theory commonplace in this culture. The knowledge of physics in Eastern Mysticism and in American Indian culture was integrated or inseparable from wisdom or life at large. It was rooted in feelings, morality or common sensings:

> The ancients were wiser, unburdened by bogus modern scientific theories.

In the world of behavioural science, the famous psychologist, Kohler, emphasised the importance of common sense. He stated, in the 1940s, that the common experience and sayings of the layman show more awareness of basic truths about human behaviour than does science. However, Kohler does not provide anywhere near such extensive and powerful evidence and examples as Capra. R.B. Joynson, another expert psychologist, does furnish much impressive data in his 1974 book, *Psychology and Common Sense*, to support the reliability of everyday sayings compared with the unreliability of expert theories of behaviour. He analysed various scientific theories like operant conditioning and personality motivation. Joynson concludes that expert scientific theories of behaviour are *trite* when measured against the common sense sayings of the layman. In other words:

> The common man knows more real psychology than experts.

Within a small but expanding band of experts including some behavioural scientists common sense is making a powerful comeback. For example, a book edited by Fritz van Holthoon and David Olson in 1987 entitled *Common Sense: The Foundations For Social Science* is excellent. The volume deals with the relation of common sense to philosophy, history, science, education, and so on and so forth. The various contributing experts show in their writings they are as keen as myself to have common sense back at the centre of things and, as the book title indicates, as the foundations of social science. It is a scholarly or academic book which sadly will probably be read only by similar experts:

> It is paradoxical some experts demand a return to common sense – the opposite of expert sense.

My own essay should not be damned by being called scholarly or academic. Even Dan Quayle, John Prescott, Posh Spice and George Bush should understand my effort. The main message of this chapter then is that you know far more about psychology and other behavioural sciences than you think. From birth, you have been constantly interacting with feelings, thoughts and experiences of your own and with those of other people. This constant weighing up of your own behaviour and that of others is what real psychology of behaviour is. To the extent that your common sense has not been squashed or corrupted by modern theories and science, you have more real knowledge than experts. We are all permanent students of behaviour. Studying behaviour is how psychology is defined, even by experts:

> We may not always be wise men, but we are always students of behaviour or psychologists.

Chapter 5

Health as a Whole

Health is the greatest of riches.

Ancient Wisdom

The National Health Service in Britain in 1998 is in a state of collapse. People at large, doctors and nurses have been complaining and feeling frustrated for a long time. In spite of this, governments have been sending out positive messages [spin doctoring] about how well their policies and resourcing strategies are progressing. Government will be the last agency to admit to a crisis in any service for which it is responsible. Operations are cancelled, patients are left on trolleys in corridors and shunted from hospital to hospital over many miles. Waiting for treatment can run on for months and months. We can no longer train or keep enough doctors or nurses. Doctors and nurses want to do a good job, but expert policies, theories and laws are making their work impossible:

Politicians and other experts can seriously injure your health.

To illustrate how we are the healthiest we have ever been, experts tell us we now live longer. On the other hand, we have been described as, 'The Sick Society'. Members of the government and other experts take the credit for any successes of the health service, but blame others for failures. In the tradition of science, the government health service is mainly concerned with physical illness, its physical causes and the material resources to combat it. Health has to be viewed as an integrated whole of bodies, minds, spirits and the natural environment. By spirit, I do not mean worshipping in the various religions. Health in spirit denotes being in harmony with the better aspects of self, society and the environment. It is a feeling of being at one with the world – of identifying and being at peace with nature. Modern society does not foster moral or spiritual health. It is too concerned with their opposites – trying to heal physical bodies by material means and resources. Imbalance is the outcome:

92

Health is good relations with other people, and things that involve minds, bodies and spirits.

That a man lives for a very long time is not particularly meaningful in itself. If a man lives to be ninety years old and has been sick in mind and spirit for long periods of time, we cannot regard him as 'healthy' in spite of his great age. Had this man been healthy in mind and spirit he would have had a better life and may have lived even longer:

Quality of life is more important than length of life.

With the advance in medical science, how is it that in Britain, we are less healthy now than in World War Two? We had fewer material resources available to us during that period. In America too, which is described as the most wealthy, modern, civilised and technologically advanced nation on earth, even measures of physical health are low. Mental and moral or spiritual health in modern civilised society plummets by the day. Common sense values are increasingly abandoned resulting in sickness of bodies, minds, spirits and the natural and built environment:

He who destroys nature destroys himself.

Diseases such as the human equivalent of mad cow disease, excess drug-taking, heart-attacks, strokes, AIDS and other illnesses associated with modern society, increase. Even diseases which were thought to be conquered by medical science, like tuberculosis, are making a comeback. Clean air, food and water are becoming things of the past. Modern man is destroying our natural environment at an alarming rate. Plant and animal species, which give existence and balance to the whole living planet, are being destroyed daily by unwise human activity:

We are more dependent on the natural environment than it is on us.

Ancient wisdom or common sense laws view man as an integrated part of the whole natural environment including his body, mind and spirit. Science and an array of experts separated man from the natural environment and followed by splitting him into the further parts, namely, body, mind and spirit. Then medical doctors concentrated on the body and the suppression of the physical symptoms of illness or disease. Stomach ulcers, for example, are treated by medical science using drugs or surgery. Ordinary people are well aware that the roots of the ulcer are to be found in the patient's life as a whole. In spite of this common knowledge, medical science continues to focus on small physical parts and attempts to suppress the symptoms of the disease:

There are none so blind as those who will not see.

The hallmark of science is stamped deeply on medical practices. The part is focused at the expense of the greater whole. Areas of specialism in medical science have concentrated on smaller and smaller parts. At one time we had an 'ears, eyes, nose and throat' specialist. Then we had an ear specialist, an eye specialist, a nose specialist and a throat specialist. Now we have even more specialism concentrating on tinier and tinier parts. Doctors are aware that all these parts are interconnected as well as being integral elements of the whole body-mind-spirit-social-environmental-cosmic system:

Medical Sciences cannot see the wood for the trees.

The culture of medical science has not had due regard for the whole, including society and the environment, to our cost and at its own peril. The training of doctors in the suppression of the physical symptoms of disease, results in their main activity being the prescription of drugs and antibiotics. The drug thalidomide was to suppress morning sickness in pregnant women. One outcome was that children were born with stumps for arms. Medical scientists who had pronounced thalidomide 'safe', called these malforma-tions in babies a 'side-effect'. Let us be accurate, rather than politically correct, these aberrations of nature were the main effects. There are many other lawfully prescribed drugs which have caused all kind of physical, psychological and spiritual disabilities as well as loss of family, friends, jobs and in some cases – loss of life itself. Rather than healing in the true sense, medical doctors have been trained by their expert tutors and governing bodies to be, in large part, professional and legalised drug dispensers:

Physician, heal thyself.

However, due to the culture of science and its masters, most doctors have felt frustrated and helpless to do anything about their lot or their feelings.

Also, medical science and doctors are still held in high regard. Being in a high status position does not exactly make for changing things. Though the stock of the medical profession has fallen somewhat over the past ten to twenty years or so, it is enjoying a small revival at the moment. Doctors and nurses are seen by the man in the street as suffering enormous pressures just as he is whilst waiting for much needed treatment. Ordinary people can identify and sympathise with suffering. An old wisdom is illustrative:

Pain and suffering seek company.

Instinct and experience make doctors aware that there should be more to their profession than the suppression of the physiological symptoms of diseases. A few doctors even recommend a return to ancient wisdoms or common sense laws in respect of health and disease. Doctors who want to use more common sense approaches are wary to do so. They could be prosecuted if they strayed from using the orthodox medical scientific theories and practices in which they are trained and qualified. Doctors are governed by expert laws, rules and regulations and codes of practice which make the use of many common sense laws and practices illegal. Another pressure on doctors is that patients have been conditioned or socialised by modern materialistic culture to expect some kind of pills when they visit a doctor. One great burden upon doctors and nurses is the number of patients they are expected to handle. Britain, along with too many other places in the world, is vastly over-populated. Many countries in the world are short of water let alone food and basic medical facilities. Over-population is grinding our health services to a halt. This state of affairs can be seen in almost all our institutions. In the health service as elsewhere, we have too many people chasing too few resources, especially treatments by sophisti-cated and expensive technologies. What is more, doctors are put under increasing social pressure to sign more and more sick notes which can lead to a variety of social benefit awards:

The more people biting at the cake the less cake they get.

After seeing the negative effects of trying to suppress the symptoms of disease, a few doctors are being more openly critical of medical science. The harmful effects of drugs get more visible by the day and the medical establishment is a key player in our drug culture. Antibiotics are becoming impotent and like drugs, have been over-prescribed. Over-use of anti-biotics has led to micro-organisms adapting themselves so they have become immune. Hence, medical science has played a major role in the development of 'super bugs' which are now overtaking the expert efforts of the medical profession. Antibiotics decrease the effectiveness of the body's own immune system so their use, let alone extensive use, has always been questionable. Apart from bacteria and viruses resisting the products of medical science, more visible bugs have also developed immunity. The chemical DDT was sprayed liberally around the world to kill mosquitoes which are associated with malaria. This chemical had many negative effects on the whole environment but malaria has made a comeback. Scientists seem very slow to learn an obvious lesson – nature bites back. Of the great over-use of chemicals, drugs and antibiotics by doctors, common sense laws have much to say. One is particularly fitting here:

Excess in anything leads to its opposite.

A simple example of this law is that if you like strawberries, you will eat some for pleasure. However, if you ate a bucket full of them, you would be sick. In other words, you will get pain, not pleasure.

Problems for doctors and nurses mount by the day. They are open to violent attacks from patients, visitors, and drug addicts searching for a 'fix'. Other trouble-makers in our 'modern' times now use hospitals and medical centres as part of their violent playground. Along with the increase in violence, medical staff are expected to do more and more work with less and less staff and other resources. Experts call it efficiency. Staff call it by less complimentary names. What is more, the explosion of paper work and officialdom is demoralising medical staff. Government is very short of common sense:

You must not flog a willing horse.

For doctors, the pendulum has swung from one extreme to another. Once they could, literally, bury some of their mistakes and cover others. However today, in our material compensation culture, doctors can be sued for anything. As a consequence, in this modern age of blame, The National Health Service has to pay much larger insurance bills to cover expenses for medical staff being sued. Some doctors, of course, should be sued and never allowed to practise. There are doctors who have been struck off the medical register for gross incompetence or serious crimes. Unfortunately, with a smart lawyer these offenders can be found practising medicine again in a relatively short period of time.

Laws trap honey-bees and free hornets.

No medical treatment can be perfect. We can all find fault with anything. To be more accurate, we can find *many* faults with anything. This is a fact, not a matter of opinion. Just imagine what greedy lawyers and politicians can do, and indeed, do, with this fact. It is easy to find faults and once these are identified, then blaming someone is also very easy. Modern expert laws, created by politicians and lawyers, mean that medical staff have to do the impossible – produce work that has no faults. If they do not achieve this impossibility, they can be sued. This is a lawyer's dream come true, but it does refute common sense law:

Nothing is ever perfect – and that includes the very best medical treatment there is.

The drugs doctors prescribe are tested and recommended by other expert researchers in medical science. Thus, when doctors issue them, they usually do so in good faith. It is the general medical scientific culture that is problematic. Doctors are bound to this culture in many powerful ways including legally, financially, socially and so on. Many feel guilty about prescribing drugs and being a party to our modern drug excesses. Doctors quite often just pass on to patients what they have been told by experts who specialise in the field of drugs. Many doctors do believe in their drugs, or as they point out, they would not prescribe them. Medical drugs are a case of:

All that glisters is not gold.

The sequence of getting information about drugs goes something like this. First, experts tell us there are no bad side-effects. This is because they do not know or prefer not to say. Next, even when many patients report side-effects, 'government experts' deny them. They use terms they think are impressive. They say, 'There is no objective scientific evidence to warrant taking action'. Whether in science or elsewhere, all objectivity means is the extent to which people agree. Objectivity is another term science has tried to make special to experts. All scientific objectivity means is that some scientists agree on something. More often than not, just as many scientific experts disagree. Court room dramas involving medical experts clearly illustrate this. In almost every one of these cases, the prosecution lawyers have medical experts who say one thing, whilst the defence experts say exactly the opposite. Common sense laws predict this. As we have indicated earlier, common sense maintains that much of our reality is defined by opposites and that includes modern scientific medical evidence in courts of law. This makes scientific objectivity or agreement about as useful as a chocolate teapot. Ironically, scientists criticise common sense laws as being, 'not objective or reliable'. The laws of common sense are very objective and reliable. Billions of people [not just a few scientists] over thousands of years [not just for a few weeks, months or years] have agreed on the validity of common sense laws. Compared with the objectivity and reliability of common sense laws, science is a non-starter:

People in glass houses should not throw stones.

As a reaction against the excesses of medicine, the common people along with some medical doctors are returning to ancient wisdoms or common sense laws in respect of health and disease. The Holistic Medical Association and other complementary medical groups have come into being in the last decade or so. There has been a rediscovery of some ancient wisdoms. In theory at least and often in practice too, alternative therapies such as homeopathy, osteopathy, chiropractice, aromatherapy, acupuncture and so forth have more regard for the whole person than has medical science. Most aspects of holistic or complementary medicine have been regarded as useless by medical science. Now, there is a little more respect for what orthodox medicine regarded as 'quack' practices. Some medical doctors actually send patients to alternative practitioners or even go as patients themselves. However, many do not admit to this for their masters such as The British Medical Council or The British Medical Association would consider such action as irresponsible, unprofessional and could punish them. There are, of course, charlatans acting under the guise of alternative practitioners, but there are charlatans in orthodox medicine too:

There is good and bad in all professions.

A few medical doctors have been so disenchanted with medical science, they themselves have become alternative practitioners. Some doctors have been wary of medical science since it began. It has gone against their inner feelings – against their better judgments, in spite of the powerful brainwashing of medical science. Paradoxically, though orthodox medicine treats physical symptoms of disease, almost all doctors admit that if they could treat the whole patient, they would be more effective. It is extremely difficult for doctors to go against their own traditions or culture even if they want to do so. Virtually every aspect of doctors' behaviour is governed by expert laws and their masters. A common wisdom and a common saying spring readily to mind here:

They that are bound must obey.

He who pays the piper calls the tune.

Orthodox medical science regards complementary medicines like home-opathy with much disdain. Homeopathy focuses more on the whole person than does medical science. In some ways homeopathy is the opposite of medical science. A term meaning the opposite of homeopathy is used to describe the mode of treatment used by orthodox medical practitioners. It is called allopathy. Let us illustrate these opposite types of treatment. With a fever, medical science tries to suppress symptoms like high temperature. Homeopathy believes the high temperature is the body's immune system trying to throw off the fever and should not be suppressed. Indeed, homeopathic medicine encourages the rise in temperature as it is the body's and nature's way of dealing with the disease successfully. That is, homeopathic practitioners give substances that in a healthy person promote symptoms of the fever like high temperature. The origin of homeopathy is often incorrectly attributed to a medical doctor Samuel Hahnemann. He was a student of biochemistry over two hundred years ago. Though Hahnemann did make the technique popular, it was a revival of what was practised in very early societies and is an example of an old wisdom that can be expressed in numerous ways:

Like cures like.

Having a hair of the dog that bit you.

Strength of the homeopathic substance which may be prescribed is not directly related to strength of effect. Rather, the opposite is true. Extreme weak dilutions of the substances used as homeopathic remedies seem more effective. Medical scientists argue that the dilutions are so weak as to contain none of the substance being diluted. However, physicists do admit to the existence of energies that science cannot explain. The weakness of homeopathic substances to achieve strong effects is consistent with common wisdoms:

Small things can have a big effect.

There is more to life than we can see.

The ridiculing of homeopathic remedies by medical science is biased, as is all science that does not coincide with common wisdoms. During the great cholera epidemic in the nineteenth century, homeopathic treatments were more successful than orthodox medicine. The Board of Health, dominated by experts in medical science, tried to hide this information by not publishing the figures of the achievements of the homeopathic practitioners. In this case, medical science was not just without morality [amoral], it was specifically immoral. There are many other instances of medical science suppressing information about the success of alternative therapies. Information about its own mistakes is a different matter. Not only does medical science suppress the symptoms of disease, if something does not fit into the belief structure of science, then experts suppress or reflect it:

We soon believe what we desire.

However, there is a criticism of homeopathy that relates to one of its claims. Homeopaths say that, even when their treatments do no good, at least they do no harm. This runs counter to a common sense law that states, there are advantages and disadvantages to everything. What homeopathy can justifiably claim is that it has not created the vast number of disasters of medical science:

One man's meat is another man's poison but some poisons can kill most men.

Another therapy that is more holistic than orthodox medical practice is The Bach Flower Remedies. Doctor Edward Bach was a pathologist and bacteriologist just before World War One. He believed the underlying negative emotional states were responsible for the physical symptoms of illness. Hence, he focused on these mental states. Bach capitalised on the strong inborn response to smell or fragrance. Drops of extracts of flowers are taken in water to deal with such emotional states as fear, depression, lack of confidence and guilt. Here again, flowers have been used in numerous ways for the purposes of healing by ancient cultures long before Bach gave his name to it. The Bach technique is based on various old wisdoms to which everyone can bear testimony:

We are what we eat, drink, breathe, think, feel and do.

There is a growth in the number of people who praise alternative therapies in reducing illness or promoting health. The fact that medical science pronounces that alternative therapies are useless cuts no ice with the many who have benefited from more holistic and natural approaches. Gradually more and more practices in alternative therapies are having to be accepted by medical science as their value can no longer be in doubt. Often, these are given more acceptable scientific names which give the impression that they were really in the realm of modern science all along. Giving a procedure a more scientific name does not make it better. It may make it more popular. People are impressed with something if it is 'scientific'. Actually, the rediscovery of some ancient wisdoms by quantum physicists did give some momentum to holistic health practices. However, as one common sense saying would put it:

A rose is a rose by any other name.

Apart from quantum theory becoming very famous for rediscovering some common sense laws, we will look at another instance where science has been forced to change its views. When I studied anatomy and physiology at a medical school, some bodily functions were regarded as being outside the individual's voluntary mental control. Heartbeat and contraction of blood vessels are examples. They were called autonomic (automatic) responses. Yogis' claimed they could control these 'involuntary' or 'autonomic' responses with their minds. Scientists said this was impossible.

Scientists tested the Yogis' claims in an experiment which proved the Yogis correct. This practice had been in common wisdoms for thousands of years. Scientists found their students could perform this feat. Experts now call it by more scientific names like 'autogenic training'. Medical science rediscovers yet one more ancient wisdom:

Mind and matter are indivisible.

The nervous system exerts control over every cell in the body and so mind is involved in everything. Not only are body, mind and spirit related, we are also intimately connected to other living and 'non-living' things. Medical science works on the assumption that disease is caused by germs. Germs are the effect of some earlier cause, which in turn, is the effect of some previous cause and so on ad infinitum. We have seen in an earlier chapter how one cause turns out to be the effect of a previous cause. There are more important things to disease than germs:

Germs are the effects of disease as well as its causes.

The same number of germs can kill one person, make another ill and leave someone else unaffected. Two examples which refute the theory of orthodox medicine that germs cause disease, concern typhoid and cholera. These cases are highlighted by Harry Benjamin in his book *Everybody's Guide to Nature Cure*. Medical researchers themselves found a report by doctors about London's Metropolitan Water Boards which refuted the germ theory of disease. In the report the doctors stated that it was typhoid fever that led to the development of the bacillus or germs – not vice versa. The cholera case involves a famous Professor Pettenkofer. He was not a supporter of the germ theory of disease. The professor swallowed a test-tube full of cholera germs in front of a class of amazed students. According to expert germ theory, the amount of germs drunk by Pettenkofer was enough to 'kill a whole regiment of soldiers'. Nothing happened and the professor said, 'Germs are of no account in cholera. The important thing is the disposition of the individual.'

The whole is more important than the part.

Health is the concern of us all. There has to be more of a unified effort to promote behaviours that contribute to health as a whole. All institutions, groups and individuals have to contribute to this end. Medical doctors and nurses are those who specialise in dealing with illness and the public is conditioned to expect a great deal from specialists. The doctor's expertise does not go much further than his surgery door and they know it. What is more, they are well aware, like all of us, that one common sense wisdom that cannot be denied is:

Prevention is better than cure.

We all have a co-operative responsibility for health and disease. Just after World War Two, a greater sense of community or shared values existed. This sense of common purpose applied to many things, including health. There was a stronger sense of community compared with modern attitudes that have seen community life crumble. Villages, towns, school pro-grammes and families used to involve themselves in more health-giving activities than we do today. Local businesses also helped promote healthy pursuits in the community. They were an integral part of it and contributed to its welfare. A sense of community is basic to social and individual health. To prevent disease and promote health, this spirit of community – of shared identity – has to be reflected in activities that bind people together. Such activities spring from common values. What people already share are inborn values contained in common sensings of what is good and bad. Common sense is a force that promotes health as a whole. When suppressed and made illegal, as it is in our 'progressive' era, the consequence is sickness:

Society's health is the individual's health and individual health is society's health.

The nature or type of community in which we live, not only gives expression to our need for affiliation, it exerts a great influence on our health as a whole. Like the sub-atomic particle, we depend on relationship with others for our very existence. Relationships or social groups also give meaning and purpose to life. Existence on some modern housing estates is a constant drain on health in body, mind and spirit. It can be a daily and violent battle for inhabitants' survival with an increasing number ending up as hospital cases. Some people get killed, others die through despair and the loss of the will to live, while suicide is a final option. Some housing estates in the USA and in other countries are surrounded by high protective fencing with security guards on patrol. Modern society destroys peace of mind and the human spirit:

Destroy the spirit and the body dies.

The urban sprawls that swallow up more and more of the English countryside shatter community life and consequently, health as a whole. Expert planners and architects, not to mention their political masters, have much to answer for concerning the nation's health. Too much of our modern man-made environment is destructive to nature, to man himself and to all living things. Experts have produced policies that create all types of illnesses. Rage is harmful stress which is connected to most modern illness, including fatal ones, and it is not just restricted to road-rage. Rage can be seen in hospitals and doctors' waiting rooms, in schools, in Jobcentres or in almost any other place you care to mention. It puts increasing burdens on everyone including the health services. Peace of mind and positive aspects of human spirit are disappearing at a frightening rate resulting in what is justifiably called 'The Sick Society'. Experts have indeed made a large contribution to the separation of man from his natural environment as well as separating man's body mind and spirit:

Expert planners and architects have made a pig's ear out of a silk purse.

We have become conditioned by the scientific society and its expert disciples to accept a world where body, mind and spirit are treated separately. However, everyday conversation shows we know instinctively that mind affects matter and matter affects mind. You will be able to think of an almost endless number of examples. I will highlight a few. 'He is going bald and he is very depressed about it.' 'She's worried to death over her mother's accident. She's lost an awful lot of weight.' If we think of our favourite food, our mouths water. Our sex glands are stimulated by our thoughts. One telling definition of sex that illustrates the power of the mind is:

Sex is ninety per cent imagination and ten per cent friction.

One term used by medical science, doctors and most of us, does not separate mind and body in relation to health and disease. It is 'psychosomatic', which means mind–body. We have been conditioned by experts to use this term in an uncomplimentary way. We say things like, 'There is nothing wrong with him. It is all in his mind. The illness is in his imagination.' One story that is told of a doctor who repeatedly told a patient that his illness was 'only' psychosomatic. The doctor could find nothing wrong with him. The patient died and on his grave-stone it read, 'There, I told you I was ill.' When a doctor says that he can find nothing wrong with you, it does not necessarily mean that there is nothing wrong with you. It means the doctor cannot find what is wrong. The doctor views his patient, as his profession expects him to do, through the eyes of medical science. If the doctor cannot find anything wrong and the patient still maintains he is unwell, it is at this point the doctor might think of the term 'psychosomatic'. If the doctor cannot find orthodox physical symptoms, he has got a problem. With his background of training in medical science, the doctor may say you have a virus that is going round. This often means he does not know what it is. Are there any illnesses that do not involve body and mind together – that are not psychosomatic? Too many experts lead us to think their knowledges are better and more infallible than they are. Doctors can be fooled more than the title 'expert' would suggest. The following is yet another example that illustrates the point. A few people with no formal medical training have pretended to be doctors and have gone undetected for months. Not only this, they received much praise from patients and doctors for doing a good job. In many areas of their expertise, medical scientists are discovering that:

Things are not always as they appear to be.

Fortunately, though medical science itself is without morality, doctors are not. In the ordinary parts of their lives, when they are members of families and other social groups and not acting as medical scientists, doctors are more free to use common sense. Most doctors are dedicated people with much integrity. Even when doctors are talking to patients, no matter how scientific they try to be, common sensings tug and intrude on their actions. They may try to push their feelings aside, as scientists insist they do when doing experiments, but common sense can never be totally denied. To the degree that medical doctors, in their professional role, do not let the findings of medical science hide their better feelings, they are more likely to be better healers. Many sense when they are prescribing a particular drug, produced from results of medical research, they are doing something against their better judgment – that it is wrong. However, they have to follow what is laid down by law:

> **Medical doctors are experts whose commonsense is banned by scientific and legal laws.**

The medical establishment is trying to make nurses more expert. This could force nurses to use less common sense for which they are famed. A common saying is that if you have something good do not try to fix it. A Russian proverb echoes this sentiment:

> **The egg does not teach the chicken.**

Medical science has rediscovered some other things that are examples of common sense laws. People can exert mind control over the secretion of chemicals in the body. Endorphins and encephalin are examples. One of the effects of these is pain relief. The mind can also consciously influence electrical activity such as brain-waves, all of which are related to health and disease. Biofeedback is the term given by experts to gadgets used to measure these activities inside the body. Medical science has also verified that the bed-side manner of doctors is more effective in healing than the pills or medicines they prescribe. This is clearly an example of mind influencing matter and matter influencing mind:

> **The greatest conjuring trick in the history of medicine is the scientific separation of mind and body.**

All of us can probably recall an instance where the bed-side manner of doctors or nurses was important to the healing process. One of the examples I can recall is about an old lady who was in hospital for two weeks. Whenever I went to visit her, she was always telling me about a Nurse Holloway. It was Nurse Holloway did or said this, that or the other. One day I arrived to find her coughing, spluttering and laughing all at the same time. I asked her what was going on. When she could catch her breath, she told me that when she had a coughing bout, Nurse Holloway had asked her if she was a smoker. The old lady had told the nurse that of course she was not a smoker. Nurse Holloway had replied, 'It's a pity you are not a smoker because stopping smoking would have helped a cough like that.' The old lady started to laugh and cough again. I told the old lady she could do herself an injury with laughing so much. As I went away she called after me . It was an old saying which recently has been supported by evidence from medical science:

Laughter is the best medicine.

The rediscovery by medical science that humour is good medicine is now in practical use in some health services. Laughter aids healing physical wounds and is another example of a mind influencing biological matter. Orthodox medicine, in its separation of mind and body, does not ignore mind completely. It has psychiatrists. These specialist mind-doctors rely mainly on the technique of 'uncovering'. This involves the psychiatrist leading the patient back in his personal history and uncovering events which may have caused the present mental disturbance. Once the patient has become aware of these events, it is supposed to heal him. This is still the main method used to help patients even though the evidence shows that the technique is generally a waste of time. Research studies show that:

Talking to and stroking your pet dog can heal more than psychiatrists.

There is no evidence, scientific or otherwise either, that psychiatrists or specially trained expert counsellors help patients as effectively as talking over your problems with a sympathetic friend, taxi-driver or a complete stranger. Let us face it, a psychiatrist is a total stranger compared with many other people we know. From documentary and other films, we already know the psychiatrist's main mode of operation. He repeatedly asks the question, 'And how do you feel about that?' Another experiment that was conducted also brings into question the so-called specialist skills of psychiatrists. Some doctors went to a mental institution and pretended to be patients. They fooled the expert staff but not the mental patients themselves. In this experiment, the mental patients turned out to be better observers and analysers of human behaviour than the experts:

Psychiatrists fool all people sometimes and some people all times, but not all people all times.

Only where they use common sense laws are psychiatrists useful in helping people. Normally psychiatrists create much dependency of the patient upon themselves which is very financially rewarding. Because of science, specialisations, and expert theories, psychiatrists or trained counsellors are less likely to use common sense laws than the ordinary man in the street. Thus, if you need help, seek a friend or some other layperson who is known for the use of much common sense. It is very interesting to note that the more trained psychiatrists a geographical region has, the more mental illness there is:

> Psychiatrists have greater need of their patients than the patients have need of them.

There is an increasing number of cases of mental disturbance and depression. How often do we hear this story? A man says his wife has left him and as a consequence, he drinks to excess, becomes depressed, aggressive and gets into trouble with the police, his neighbours and almost everyone who crosses his path. Here, the man rationalises the cause or blame for his downfall to the departure of his wife. On closer examination, the reverse of this is closer to reality. It is often the excessive drinking, aggressive behaviour and depressions that made his wife leave in the first place. There is much evidence to support such instances of shifting the blame for such anti-social behaviour completely on to other people. Expert theories and laws encourage people to take less and less responsibility for anything and this is true in respect of health and illness. Too many of us deny the wisdom of the following ancient common sense law:

> Man is the architect of his own misfortune.

Like science, generally, medical science is overrated. Even so-called medical break-throughs, for which medical science has taken the credit were practised in ancient civilisations. For example, Edward Jenner's work in 1796 is quoted when vaccination is spoken of by medical experts. People from early civilisations put scabs of victims of disease into the nostrils of healthy individuals to give them a mild form of the disease so they would become immune to the full-blown disease. That is, they used the vaccination principle long before modern man was born. Similarly, Alexander Fleming's name crops up in association with penicillin. When

Fleming stumbled upon the antibiotic in 1928, he too, rediscovered an ancient Egyptian practice. Egyptians used to put mould on wounds to help them heal:

Nothing is really new in this world.

Due to the over-emphasis on matter or materials by government, medical science and many of us, there are complaints about lack of material resources in The National Health Service. As we have seen, we are well aware that many sicknesses including physical symptoms, stem from the state of societal values or morality. Greed, violence, pollution, overcrowding, injustice, lack of responsibility, bureaucracy and other excesses are the origins of sickness in body, mind, and spirit. As we have become materialistically richer, our health as a whole has got poorer:

Trying to provide material answers to moral problems is an expert solution, not a common sense one.

To make medical science more acceptable to the majority it has developed, throughout its history, a culture that takes more credit than it deserves. Improved social conditions and hygiene, rather than medical expertise, had much to do with the diminution of disease during the past few centuries. Today, the social condition of overcrowding is unhygienic or polluting to health in body, mind, spirit and habitat. Excess population is connected to all other pollutants. The list of them seems endless. All our senses are under attack. There are very sore sights for very sore eyes. We are jostled by bodies and cars. Our ears are pounded by ghetto-blasters and in-car, in-house, in-mail and in-anything stereo-systems. We cannot escape in our own homes any longer and the same is true at work and at play. Pollutants are everywhere. They are in the food we eat, the water we drink, the air we breathe and in all our bodies, minds and spirits. Great excesses of physical and mental pollution are taking a great toll on health and place an expanding burden on health services:

Cleanliness is next to godliness.

Years ago, when I believed that science was vastly superior to common sense, I was giving a lecture to some postgraduate students on research methods in science. Part way through I paid the usual lip-service of experts to common sense by saying, 'Common sense, of course, is very important.' One student said, 'Common sense is full of inaccurate rubbish and old-wives' tales.' To play devil's advocate, I said, 'Well let us take a common sense saying such as, all things are related, and see if it can make some predictions.' As we have mentioned in an earlier chapter, making predictions is the main aim of all sciences. I had noticed in the morning my old car was puffing out great volumes of fumes that were easily seen on that frosty day. Hence I said, 'Let's look at car fumes. We know they are harmful to health. Some people use them to commit suicide. If all things are related, car fumes will have an effect on all illnesses. This is one prediction then. Another prediction is that experts will discover one disease affected by car fumes. Then they will discover a few more and so on until they come to the conclusion that car fumes affect all illnesses.' These predictions are coming true. Government experts have admitted to a few diseases that are affected by car fumes such as asthma and bronchitis. Eventually, since common sense says all things are related, it will become obvious that all illnesses are affected by car fumes. The rejection of common sense laws by all our institutions, including science and medical science, is the greatest error of modern times. An ancient proverb is very fitting here:

Though wisdom may be abandoned, it cannot be falsified.

The predictions I made were not clever or obscure, they are obvious to everyone. Common sense is a blinding flash of the obvious. However, it was not until around 1998 in Britain that government experts pronounced that car fumes posed 'a significant hazard to health'. An old milkman told me when I was a young boy that, if enough people got cars, the fumes would kill lots of people. His prediction was correct. On reflection, perhaps I stole my prediction about car fumes from the old milkman. As we have seen in an earlier chapter, one cause is also the effect of an earlier cause, so car fumes are both a cause and an effect. For example, car fumes are the effects of man's desire for material things, while at the same time, car fumes are also the cause of illnesses. Walking along a street in today's modern towns and cities is like walking in a giant exhaust pipe. Government spin doctors make unleaded petrol sound like it is good for you. It is lethal. In the present context, the ancient and common sense law would read:

All things are related to health and disease.

Eating habits are related to health and disease. Since all things are related, we could choose anything at random and relate it to health and disease. Let us do this. Let us just pluck something out of the air at random and see how it is related to health and disease. How about a pig's tail? A pig's tail is related to a pig's body, parts of which are used in human transplant and in human diet. These have effects on health and disease. However, after that little diversion, we will talk a bit more about eating habits. As we have stressed numerous times, common sense laws insist that much of our reality is defined by opposites. The opposite of over-eating is fasting. This practice has been used for thousands of years and has been passed down the ages. Today, it is still practised in some cultures and religions as a positive aid to health. Fasting detoxifies body, mind and spirit. Indeed, purification of body, mind and spirit defines health. Fasting is nature's own way of helping itself purify the whole person. When we are ill, the desire to eat is shut down or off. It is nature's method of getting back into balance. Excess in fasting, like over-eating and any other behaviour, is harmful. It can result in much illness and death. Anorexia nervosa is one example. One wisdom that spells out guidance in relation to fasting, over-eating and many other behaviours is:

Moderation in all things.

Genetically modified food is a bone of contention. The British Prime Minister, Tony Blair stepped into the row in February 1999 and said he was happy to eat genetically modified food. He went on to say that it could be healthier, tastier and cheaper. New genetically modified food-stuff is consistent with the 'new' in the political party's revised title, namely, New Labour. At least the Prime Minister is putting genetically modified food where his mouth is. However, he may have to eat his words also. Government emphasised that the safety of the people was paramount. You can guess what this means – more laws and less justice. In respect of genetically modified food, the government has promised 'comprehensive legislation' as soon as possible. Genetically modified food could make the following story come true. A doctor answered a knock on his surgery door. When he opened it, he saw the Prime Minister with a frog growing out of his head. After composing himself, the doctor asked what he could do for him. The frog replied, 'Get this fool off my tail-bone.' A common saying is relevant here:

> **Many a true word is spoken in jest.**

Genetic engineering has already caused devastation to some people in the United States of America. What was billed as a perfectly natural sleeping pill turned out to be genetically modified L-tryptophan. Only on the market for several months, it killed thirty seven people and made 1,511 seriously ill. Some were disabled. Others suffered slow agonising deaths, paralysis, swellings, broken skin, loss of memory and heart problems to mention some of the effects. Genetic modification of humans including cloning has been described as immoral by some experts in science, in government, in religion and in most other institutions. For people who think that because some powerful experts have denounced genetic modification of humans it will not happen, they have another think coming. If human cloning has not already been done somewhere already, it will be and sooner rather than later. Whenever experts see that something is possible, they invariably do it:

> **Nature is conquered by obeying her, not by trying to conquer her.**

Perhaps the Prime Minister has a hidden political agenda by recommending genetically modified food. He might think this is a way to deal with the population bomb and its many associated problems. Government policies and laws seem to be increasing all the things his political party claims it wants to decrease, including unwanted population expansion. Radiation poisoning may result in a nightmarish thinning of the population. Politicians informed us that nuclear energy was the way to the future. It was progress and good for us; it was being modern. When the Chernobyl nuclear plant in Russia began a melt-down, it affected the environment and posed health problems here in Britain. Government experts admitted to a few 'minor' observations like the contamination of a little grass and animals' milk in the odd place or two in England. Our own nuclear plants have problems and leak radioactive materials into the environment including streams and rivers. The official government expert line is that the radioactivity levels in our back gardens are minimal and do not pose a threat to health. Government is rather shy and unforthcoming about the fact that the containers in which they bury nuclear waste, have a much shorter life-span than the radioactivity itself. This is not to mention the various possibilities of accidents to the containers. So confident have British politicians been about expert theories, we struck a business deal with some of our European 'partners' for them to bury their nuclear waste in Britain. Now, we could have foreign trucks, as well as our own, trundling through our towns and countryside loaded with nuclear waste all in the name of being good for the economy and Britain. Thus we are, literally, storing up health problems for the future in addition to the ones we have at present. One positive outcome of the Chernobyl disaster was it re-emphasised that, though we may appear to be separated in space and time:

We are all interconnected and dependent on one another for health and existence.

As well as the possession of nuclear technology, experts have developed other sophisticated tools which will continue to have great impact on health and life at large. New technologies are being carried to excess as they are elsewhere. In a materialist world, there will come a time when medical science can dispense with doctors and nurses and have machines to do operations, prescribe drugs and other medicines. Excess technology is anti-health, anti-social and anti-nature. Its development and use in medical science gets faster and faster by the day:

Fools rush in where wise men fear to tread.

One medical doctor readily admitted in a television interview that The National Health Service is geared to the use of 'glamorous' progressive high technologies and not to basic care. Another move away from basic care and one more nail in the coffin of common sense was the influx of specialist managers and administrators into hospitals and medical practices. This was done to 'rationalise' the delivery of health services. Before, during and for a period after World War Two, specialisation had not submerged common sense to the degree it has today here in the late 1990s. Wards in hospitals were run by nurses, sisters, staff nurses and matrons and they were admired the world over for the excellent job they did. They were famed for their common sense. Their reputation was so high they were elevated almost to divine status. Ministering angels is what they were called and with great justification and feeling. Nurses organised and fulfilled the needs of sick and dying people with great care, grit or determination and with much good humour to very good effect. They nearly always got the best out of people in what are the most difficult of circumstances. If this is not management of the highest order, what is? Whenever nurses move out of nursing to some other job, their new employers are impressed with their management skills:

More expert management, less common sense health care.

Nurses are first rate managers when allowed to be so. In earlier times, before specialist managers were brought in, matrons and nurses ran hospitals to far better effect than experts. Matrons and nurses ensured that those who did sloppy work had good cause to be fearful. Modern experts and laws dictate that no one should ever be fearful at work. This flies in the teeth of common sense laws. People should be fearful of doing sloppy work or engaging in any other kind of bad behaviour. Without knowing fear, its opposite, boldness or fearlessness, has no meaning or existence. There are many ancient wisdoms or common sense laws that speak about sloppy work and bad behaviour. One example is:

If a job is worth doing, it is worth doing well.

As we noted earlier, research shows that 'bed-side manner' is more important in healing than the medication prescribed. Therefore, it is not surprising that nurses are major contributors to the healing process. Nurses get to know more about the whole patient than do doctors. Patients confide and discuss all kinds of their inner-most feelings with nurses, such as family, friendships, work, leisure, living conditions, finances and so forth. Nurses listen patiently and sympathetically while applying common sense laws. One of these laws which nurses use and is often foreign to some experts is:

He who listens most, learns more.

Though nurses are some of society's best healers, so are ordinary people. Children run to parents and ask for a grazed arm to be kissed better. We heal by touch, hugging and by good social interaction with others in a pleasant natural environment. Not only do we heal others, we heal ourselves. More often than not we know what is good and bad for our health in body, mind and spirit even if we choose to do what is harmful. Some other acts of healing concern nature and the environment. For example, some farmers are reverting back to using wiser modes in agriculture. They have been party to expert theories and practices which have wreaked havoc on everything directly or indirectly. An increasing number of farmers have given up using pesticides, hormones to bulk up their cattle and the tearing out of hedgerows and dykes. They are returning more to common sense laws:

Healing and disease are in the hands of everyone.

Governments and other experts make choices about who receives various types of treatment and also when they are treated. Since the material resources are limited, this means that experts choose who shall be left to suffer, who shall benefit and who shall live and who shall die. Experts are reticent about this inevitable truth and say things like, 'All people should have equal access to the health service in relation to their needs.' What they should have and what they actually get are different kettles of fish. Do experts issue contraceptives to school children to prevent unwanted pregnancies and slow down the exploding population bomb, or do they shorten the waiting list for hospital treatment? Experts have had more than half a century to create a good health service and their expert theories have been found to do grievous bodily harm, not to mention the battery of minds and spirits. Decisions about who receives what treatment and when should be made by a randomly selected group of Justices of The Peace from the local community. Any disputes between medical staff and patients would also be dealt with by them. Expert lawyers would not enter the picture. Justices of The Peace would use common sense laws to handle all situations:

Justice in health service must be in your own hands.

One piece of evidence which must be galling to politicians and medical science concerns Christian Science. Followers do not use medical science or medical doctors. Christian Science basically believes disease is in the mind and people are made healthy by the healing of their wrong-doings or sin. Medical doctors and medical science regard Christian Science as 'unscientific and dangerous'. A medical scientist researched Christian Science. He was Dr G.E. Wilson, an autopsy surgeon in Seattle, Washington. At the time of Wilson's investigation, medical science felt it was on a high peak. It was in the golden era of the 'wonder drugs' such as sulpha, penicillin, and so forth. Dr Wilson however, found that in spite of the great confidence of medical science at the time, members of Christian Science groups were no worse off in terms of death rate. He presented his findings to The American Academy of Forensic Science. As you can imagine, the members of the academy were not too pleased. Christian Scientists do, of course, use numerous common sense laws such as:

Do unto others as you would have them do unto you.

Honesty is the best policy.

I would imagine that the government wishes it could get its spin doctors to convert the whole population of Britain to Christian Science. In this way, the government would be able to dispense with The National Health Service completely. Billions of pounds would be saved and the nation's health could be no worse off. One problem for government would be that it would put many medical scientists, lawyers and politicians out of work and increase the unemployment figures:

One thing leads to another.

Medical doctors have saved many lives, of course, particularly when the 'physical' is sensibly and justifiably focused. Doctors have stitched wounds, set bones and done surgical procedure that have changed lives for the better. Restoring sight by surgical intervention is illustrative. There have been counter-productive surgical procedures also. Frontal lobotomy is one. Statistics related to the surgical removal of cancers such as mastectomy do not present a very good picture in the majority of cases. Figures for radiation therapy are also less than convincing. Even when doctors have put shattered bodies together again after, say, a road accident, recovery is still strongly related with the mind and common sense nursing or after-care. When things go wrong for medical doctors, it is not for want of trying. Generally doctors do what they do in good faith. They want the patient to recover as soon as possible just like the patient. Nonetheless:

The road to hell is paved with good intentions.

To review then, medical science has the same faults as science at large. It has separated knowledge from morality and focused knowledge. Such knowledge loses its meaning when detached from morality. Medical science has also separated mind and body and emphasised the physical at the expense of the mental. It stresses the part to the detriment of the whole or the individual to the detriment of society. There is nothing wrong with examining smaller and smaller parts so long as the whole is borne in mind. In fact there is a common sense law included in an earlier chapter which states that the whole is reflected in the parts. However, if you want to see the wood (whole picture), as science strives to do, it is unwise to stay with your nose pressed up against a small part of the bark of the tree. If you get too close to the bark, you might not even see the tree let alone the wood. Medical science, as is the case with all science, does not appreciate the true significance of opposites or paradoxes which define reality. However, since the queen of science, physics, discovered some common sense laws in its quantum theory, medical science is having to take a little more notice of common sense laws. Basically though, medical science is still much at odds with common sense laws:

Medical science is no substitute for common sense.

Like many other institutions the government's increasing direction or interference is creating huge problems for the National Health Service. It is amazing that politicians believe they know how to run hospitals better than matrons, doctors, nurses and people in the local community. Matrons, doctors and nurses were honourable people who were efficient. Increasing managers and other bureaucrats at the expense of more doctors, nurses and basic equipment like beds and disinfectant is typical of modern governments and 'progress'. Politicians should not be telling matrons and nurses how to run hospitals, they should be asking them how to run hospitals (or even government) effectively. Having nurses get degrees has not increased their use of common sense. Indeed, some nurses have been forced into acting increasingly as mercenaries like too many personnel in modern institutions. One expression of an old wisdom directed at achieving worthy and honourable goals was, 'If at first you don't succeed try, try again.' This old wisdom has been modernised:

*If at first you don't succeed, give up or become a politician
or manager.*

Who would have thought that we would have gone from training our own excellent doctors and nurses to taking them from third world countries which are in desperate need of keeping them? Worse still, (you couldn't make this up), at a time when we are short of doctors, we can't find jobs for our own newly trained doctors. Ronald Reagan drew humourful attention to health workers and politics. After he had been shot by a would-be assassin and was in the hospital theatre about to be operated on by medical staff, he said with a big grin, 'I hope you are all Republicans.' I can't remember if the man who shot Reagan was a Democrat or Republican sympathiser.

Now back to that British political creation, the National Health Service for a few final observations. I and most of the rest of the population were led to believe that the National Health Service was a monumental achievement of politicians and that, prior to its creation, health care for the vast majority who could not afford it was virtually non-existent. This is an inaccurate picture. Before the National Health Service, hospitals and health systems were built and developed by an array of different charities, philanthropists and other volunteers. When the National Health Service came into being its political masters started closing local hospitals, clinics, surgeries and the like, which continues today. Hospitals and other health services have been 'rationalised' or 'modernised' like other services such as the railways when the Conservative government was in power. Politicians cannot leave well alone. Health tourism such as AIDS victims is expanding and dangerous. It is sapping the energy of the native British psyche and sense of fair play. The majority wish to remind experts of a common wisdom:

Charity begins at home.

Before the National Health Service were the days when the better off saw it as an honourable duty to help and look after the less fortunate like the poor and the sick; it was a common sensing. This generosity of spirit has diminished with increasing government directives. Our country, including the National Health Service, would be in a far greater mess than it is were it not for current voluntary organisations and charitable individuals. Also, in earlier days when politicians were unpaid volunteers, they were much more effective and honourable or moral than modern career politicians:

Volunteers exhibit traditional common sense values such as
giving, sacrifice and helping the less fortunate.

The roles of medical doctors as well as other professional healers, alternative, holistic, complementary, integrative or other kinds, must be put into perspective. Some figures show that around eighty per cent of people are self-healers or self-prescribers of medicines. Other reports show that seventy per cent of illness or injuries are functional and get better basically on their own; ten per cent of illnesses are incurable which leaves about twenty per cent of illness and injury to the medical profession. Of these twenty per cent doctors do well to cure half of them. There is an increasing number of self help groups and it is perhaps a good job too with what the government is doing to the health of Great Britain. Of course expert advice is not all it is cracked up to be. We can place too much trust in experts, including health experts. Consultants can give vastly different treatments for a given condition. Some recommend rest for particular heart problems whilst others advocate exercise. Health experts tell us vitamin B supplement prevents heart attacks and strokes; later they tell us the opposite – that vitamin B supplement causes heart attacks and strokes. Health experts particularly consultants, are regarded as shining lights but:

All that glisters is not gold.

It is common sense to view health as a whole rather than a separate service or institution. It is difficult to think of any animal, vegetable or mineral that does not affect health. Everything you can think of in the world and universe influences everyone's health in body, mind and spirit for good or ill – not just food, drink, exercise, work, leisure and friends, but cars, flowers, crops and so on ad infinitum. Thus, the health of one is the responsibility of all. Holistic approaches that integrate traditional, biomedical approaches with complementary or alternative practices such as acupuncture, yoga, osteopathy and various other systems, seem commonsensical:

Health must be seen as a whole because the common sense
law is: all things are connected.

CHAPTER 6

Family Diversity and Unity

Charity, responsibility and other values begin at home.

Good families are founded on common sense, not expert theory

As I have tried to illustrate, expert laws and modern science have had a great impact on common sense and justice which are basic to all good institutions including the family. Expert laws are dictating how we should be treated and how we should behave towards others even in our own families, as if we did not know already. Even anti-social families know how they should behave. They clearly recognise what is bad behaviour and are quick to shout about it when they are on the receiving end. The fact that they indulge in bad behaviour does not mean they are unaware of its opposite – good behaviour. Many people know that smoking is bad, but it does not stop them smoking. A minority of anti-social families have been allowed, by expert laws, to exert too much power over the majority of good families. Unfortunately the anti-social minority is growing:

With false laws the exception can become the rule.

Not so long ago, politicians were telling us that it was a small minority of children taking illegal drugs. Now a report informs us that over fifty per cent are involved. The continuing production and spread of expert laws and science, both of which contain rationality divorced from wisdom, is changing the structure and function of the family. The characteristics of expert laws and science are taking over instinctive family values. Now, in a growing number of families, there is great focus on the part or individual self at the expense of the greater whole or family, the larger community and society. Too many families are getting like science itself, separating out and rejecting wisdom, morality or common sense. Just as physics concentrated on objects and matter, which gave impetus to materialism, the family has become more materialistic also. Zsa Zsa Gabor more than hints at the importance of materialism when she tells us wryly, 'I want a man who is kind and understanding. Is that too much to ask of a billionaire?' In modern times we can see that:

> Science's hallmarks of lack of morality and materialism are stamped on the family.

Fortunately, some good families have been influenced less by expert theories and laws than others, but experts' impact is becoming more and more visible. Resistance to expert theories affecting the family is becoming increasingly illegal. Common sense cries out against expert theories, but it is being choked by the constant production of expert laws. Some families have been willing accomplices to expert theories and laws and have provided momentum for their production. Expert laws suit the purpose of a minority of bad families and the aspirations of experts to fame and fortune. Political ideology not only favours the individual and his rights over the best interests of the family group, it also favours minority families from hell at the expense of the peaceable majority:

> He hurts the good who spares the bad.

To illustrate how expert theories, science and laws have affected parents and children, I would like to tell a few personal stories about families. I have little doubt that you will have had similar experiences. The other day, I went into a newsagent's shop. Outside was a boy about four years old sitting in a pushchair. A large lady in her early twenties holding another one-year-old child was being served in the shop and was his mother. There were some seven or eight other people in the shop. The boy outside started pounding on the shop window with his clenched fists. He was doing it so violently that some customers in the shop began whispering 'He's going to break the window and cut himself to pieces.' The old lady shopkeeper called out for the boy to stop. After she had done this three times without effect, the boy's mother said, 'Oh leave him alone. He can't help it. He is too young to know any better.' In what she said, his mother was stating the exact position of expert legal laws, science and modern political theory:

> The mother was reciting expert legal law. her son was too young to know right from wrong.

She echoed the value-free view taken by science that
beating on a window is a fact, neither good nor bad.

The mother was quoting our modern political ideology and
legal laws which stress individual rights and freedom.

Some people are wise and some are otherwise.

Some experts, like lawyers, would rationalise the mother's behaviour by saying she was putting into practice the Christian ethic of 'forgiving' her son as well as conforming to expert legal laws. She was not forgiving her son as much as chastising the shop owner. There was nothing to forgive her son for as she saw no wrong in what he was doing. She had several opportunities to stop him but she made no attempt. Her aggressive voice and manner showed she was angry with the shop keeper for daring to criticise her son's behaviour. From what was said in the shop by the other customers when the mother had gone, her behaviour was not in keeping with the mother acting in a Christ-like manner. They were amazed at the violent behaviour of mother and son and surprised that the mother said nothing to restrain her offspring. Because a child persists in doing wrong does not mean he does not know he is doing wrong. Children can enjoy doing wrong and so can adults. Experts argue that it is just a matter of opinion as to what is right or wrong. Common sense laws disagree with this view:

Doing something we would not like done to us, is wrong.

Another example of overstressing individual rights or the expression of self concerns two married friends of my wife. We visit one another and once we stayed overnight at their house. They have a six-year-old boy who stays up watching television until eleven o'clock at night. From about nine o'clock, his mother would say every ten minutes or so, 'Just another five minutes and then you'll have to go to bed.' This went on for two hours. The boy came up with all kinds of reasons to stay up longer. After going up to bed at eleven o'clock, he came downstairs four more times before midnight because he was thirsty, could not sleep and so forth. According to his father, this was his regular routine at night. As it was a small house my wife and I slept on a make-shift bed in the living room. At six o'clock in the morning, we were rudely awakened. The television was on and the son was sitting in a chair watching it. I asked, 'Do your parents know you are down here watching television?' Without taking his eyes off the screen, the boy replied, 'Oh yes, I always watch at this time in the morning.' When the parents got up at eight o'clock, *I* enquired, 'What is this early morning television viewing about?' The mother said, 'I know it is awful. It is disgusting that the BBC allows programmes to come on so early in the mornings. I mean you've got to let them watch if they are awake haven't you?' Expert theorists and lawyers could not have bettered this mother's piece of rationalisation in justifying individual rights or freedoms:

Give a child an inch and he will take a mile.

When the same family came to stay with us, on their arrival we went into the kitchen for a cup of tea. The young son immediately went into the living-room and switched on our television. I went and switched the television off and told the boy that to come into someone else's house and put on the television was not quite the thing to do. Off he dashed to the kitchen and returned with his mum who said, 'Do let him have the television on, it is his favourite programme.' This child had a lot of 'favourite' programmes it seems. Another example of polite children concerns some of our relatives. One family visits and within a short time of their arrival the children are into almost everything. They root in drawers, in bedrooms and in any other place their fancy takes them. Once, they located some Christmas presents we had hidden a month before the festive season. These presents were not even for them. The parents did not take the slightest bit of notice of their children's behaviour. One rationalisation parents use to excuse rude behaviour is, 'Well, kids will be kids.' This reasoning is becoming more wide-spread and is applied to increasingly bad forms of behaviour. Next, is an observation from William Perm followed by an old wisdom:

Men are usually more careful about the breed of their horses and dogs than of their children.

Good manners make good friends at no cost.

Our modern age of reason or rationality divorced from common sense or wisdom is reflected in the behaviour of both the mother and son I mentioned in relation to excess television viewing. The same mother has developed another habit with her son that achieves the opposite of what it is supposed to do. The son throws violent tantrums when he cannot get his own way at home. His mother regularly spends two hours or more talking his tantrums through with him. What these lengthy sessions amount to is the boy screaming answers to his mother's endless 'Why' questions. She does this in order to *understand* the tantrums. Providing reasons for anything can go on forever as we have shown earlier. It gives her son great practice and skill in rationalising his very bad behaviour. Perhaps his mother is giving him some extended practice in rationalisation so that he can become a professional politician or lawyer. Tantrum or rage behaviour is increasing. Only yesterday I saw a boy about four or five years old in a busy town centre pleading with his mother to buy him something. When the mother said he would have to wait until she could afford it, the boy went mad flailing around and screaming foul-mouthed abuse at his mother. She kept shouting that he must wait. The boy screamed amidst his tears 'I want it now, now, now!' This reflects one value that is becoming more widespread in modern society – immediate gratification. Some onlookers were amazed. Others just said, 'It is the way of the world today isn't it?' More parents and members of the public have been forced to accept such behaviour though it goes against their common sensings. We have been conditioned to accept bad behaviour. We have had little choice in our modern 'progressive' society and many people are in despair. Expert theories have outlawed our instinctive values for good family life:

Freedom of the child is bondage of the parent.

One man's meat is another man's poison.

I asked our friend, the mother of the boy who watches early morning and late night television and has regular tantrums, how he liked school. She said he liked it and got glowing school reports, but he moaned about the strictness of the teachers and was afraid of them. I asked if he had tantrums at school. The mother said, 'Oh no, he wouldn't dare. He is too scared of his teachers and what his friend might say.' She told me the headmistress was surprised he had tantrums at home. At school the headmistress and teachers regarded him as a model pupil and could hardly believe he was capable of such behaviour. The mother went on to say, 'I haven't told him I let his head teacher know of how he acts at home or he would throw a fit.' I suggested a certain amount of fear he experienced at school might be quite a good thing for him. The mother replied that she did not believe pupils should ever fear teachers in any way. Can being unafraid or fearless have any real meaning without experiencing its opposite – being afraid or having fear?

> Those who are prepared to tolerate bad behaviour will surely get it.
>
> You reap what you sow.

At the outset, children are very self-centred and can continue to be so if allowed and rewarded for such behaviour. Common sense and experience tell us that this is not because they are completely selfish. This would be against the common sense law of opposites. Children's behaviour is more concerned with curiosity and the exploration of their boundaries of influence to see how far they can go. In the world of the young child, parents are all-knowing and all-powerful and to be able to manipulate these main sources of power along with other adults is success and power indeed. Crying is attention-seeking and a source of power. It brings parents running. When rewarded, crying becomes a habit and for the child, a successful one. Unfortunately very bad behaviour can get far more attention than good behaviour. If bad behaviour is not discouraged, it develops and expands. Ancient wisdom and common experience have always recognised the constant testing out of parents by children:

> Children will be as good or bad as parents expect or allow them to be.

Children should not be expected to behave like angels, but behaviour of too many of the modern generation is very destructive and violent to all concerned, including themselves. Even in earlier times when children's behaviour was a great deal better than it is today, F. Lebowitz said, 'All God's children are not beautiful. Most of God's children are, in fact, barely presentable.' Modern families reflect the practice of expert theories and science of focusing one side of two opposites. There is much freedom without responsibility. One common illustration of this is that there is an ever growing number of anti-social people who have children knowing full well they are incapable of looking after them. Some of them are school children themselves. Some of them readily appreciate they are unable to look after themselves, never mind having children, but produce offspring anyway. Their expectation and plan is for the majority to support their irresponsible or anti-social activities. Such an expectation is grossly immoral, not to mention the degree of promiscuity involved. One boy barely sixteen years old is already the father of two children by two different girls, themselves hardly in their teens. When interviewed this boy's father said, 'I don't know what all the fuss is about. We are all comfortable with what happened.' Another fifteen-year-old girl became pregnant by an eleven-year-old boy and stated that she thought the boy would 'make a good father'. Common sensing or instinct makes us feel angry that we are forced to shoulder the burden of irresponsible people which politicians and their laws make us do. Our inner feeling tells us that the family should take responsibility for the behaviour of its members:

Charity begins at home.

This common sense law has been overthrown and outlawed by experts. There are all kinds of policies, laws, theories and rationalisations to reward and encourage anti-social families. A simple example is that if unmarried girls, some of whom are hardly out of school, have a child, they can be put at the top of a council house list. Responsible married couples are downgraded on the list and have to wait for a house. At the rate single girls are producing children with absent fathers, normal married couples will have a mighty long wait for a house or apartment. Expert policies and laws separate or split up families into smaller and smaller parts which reflects modern science. An ancient Chinese proverb is fitting here. Virtually all cultures have numerous sayings with exactly the same meaning. In this context it reads:

Promiscuity brings family sorrow.

Not only do experts force us to support and reward antisocial behaviour, their laws also dictate the language we use to describe it. It is politically incorrect to use such terms as unmarried mothers or fathers, we are obliged to call them 'single parent families'. This, of course, puts some good citizens under the same heading of 'single parent families'. A woman may have struggled to bring up a family because her husband has been killed or died as a consequence of some expert laws. Such a person should not be classified under the same name category as promiscuous, irresponsible or selfish people who are a great drain on the rest of society. Expert ideology specifically promotes individual rights or freedoms and the expression of self as desirable goals. Theories and laws of experts have edited shame and other essential feelings out of life's script. This is a charter for anti-social and promiscuous families which could hardly suit them better than if they had written it themselves. Modern ideology has produced great imbalance or disharmony in modern family life. The natural feeling of the majority of good families is that the anti-social behaviour of irresponsible parenting and expert laws which make them support such activities are shameful and immoral. The present state of affairs flies in the face of common sense laws:

Without shame there can be no pride.

Most systems in our society are based on expert theories and laws which work against the welfare of the normal family compared to anti-social families. To justify their position experts rationalise their policies by saying that all families are different and so there is no such thing as a normal family. One government minister said, about the withdrawal of tax allowance from married couples, that the allowance was 'offensive to other types of relationships'. If normal married couples were not forced to sponsor other types of relationships, such as the promiscuous and irresponsible production of children, they would not need an allowance in the first place. It is only a fraction of what they are made to contribute, in one way or another, to the upkeep of a growing tide of children of 'single parent promiscuities'. This is another wisdom that all cultures have:

Good families beget good societies, bad families beget bad societies.

Common sensing or wisdom means shared feelings or values that are alike. Modern fleeting sexual encounters are separate from wisdom and do not reflect the better side of our nature. Even the majority of promiscuous people are seeking a lasting relationship that can provide a special identification which gives the opportunity to express the better parts of their nature. This is far more fulfilling to people. Promiscuous people, at some time or other, admit to the great agonies of their lives. Expert theories and laws pander to the worse or immoral sides of our being. Like many other wisdoms, the following one is losing much of its meaning. Repentance and conscience are seen as old-fashioned and out of date in our modern society with is modern laws. It is particularly relevant to brief sexual encounters or any other anti-social behaviours:

Act in haste, repent at length.

Normal families are defined by the majority's feelings and values, not by experts and other vocal minorities. The common sense laws of the majority are also the best guides for what is acceptable social behaviour, including the behaviour of families. Good families seek to express the better aspects of their nature and this is based on wisdom, not rationalisation separated from common sense laws. In a nutshell, good family life is founded on common sense. When it comes right down to it, experts find it difficult to disagree with this obvious observation. Politicians and other experts stress how important good family values, with committed husbands and wives, are to the stability and success of society. On the other hand, they manufacture laws and policies that destroy good family values and promote and support promiscuous and irresponsible parenting:

You cannot have your cake and eat it.

The most famous and influential expert on children and families is Doctor Benjamin Spock. He, like politicians and lawyers, was an expert who paid lip-service to morality in respect of children and families. His writings are regarded as 'The Bible' for child rearing and good parenting. Though he has an extensive band of disciples, some criticise his theories for allowing far too much freedom for children. His works show he is a great believer in rationality or finding reasons for bad behaviour. The friend I mentioned earlier, who spends hours indulging her son's extensive television viewing habits and his tantrums, uses Spock's theories:

A little knowledge is dangerous, expert knowledge can be fatal.

An example of Spock's lip-service to common wisdoms concerns his theories compared with what he did in practice. His disciples say his theories are full of wisdom and common sense strategies. However, according to a report, Spock's son states that in bringing up his own family, this world famous expert did the very opposite of what his theories recommended. As a father, Spock was a cruel tyrant who created great misery for his son and family. According to his son, Spock was responsible for driving his wife to drink. He led his adoring public to believe he ran his own family in keeping with his widely acclaimed theories. For Spock, like many other experts and an increasing number of the general population, image becomes more important than substance, truth or wisdom. Not only does Spock ignore some common sense laws in his written theories, he defied even more in bringing up his own family. You will, no doubt, be able to furnish a number of them. One might be:

Practise what you preach.

Though Spock's theories reflect some of the usual expert excesses and defy their share of common sense laws, they do contain certain recommendations that coincide with common wisdoms. For example, he advises parents to use their instincts in bringing up their children rather than expert theories. Many, of course, regard Spock himself as an expert. Because Spock did not put into practice his theories with his own family, we should not be blind to the fact that he recognised the importance of some common sense laws or instinctive values in his books. At least he did not deliberately set out to degrade and exclude common sense values or morality as expert science does. Even Einstein, who was a great believer in common sense, did not apply it to his own family as much as he hoped he would. To some degree or other, we are all guilty of paying lip-service to common sense laws or morality. We can all talk a better game than we play. The degree to which lip-service is paid to common sense laws is very important for it indicates how wise or otherwise a person is:

Actions speak louder than words.

Paying lip-service to common sense laws is part and parcel of human nature. It is not new. What is of concern is the rate of increase of it and its use by more and more people. Virtually everyone will readily admit that letting a child have its own way too much spoils the child and is bad for it. When a child asks its parents for some consumer article or to do something an inner voice often warns that to let the child have its own way is wrong. In spite of this feeling, parents allow the child to have its wish and then rationalise the decision with all sorts of logical reasons. One common one is that other children have not been denied such requests and you do not want your child to feel different and deprived. Big things can develop from small things, as an oak tree from an acorn. Similarly, gross behaviour in children can grow from small acts. One ancient saying that is relevant to children asking for things is:

> If you give children an inch, they will take a mile.

Rationalisation by parents and children is the main form of justification for paying lip-service to common sense morality or ignoring it altogether. Parents and even very young children know what they should and should not do in situations requiring moral judgments. It is the ability to tell right from wrong in human nature that led to man's development and evolution. This is a general characteristic of nature. The fact that you can give an example of an exception to any rule does not mean that the rule or law is no good. Citing an exception to a rule and then concluding that the law is meaningless is a regular but fallacious argument used to make common sense laws seem useless. It is a strategy much used by politicians, lawyers and others striving to get their own way. Using a few exceptions to claim the rule is wrong is another illustration of detaching rationality or reasoning from wisdom or common sense. One common sense law states clearly:

> There are exceptions to every rule.

In its origin, as indicated earlier, rationality was an integrated part of human nature and ability, but when separated from its roots in wisdom, which is a speciality of experts, it is very harmful. It is characteristic of modern family life which focuses the part at the expense of the whole. Individual rights and the importance of self are excessively stressed to the detriment of the family, and larger groups like the local community and society as a whole. Where is there a single expert law that improves on common sense laws in relation to the well-being of families, parents or children? If common sense laws were used instead of expert laws and theories, families would be far better off physically, mentally, morally, spiritually, financially and in any other way you care to put it:

There is no substitute for common sense in fostering good family life and values.

Not so long ago, when families fell down in taking responsibility for their immediate family members, other relatives together with agencies like the school and members of the local community including the police, helped put matters on a better footing. This was in the days when common sense held more sway and there were far, far fewer expert laws. Most families worked in co-operation with one another, with the school, with the local community and its policeman in dealing with bad behaviour of children:

Shared values are the strength of family, community and society. They reflect human nature and common sensings.

Now shared values have splintered into individual wants, tastes and rights. This often means it is every parent, teacher, child, policeman and community member for himself. R.W. Emerson makes an interesting observation on the cult of the individual. He says, 'We fancy men are individuals; so are pumpkins.' Along with the philosophy of stressing individual human rights and freedoms have come brutal and violent children, some well below the age of ten years who are virtually professional criminals including murderers. This behaviour is spreading. Expert theories and laws have resulted in corrupting the innocence of childhood and the better nature of children. Some youngsters do not even bother to pay lip-service to morality, they make a virtue of violence and immorality. In ancient cultures and even in later times, in the American Indian culture as well as our own society, paying lip-service to or ignoring common sense morality was the exception to the rule. Things are changing for the worse:

Bad behaviour that used to be an exception to the rule is fast becoming the rule.

Over recent decades then, we feel responsibility for family life and children has been taken out of the hands of the family more than at any other time in our history. This shift of responsibility accelerates by the day. Common sense has been rejected in disciplining unruly children. Expert laws have replaced common sense. Responsibility for children no longer belongs to the primary socialising agents of the family, relatives, the school and the community including the local policeman. Political law-makers and their agents such as judges, lawyers, psychologists, social workers and even The European Court of Justice have taken over. Moral welfare including the discipline of children is being taken out of the family more and more with each passing day. The slightest disagreement that even a very young child might have with its parents can involve many official bodies, agencies and personnel created by government and its expert laws. This is particularly true if the child wishes to cash in on all the expert legal rights available to him. Even the most trivial cases can go on and on in true legal fashion. Rather than involving all these counter-productive agencies, any family problems that are not resolved by the family should be dealt with by eleven randomly selected Justices of The Peace from the local community. Apart from getting much more real justice, the time and number of people involved would be drastically reduced:

Too many cooks spoil the broth.

There are many examples in the media every day of expert laws making parents' decisions illegal. One boy in Britain who objected to his parents' mode of discipline is taking his parents to The European Court. Another parent who wanted to cane his son for threatening to stab a younger brother is in danger of being prosecuted as experts regard caning a physical abuse of the recipient no matter how horrific or brutal the crime. Today there is another case where a fourteen-year-old girl had a row with her parents about an older boyfriend who, incidentally, turned out to be a criminal. She put herself into local council care against the wishes of her parents and it was all legal and above board. The police were powerless to do anything. The girl became pregnant. The lady columnist reporting the story in the press asks the common sense question that is on everyone's lips:

What sort of law allows families to be treated like this?

Expert theories and laws encourage children to leave the family home and indulge in many self-destructive and anti-social behaviours. More and more children are running away from home at a younger and younger age. It is a modern day adventure for too many of today's youth. The excitement of the big city can be compelling in a society that worships glamour, sex-gods and 'having a good time'. With the modern obsession for self expression and individual freedom, parents have little influence over children who choose to behave badly. These children use expert laws to justify their actions. Running away from home, for example, has been rationalised with all manner of reasons. You will be familiar with many. Some are as follows:

Some Common Reasons Given For Leaving Home

My parents always wanted to know exactly where I was going whenever I went out.

My parents and I just did not get on.

My parents would not let me play loud music after midnight.

There was nothing for young people to do where I lived.

My parents didn't like the people I hung around with.

I know I'm only thirteen and my boyfriend is twenty but my parents have no right to choose my friends.

These rationalisations lack wisdom and experience, but they reflect expert theories and legal laws. If you so choose you can find a reason for anything upsetting you. Youngsters can select any piece of parental behaviour and use it to rationalise leaving home or any other activity they wish to do. Some youngsters do not bother with other rationalisations or reasons, they just chant the experts' modern philosophy which is enshrined in legal laws:

I am an individual and have the right to do my own thing.

If my parents don't like it, tough, that's their problem.

Such behaviour leaves even good parents wondering where they went wrong. Experts can usually tell them, their theories see to that. It is interesting to observe the children of experts on human behaviour. Though I could cite you many examples from my own experience, I shall restrict my illustration to two cases. About the beginning of the permissive society in the early 1960s, I knew two famous professors of psychology. Both were devout believers in free self-expression for their children. When I knew them, one had a four-year-old boy and the other had a little girl of the same age. Both were allowed to do anything that was not physically harmful to them. They were allowed to draw on the walls of the living-room, throw pots and pans around and most other things that the majority of parents would not allow. When the little girl was thirteen years old she made headlines. Virtually a whole rugby team was taken to court for having sex with this girl in one single evening. The girl had been more than a willing party. When the little boy was fifteen years old he was accused of stabbing someone and has spent most of his life since then in various mental institutions:

Too much freedom destroys lives.

When promiscuous teenagers have children, many regret it both sooner and later. They themselves experience being on the receiving end of the kind of behaviour they made their parents endure. Their own children are anti-social, anti-parent and can run away from home at an even earlier age. These children also have an additional rationalisation string to their bow and can point out to their parents: 'Well, you can't talk, you ran away from home and had me when you were fifteen.' Some parents might wonder if there is not some truth in Patrick Murray's lighthearted comment that, 'Teenagers are God's punishment for having sex.' God does not have to be brought into it, promiscuous sex brings all kinds of punishments to the participants, the offspring, the families and to society at large:

The apple doesn't fall far from the tree.

It would be a mistake to assume, as too many experts and their disciples do, that youngsters who are promiscuous or run away from home do so because they have bad homes. Even if they do actually come from a bad home, other members of their family should be responsible for providing accommodation and support. This is what families are for in the structure and function of a good society. The burden should not immediately be thrust upon the majority who are strangers compared with family members. Family such as parents, brothers, sisters, grandparents, aunts, uncles, cousins and the like have to take responsibility for its own members when they fall by the wayside. Next in line to provide help should be friends of the family.

Only in emergency circumstances, such as having no living relative or friends, should the majority be called upon to help. There are many common sense laws that relate to this. Two are:

Charity must begin at home.

A friend in need is a friend indeed.

Experts would claim that it is only in emergencies that the majority are called upon to help. However, politicians, lawyers, social workers and the like rationalise what emergency means to fit their own theories and agendas. These are not to the benefit of the majority families nor do they benefit the anti-social families and children they are supposed to be helping. If expert policies and laws were any good, things would be getting better, not worse. Some youngsters who leave even a bad home often associate with people far worse than those they ran away from in the first place:

Running away from home can be jumping from the frying pan into the fire.

Youngsters claiming they cannot get on with their families are too often putting forward a rationalisation which really means they could not get their own way. Most youngsters have numerous blood relatives and if they are unable to get on with any of these, it often says more about their own behaviour than that of their relatives. Sometimes anti-social children, together with their expert supporters like lawyers and social workers, use an old common saying to justify their case. It is:

You cannot choose your family or blood line.

What they do not mention too much is the opposite of this which can have more relevance to the more wayward and selfish children. It states:

Parents may choose their friends, but not their children.

More expert laws on rights are being planned for us in respect of runaways and the homeless. The leader of the Labour Party, Tony Blair, is reported to have promised before the 1997 election that should the Labour Party get elected to office, homeless people or street dwellers would have a *right* to demand a permanent home. The major message is already clear enough, if you are single, to get a new home, get homeless or pregnant, or better still, pregnant and homeless:

What is legal is getting more immoral.

Children go into care homes on the say-so of expert theories and laws. They can be in far greater danger in these places than in a very bad parental home. The experts' professional care homes are all too often a hot-bed of almost any behaviour or crime you could imagine. There have been deaths from stealing cars and 'joy-riding', from drugs and from other assorted modern pleasure-seeking activities. Under-age sex is rampant as well are numerous forms of sexual depravity. One daughter from a middle class family took advantage of the expert rights that are available to her in the social welfare system to get into care. She is twelve years old and is associating with a twenty six year old drug-pusher and goes shoplifting instead of going to school. If children wish to indulge in any kind of depraved or criminal behaviour, a care home is the place to be. In practice the children can have complete authority in these homes. The majority want the behaviours that lead to children being put into care homes dealt with long before it gets to the care home stage. Experts, of course, say they want the same, but their laws make it impossible. Expert laws have also made the staff in care homes unable to do their jobs in any common sense fashion:

Putting children into care homes is like using petrol to put out a fire.

Prevention is better than cure.

There seems to be no limit to the lack of common sense of experts. Their decisions are breathtaking to the majority of people. Our anger and frustration are showing in the number of incidents of frayed tempers everywhere in everyday life. Angry reactions of ordinary people are becoming a norm, if they are not the norm already. The majority of staff in care homes want to change the situation for the better, but they, and the police from whom they often try to seek help, have their hands tied by expert laws and theories. Everyone concerned can do little or nothing to stop these children running riot. Expert theories and laws enshrined in The

Children Act is another example of more laws, less justice and good behaviour. It gives unrestrained choice and action to children. The Children Act, designed to protect children, gives them power to destroy and be destroyed:

> Too much freedom and power corrupt.

Expert theories and laws foster the attitude that at the first sign of conflict, blame someone and runaway or contact a lawyer or some sort of social worker. Some family conflicts, of course, can develop into serious abuse. It is not always the parents who do the abusing. Some mothers in growing numbers are complaining that their sons and daughters punch and beat them. When conflicts cannot be resolved by the family members themselves, ordinary people in the community can detect and deal with it more effectively than detached experts with their complicated laws. All cases of family conflict such as abuse should be handled by randomly selected Justices of The Peace from the local community along with any other sort of dispute or crime:

> Expert laws on individual rights aimed at reducing family
> conflict has greatly increased it.

Conflict itself, like its opposite, harmony, is part and parcel of everyday living, including family life, and good family life at that. It is in the family that we learn how to handle conflict which is an essential ingredient for effective interactions that relate to respect, responsibility, and other values. If you cannot live with conflict, problems and struggle, you cannot live life at all. Many old wisdoms make this point. One of them is:

> You have to take the rough with the smooth.

From the very outset, there is conflict between baby and parents. Even before birth, the child can keep the mother awake, make her sick and cause many upsets to the family routine. After birth, there are conflicts about feeding and sleeping times which can go on through infancy and into adolescence and even into adulthood. Some new parents seem to give the impression that most inconvenience or upset with children happens in babyhood with having to change nappies and do most other things for their extremely dependent infant. Parents can think that when their child starts school, their problems will diminish and they will have much more time to themselves. As time goes by, parents realise that how the child was treated and disciplined in the very earliest of days is very important to later behaviour and attitudes. In other words, they realise the truth of many common wisdoms, two of which are:

> **The child's most important attitudes and behaviour are developed at his mother's knee.**

> **The child is the father of the man.**

Some friends of mine who are parents show how conflict can develop from the very day a child is born. Mary and John got married and after two years had a son Charles. His mother fed the baby by the 'feed-on-demand' method. This feeding system is the one recommended by Doctor Benjamin Spock, the child expert. He reasoned that this was a good method as it stopped the baby crying. Every time the baby cried Mary, his mother, picked him up and offered him food. Sometimes he was not hungry, he just enjoyed being picked up and getting warm attention. He did not just cry for food, he cried for anything he wanted as he became more aware of his surroundings. After a while, the crying was sometimes modified to a whine. If the child did not get immediate attention and what he wanted, he would turn it into a full-blown cry or scream: Two wisdoms give good advice:

> **If you reward a child's whining, you'll get whining.**

> **Excess feeding-on-demand to satisfy the child leads to its opposite – dissatisfaction.**

Mary, the mother, says she could not go out to work even if she wanted as her son is so demanding. She takes her son shopping every day as it is her favourite pastime. Her son, Charles, uses his crying, whining or screaming to get his mother to buy him a toy or some other present every day. Their house is packed with toys. Even the bathroom and bath are jammed with them. Toys are literally piled around in every room, hallway, shelf and even the conservatory and shed are full of them. It is impossible to sit down in a chair without first removing some toys. The grandparents and other relatives compete with one another also to give Charles more and more expensive presents. I was there once when the boy's maternal grandparent brought an expensive aeroplane as a gift. He took it out of its box, gave it the most cursory of glances, then played with the cardboard box in which it came. There are several common sense wisdoms that relate to excess of things including material gifts and selfish demands. One of them is:

> When a child is given everything, it is likely
> to value nothing.

Mary does not like much of her son's behaviour and issues threats such as, 'I won't take you shopping if you are not a good boy.' She rarely carries out any of her many threats. Due to the constant attention demanded by her son, Mary is unable to do the normal tasks about the house. There are piles of unwashed and un-ironed clothes in great profusion. If you have a cup of coffee, you have to wash a cup and make the coffee as the mother is too busy running around after her son. All this, of course, upsets the husband when he arrives home from work and has to cook the evening meal after he has washed enough pans and crockery to do so. The husband is more strict with his son, but the boy spends most of his time with his mother. Even his father has come to accept some of his son's habits though he moans about them. He says, 'Ah, what can you do? It is a sign of the times I suppose. Sometimes I feel like W.C. Fields, I like children – preferably boiled in oil.' There is great strain in the family and marriage due to the boy's behaviour. Though the mother has been the main socialising agent for the son, the father has to shoulder his share of the responsibility. The line heard from numerous comedians that, 'Children are the ruination of the adult classes,' is becoming more of a serious observation in modern society:

> Many a true word spoken in jest.

I visited the family after the son, Charles had been going to school for six months and asked his mother how he was getting on there. She said that he thought it was alright, but she could not get him out of bed in the morning and he was always late for school. What follows is a conversation I had with his mother, Mary:

Me: What are you doing to get him out of bed in the morning?

Mary: Well, I keep telling him he should be at school by 9 a.m. like all the other little boys and girls, but he still won't get out of bed.

Me: What does the school have to say about it?

Mary: I have been up to school and we have reached a compromise.

Me: What's that?

Mary: Well, the school has agreed that he can go to school late on three mornings out of the five.

Me: How is that working?

Mary: I still can't get him out of bed on time.

Me: What time does he go to bed at night? [Actually, I already knew.]

Mary: Well, you know he likes to stay up until we go to bed. Sometimes he does fall asleep before we go. I have tried to explain to him for years why he should go to bed earlier.

Me: Perhaps you should borrow my cat. If I stay in bed after the alarm clock goes off, my cat bites my toe as it his feeding time. It is painful, but it gets me out of bed and I do not stay in too often after the alarm has gone. If my cat can train me, perhaps you should take a leaf out of his book:

There can be no pleasure without pain.

Mary, of course, does not like her son going to school late or many of his other behaviours and with the passage of time issues more and more threats. The son has learned that when his mother says, 'No', to his demands, she gives in if he whines or cries long or loud enough. This behaviour is becoming far too widespread in modern society and the whining or petulant outbursts, to get what one wants and immediately, is not just restricted to children:

Empty vessels make the most noise.

The husband of another couple, Mike, complains to me about his twenty-year-old daughter. She does very little to contribute to the family home where she still lives. As she puts it, 'I just want a good time, to do my own thing and party as much as I can.' When at home, she expects her parents to wait on her hand and foot and leaves her dirty laundry and other articles strewn all over the house. Mike knows what he *should* have done. He tells me that children should be involved in jobs around the house from the time they are tiny tots. In this way the family is more cohesive and responsibility gains real meaning. Although Mike's daughter earns as much as he does, she will often say, 'I can't pay anything to the family coffers this week, I need the money for a new dress, shoes' and so forth. Mike is always quoting old wisdoms at me in one way or another. Some are:

> Too much freedom can be worse
> than too much discipline.
> You've got to train children when they
> are very young; it's too late at twenty.
> Sometimes you can be too kind
> for their own good and yours.

Allowing children vast amounts of freedom would be understandable if it were good for them, even if it were harmful to parents. This would be an acceptable form of sacrifice from the parents. However, a great amount of freedom is bad for both children and parents:

> Sometimes you have to be cruel to be kind.

I remember going to Mike's house when his daughter was eight years old and I have witnessed many similar incidents. Like many children who are allowed to do it, Mike's daughter adopted a whining, pleading tone when she wanted to get her own way. On this particular occasion, she wanted to go to a 'pop' concert with her friend and her parents. She asked her father if she could go. He snapped firmly 'No, certainly not.' She asked him nine times and gave numerous reasons why she should go, including one that her father was the only dad who would refuse such a request. She also claimed that she was the only one in her class at school who had never been to a 'live' pop concert. After the ninth time of asking, her father said begrudgingly, 'Oh go on then, you can go.' After his daughter had left the room, Mike turned to me and said, 'Well her best friend is going and I don't want to appear mean.' This was a regular pattern of behaviour. Mike would refuse a request that was against his better judgment for eight or nine times and then give in to the persistent whinings and rationalisations of his daughter. From these exchanges, the daughter's main learning was that her father would give in, particularly if she could make him feel guilty:

> In modern society, if you whine long and loud enough you get your own way.

The friends I have mentioned have learned as parents that without common sense discipline, true freedom does not exist. Unbridled freedom leads to unbridled violence and destruction. Just yesterday, two twelve and thirteen-year-old girls were given a two year custodial sentence for kicking to death another girl of their own age. The dead girl had been trying to stop a fight. The parents of the dead girl, the police and most of the rest of the population were very unhappy about the length and type of sentence. One expert lawyer rationalised the shortness of the sentence by saying the kicks to the skull were not intended to kill, therefore the death was accidental. It is amazing that professional lawyers have been tolerated for so long as the following proverb or its equivalent has been around in all cultures since lawyers were lawyers:

> The law is an ass.

In point of fact, asses would justifiably be offended. Sometimes other people in the local community try to compensate for lack of common sense in expert law or in the home. Expert laws and theories not only prevent this, they punish the helpers for their efforts. One of today's news stories concerns a headmaster who tried to restrain a ten-year-old boy who went 'berserk' after a fight. The boy's father complained to police and the headmaster was arrested for assault, even though he had used an accepted technique of a bear-hug to stop the boy flailing around. In another case, a local doctor chased off some youngsters after they had opened his surgery door and thrown stones. A parent turned up, not to apologise, but to threaten the doctor with physical violence:

> Like father like son.

Another couple I know were walking along a street of what for years had been described as a peaceful town, It was 11.30 at night. Two ten-year-old boys were sprawled out near a wall drinking from a bottle of vodka and

1. Wes aged 3

2. Wes (left) best man at his cousin Les's wedding

3. When we first started to 'walk out' 1976

4. USA 1978

5–6. Ever the joker!

7. *Wedding 30 May 1992*

8. Wedding 30 May 1992

9. 1978 with our cat Boot

10. 2006 Wes entertained Celi, a Welsh friend's dog, in their car

11. Our last trip to Venice circa *2000*

12. Winchester water meadows circa *2004*

13. 1998

14. Pitlochrie 2001

puffing away at cigarettes. They got up and lunged toward the couple and demanded money. When they were turned down, they threatened violence in foul-mouthed language. The adults reported the incident to the police. A few days later, they checked at the police-station what had happened. The police said they had been round to the boys' homes and warned them that their behaviour was 'inappropriate'. The couple asked what the parents had said. The police said they had visited the homes on several occasions in the past concerning similar complaints adding that, basically, the parents were worse than their children. One policeman pointed out what we all know about our expert legal system. He said:

> Under present laws we police can do nothing.
>
> We call all young criminals – the untouchables.

Many parents, in spite of much of it being made illegal, still hang on to much common sense in their family lives. Our friends Tom and Sue are examples. They have two children who are positive, happy, confident and skilful. From the very beginning, they expected and insisted on good behaviour from their children. If there was any whining, the child was told cheerfully but firmly to, 'Go to your room and come back when you feel happier.' When the child returned, Tom would say, 'We just love to see that smiling face darling.' He would pick her up twirl her around while kissing her. From the outset, when the child was going to do something harmful like getting too close to a fire, the parents would say, 'No, no, no.' If the infant persisted, she would be given a short sharp smack on the hand, leg or backside. After a very short time, slaps were unnecessary. The children have very few toys from shops. They make things with their parents out of cardboard, wood, cloth and all manner of materials. A common wisdom informs us:

> What children make themselves, they appreciate the most.

Once I was there and after a meal, a four-year-old asked, 'Should I get the chair daddy?' The boy got on a chair near the kitchen sink and with his father washed the dinner plates, saucepans and other utensils. The child loved it. It was great fun and father and son asked each other all sorts of questions such as, 'I wonder how many cups of water it would take to fill this saucepan, can you guess? Why does cold water not shift grease as easily as hotter water?' It was an enjoyable situation as were mealtimes themselves where all types of meaningful interactions, learnings and experiences were gained by parents and children. There was no eating while watching television. Sue, quite rightly, maintains that mealtimes are important family occasions for sharing feelings, ideas and experiences. In the home of Tom and Sue viewing television is a small incidental supplement to family life, not the focus of it. I pointed out that some experts saw smacking as physical abuse. Tom replied, 'That's nonsense. People know the difference between a smack to chastise and physical abuse. Laws do not deter those people who are bent on abusing their children anyway.' I once asked Tom and Sue to sum up their philosophy in bringing up children. Their replies were all, in one way or another, ancient and common wisdoms:

From the very beginning, start as you mean to go on.

Do not use a threat that you will not carry out.

Early chastisement means less need for it later.

Be calm particularly when dispensing chastisement.

Encourage being positive, cheerful and humorous.

Families who work, play and laugh together, stay together.

There are advantages and disadvantages both to having a stable long-lasting marriage and 'playing the field'. However, people who have all kinds of affairs, such as Frank Sinatra, still show they yearn for a happy long-lasting family relationship and marriage. In modern society, people can add to their fame by being promiscuous and then boasting about their conquests and sexual prowess through the media. Sooner or later, these same people admit their lives have been empty, lacking any real meaning and are desperate and pathetic – even suicidal. Stories in the media bear testimony to this every day. There are many other disadvantages to having many different sexual partners. Sickness in body, mind and spirit associated with not having good relations with children and ex-partners or having them hate you and make a mess of their own lives, are examples. Man, over his million years of evolution, is instinctively aware that long-lasting family associations are best suited to the welfare of his children, his other family members, the social order at large and also to his own well-being. There are many common wisdoms that support this human characteristic:

A good family is the greatest of riches.

You cannot have your cake and eat it.

Experts have rediscovered something about marriage that everyone else already knew. Their evidence shows that people who live together as opposed to marrying are four times more likely to split up. When those who live together marry, they face lower chances of success. Children of single parent families have more illness, do worse at school, are more likely to be unemployed and turn to crime. In spite of this, The New Labour Government kept producing new legislation that punishes traditional families and traditional family values. Even when marriage and traditional family values were held in high esteem, say around the time of the Second World War, there was always some sexual promiscuity about. Billy Holiday the famous singer born in 1915 said, 'Mom and pop were just a couple of kids when they got married. He was eighteen, she was sixteen and I was three.' Sexual promiscuity has some advantages. For example, if there is a serious imbalance between males and females and the population is dangerously low, having several partners could be beneficial. Even in this situation, the downside is it can be accompanied with much violence. In a period when we are grossly over-populated, is particularly dangerous:

Government policies and laws support and encourage promiscuity.

Because it is biologically possible to have children, does not mean it is a right. It is also biologically possible to kill and maim, but it is not a *right*. Rights that have real meaning and wisdom have to be earned. Experts have created all kinds of rights that are against the common sense and will of the people. The bottom-line argument used by experts is that we cannot leave these irresponsible parents and their unfortunate children out on the street. Such rationalisations really mean that the government is quite prepared to leave good families out on the street, allow old people to die of cold or starvation in their own homes and other good citizens to suffer all kinds of hardship at the hands of anti-social families. Available resources are limited. Resources are poured into irresponsible families at the expense of sensible ones. Only yesterday, a press report spoke of a fifteen-year-old boy who is costing the tax payer 90,000 pounds a year. This would support five ordinary families in a manner above their normal income. The boy lives in a cottage in a lovely part of the country with a car and driver at his disposal. It takes five social workers to look after this boy. Common sense law insists:

> When there is a choice between good families and
> irresponsible ones, the good ones must prevail

Some glimmer for change exists. More protests are heard from the majority, which in essence means we have to revive common sense values in respect of everything, particularly in respect of families for they are the foundations of any good society. Even some politicians and lawyers, including left–wing liberals, are beginning to realise that expert theories and laws embodied in the welfare state are having the opposite outcomes to the intended effect. Policies are splitting up traditional families and destroying the moral fabric of the nation. The majority of politicians and other experts seem to be notable exceptions to the common saying:

> We live and learn.

Today, more than ever, political correctness hinders the few experts who feel the welfare state is a disaster. They are not allowed to deal with such questions as sexual immorality which has led to over-population, an increase in violence and many other ills. Experts regard sexual morality as a personal matter and they do not wish to be accused of interfering with individual choice, rights and freedoms. Paradoxically, expert laws have been the most disgraceful and comprehensive intrusion into the personal freedoms of ordinary families in living memory. Using common sense laws would clearly demonstrate the great harm that expert laws and theories have created. The experts' justification of their own laws by rationality detached from wisdom illustrates another ancient and common saying:

> Politicians defend what gives them power, namely, laws,
> more than they defend the truth.

The welfare benefits system works against the interests of ordinary common sense families. It has to be dismantled and replaced by practices based on common sense laws. Only in exceptional circumstances should families be allowed to apply for benefits to be paid by the majority. Decisions on the applications would be made by randomly selected Justices of The Peace.

Families must be held responsible for looking after their own. They would be held accountable and have to pay for their irresponsible behaviour and not rely on the majority. Putting responsibility where it belongs, back with the family, provides incentive not to indulge in indiscriminate relationships and other anti-social acts. The majority want more discrimination against irresponsible behaviour, not rewards for it as expert law provides. Nature itself is striking back at promiscuity and over-population. Sexually transmitted diseases are rampant and on the increase. They are creating more sickness, more deaths and more infertility. Common sense laws achieve the best system of fairness or justice that is available to us:

More expert laws, less family justice.

The old fashioned view of children was that they should be seen but not heard. Too many children have been allowed to be so objectionable and violent that many people would wish for a modern wisdom to be, 'Children should not be seen or heard' or perhaps better still in view of excess population, 'Children should not be.' A modern wisdom that reflects today's reality is:

Children can do what they like, when they like, for experts are dispensing with wrong-doing and punishment.

Younger and younger girls and boys are producing children of their own. Some see it as a good career move as they can be supported by many unknown people – the tax payers. For an increasing number, benefits or state welfare has become a chosen life style. People can be financially better off by not working than hard-working families. Some couples can be even more well off if they separate. Divorce is the new marriage. One modern wisdom we are hearing more and more often is:

It is foolish to work when the state will support you and your children no matter how many.

Some families boast about making the state support them. One lady with eleven children by several different men seemed, like the government, proud of such welfare support and actually said, 'Why shouldn't the state support us?' Guess how much money it cost to keep them. Do not just count the financial cost – although this is breath-taking, add in the social and moral price. Experts and in particular politicians, with the rise in human rights legislation and political correctness, have conspired to downgrade families and upgrade their replacements. The traditional family with husband, wife and children is being driven out of existence by the liberal elite via tax legislation or reduced benefit, along with other various policies and laws. The norm for modern families is becoming women having several children by different fathers and men having several children by different women. This anecdote represents the experience of a growing number of children. One little girl of six asked of another girl in the playground at school, 'Who was that man who brought you to school?' The other girl replied, 'Oh, that's my daddy.' The first girl said, 'We had him for our daddy last month – we miss his giro (welfare benefits).' A growing modern wisdom is:

> More and more infants expect that different children of one mother have different fathers.

Other modern 'families' are gay couples who are getting more positive attention or better rights than traditional families. They can adopt children or have children by artificial insemination of women and by rent-a-womb by male homosexuals. It is politically incorrect to criticise all types of modern families except traditional ones. There are many other possible developments for modern families; apes crossed with humans could become aphomos, humans crossed with donkeys could be called donkmans or womdonks. The possibilities are endless and I'm sure you can suggest many more. How about a name for a species which clones politicians – blairwonkies or bushwackys? Crossing humans with machines could produce what might be known as homotechs. Experts on political correctness are banning words that relate to traditional families such as husband, wife, marriage, father, mother, brother, sister plus numerous others like shame, infidelity etc. in case these words offend others. Some experts and activists may achieve a ban of words like paedophile and incest. Already the argument is being repeated that children have the right to choose to have sex with who they like whether it be adults, parents or brothers or sisters. Freedom is all. Even the word family may disappear because of its historic background if experts think it offends some minority groups. What words could replace family for our post modern group –

pleasure units or state breeding groups? Come on, you can do better than me; I'm not in a very productive mood this morning:

Political correctness is a powerful tool for social engineering and the traditional family a prime target.

CHAPTER 7

Education, Common Sense and Nonsense

True education is the leading out of wisdom.

Ancient and Common Wisdom

Education has gone downhill over the past forty or fifty years. As usual, government wants to have it both ways. We are told that academic achievement is rising year after year and at the same time, we are informed that more schools are failing than at any other time in their history. In one experiment, pupils who had passed present day examinations were given examinations papers from thirty or forty years ago. Pupils failed examinations papers from thirty or forty years ago in spectacular fashion. The two sets of examination papers were in the same subjects and were for the same qualification.

Questions about so-called rise in academic performance

Have pupils suddenly grown more in expert intelligence?
Are pupils working harder now than in the past?
Are teachers better now than years ago?
Are examinations easier nowadays?
Are markers of examinations more generous today?

There are many people, including experts, who are well aware that television, entrance qualifications on to degree courses and examinations or other school assessments have been 'dumbed down'. Government experts use statistics to 'prove' something whilst others use them to 'prove' exactly the opposite. One saying that is being used more frequently is:

There are lies, damn lies and then there are statistics.

There are more people going to university now, but it could be argued that this is exposing more students to expert theories and creating more experts. Getting more people into universities is not all it is cracked up to be. Bill Bryson makes a telling comment on modern university life. 'In my day, the principal concerns of university students were sex, smoking dope, rioting and learning. Learning was something you did only when the first three weren't available.' Education reflects and is reflected by society and modern society is not in good condition. There are those who are not so open to expert conditioning. They make more realistic judgments of expert theories which are the main diet of schools and universities. Who said:

> The only gap in my education was when I was at school
> or university?

In education, expert theories and knowledges have been separated from wisdom and over-emphasised. This has had many unfortunate conse-quences as wisdom is the essence of a good education. Under the direction of expert policy makers, there has been far too much concentration on trying to force expert theories, knowledges and practices on to teachers and pupils rather than leading wisdom out which is the true meaning and purpose of education. Though we have been strongly conditioned to accept expert theories, the reality of true education still surfaces in all kinds of places. For example, in the book, play or film, *The Prime of Miss Jean Brodie*, we have, 'To me education is a leading out of what is already there in the pupil's soul. To Miss Mackay it is the putting in of something that is not there, and that is not what I call education, I call it intrusion.' This coincides with many common sense laws one of which is:

> Expert knowledge is no substitute for inherent wisdom.

No matter how they dress it up, education is mainly about memorisation and regurgitation of expert theories, knowledges and opinions. Such a process is a copy-cat type of training rather than an education no matter how informal teachers are. There are expert right answers to questions that experts have devised and you have to learn them one way or another to succeed. When I was seventeen years old, I told my uncle proudly that I was going to be an expert. He told me a definition of an expert that is becoming more common and shows the annoyance of the layman. My uncle, who was a bus-driver, said:

> An ex-spurt is a drip previously under pressure.

Experts in educational establishments have become increasingly political and some lecturers have aspired to and indeed got to be Members of

Parliament or local government officials. The running of places of education like Polytechnics has grown highly political itself. There seems to be more time devoted to politics than to education in some places of learning. One lady who lectures in English complained about it. She was harassed by other members in her department because they said she did not interpret English literature enough to give its rightful left-wing political slant. At national government level, education has always been a political football. Politicians know that parents have as one of their main priorities a good education for their children. Politicians keep changing the educational system to make themselves feel useful and to let us know they are there. What experts regarded as bad a few years ago is now good and so on and so forth:

Change is not always for the better.

Schooling is a political instrument of manipulation and control. Experts use education to maintain and increase their power. They reward the more informed or educated in expert theories and knowledges with the bait of gaining greater access to resources and status than are available to the majority. It is not in the interests of experts to admit that true knowledge and wisdom exist in the everyday sayings and experience of the mass of ordinary people. Such an admission would make many political and legal experts, together with their theories and laws, redundant. The main rationalisation to justify their education theories and practices is that expert knowledge is much superior to common sense knowledge. Misguided educational ideologies of experts have produced much wasted effort, indifference, antagonism and violence in schools both for teachers and pupils. Unfortunately, expert theories have made too many potentially good teachers into frustrated followers who often do more harm than good. Teachers, unjustifiably, have been made the scape-goats for the failed expert theories of their political and academic masters. However, many teachers have been willing followers, but we are supposed to obey experts are we not? This is not to suggest there are no good teachers. What I am saying is that expert theories and practices have made many teachers appear in a bad light, when under common sense conditions, they would do a good job. J.M. Keynes expresses one of the criticisms that experts have forced teachers and pupils to endure. This description was used even when education was far better than it is now, so modern education would deserve much worse:

Education is the inculcation of the incomprehensible into the indifferent by the incompetent.

There are many examples of indifference to expert policies and knowledges in our modern education system. A professor asked one hundred students at one of our newer universities in the final year of their degree course how many really enjoyed the learning process itself. They were told not to write their names on the response sheet so that answers would not identify individuals. Only three out of the hundred said they really enjoyed the process of learning itself. University students are those who compete and choose to continue learning expert knowledges and become experts themselves. The professor asked the same students why they came to university if they did not enjoy learning. The two main responses were to get a degree and to have a good time. Much of the learning as defined and practised by experts was something to be endured rather than enjoyed. The following quotation has a somewhat different meaning today with its excesses than it did many years ago:

College is a fountain of knowledge where students gather to drink.

As I write this page, I am in a coffee house and a young student in his early twenties enters. I have known him since he was a small boy and he is in his second year at university. After the usually greetings, I ask him if his university is a fountain of knowledge at which students gather to drink. He pauses, smiles and replies, 'It depends if they have a good student bar. Some students like to drink in pubs in town.' I said that I meant to drink from the fountain of knowledge. He retorted, 'I don't think many students would look at it that way. Students just want to have a good time. You only go to university once. Some students regard work as a bind. There is a growing number of students who pay outside people to write their academic papers for them. Since many degrees are now awarded on continuous assessment, it is possible to get a degree without doing a stroke of work. I understand selling academic papers to students is becoming big business in America.' I asked, 'Don't you think that it's immoral – cheating I mean?' He replied, 'Well, I don't do it myself, but those who cheat say that if big business, lawyers, politicians and many other leading establish-ment figures are up to their necks in it, why not us? They encourage us to get qualified and become successful like them. We are just doing as they say. Who in today's modern world gets to the top without being immoral or cheating? Just name me some. In fact, it is a necessary requirement, isn't it?' Experts preach what they do not practise:

> Lead by example.

Expert theories have ruined the innate desire for learning. The observation by W.C Sellar and R.J. Yeatman is illustrative, 'For every person who wants to teach, there are about thirty who don't want to learn.' Another measure of indifference and antagonism to expert education is truancy. It seems to increase by the day. This very morning there is a report in the newspaper of a fourteen-year-old boy who has not been to school for well over a year. He spends most of his time in bed or watching television. No one amongst the various authorities is able to do anything about it. Experts and their laws have created this situation. To entice truants back to school, some headteachers have decided to play 'pop' music around the school corridors and other places. Modern 'pop' music is more associated with violence, drugs, promiscuity and bad language than any other part of our culture. Playing 'pop' music at school is like throwing a lead life-jacket to a drowning man. A common saying fits this situation, though it is not a wisdom, especially if you examine what education is endorsing. It is often a much-used rationalised excuse for joining in some immoral action:

> If you can't beat them, join them.

At least, by using modern 'pop' music, we cannot accuse these educators of ignoring one accepted aim of education – that of preparing pupils for living in present-day society. Our culture is increasingly taking on the values of the 'pop' music culture and nowhere is safe from it, even in schools. The values of 'pop' music reflect those of science. It has no morality and is increasingly supported by expert laws which reflect modern political ideology:

> Pupils are being well prepared to take their place in a
> society that does not distinguish between good and evil.

One of the most famous private schools in Britain, like many other schools, merely pays lip-service to the aims of education that deal with good and bad behaviour. Whereas schools used to aim at improving society, they now reflect it. Some senior boys at this renowned school complained to the new headmaster that his excessively free regime had led to a decline in the good behaviour of the pupils at the school. They asked for more effective sanctions to be taken against bad behaviour. The headmaster said, in effect, that the chastisements used in the past no longer were acceptable in the outside world and it was the purpose of the school to reflect these changes. This was, he pointed out, the correct preparation for pupils to enter modern society. After seeing the conditions of modern society, you would think the headmaster would want to stick by the traditional purpose of the school. One of its original aims was to develop the moral character of its students and, hence, make a contribution to the *betterment* of society. Good moral character used to be basic to everything that went on in all schools throughout the land. It was expected and taken for granted by staff and pupils alike. Even those who were not academic highfliers were well-behaved at school. The moral aspect of education has been eaten away by expert laws, first in state schools and then in private schools. The senior boys in the famous private school seemed to be more concerned with the degeneration of values and standards in the school than did the headmaster. As in most schools, disruptive pupils are in a minority, but a growing one. It must also be appreciated that it only takes one pupil to prevent a whole class from functioning:

> It only takes one rotten apple to spoil the whole barrel of apples.

In the famous private school the whole student body, including the badly behaved ones, knew what was required to improve the situation. Soon expert laws will have outlawed all sanctions against bad behaviour in schools. The common sense remedies suggested by senior pupils show the young still retain their instinct for what is right and what is wrong. It is interesting to note in modern decades that whenever pupils are asked about discipline in their school, the majority invariably opt for stronger measures:

> Out of the mouths of the young comes inherent wisdom.

Expert laws and rights are the choice of the anti-social minority. This situation is harmful to teachers, pupils and everyone. Some teachers and pupils have gone way beyond the stage of indifference. They are frightened and desperate. Most teachers and pupils start school being very keen to do well, but with increasing pressure of expert theories and officialdom, too many are made to feel incompetent and helpless. They are fast losing hope. Things get worse with every incomprehensible expert law that defies common sense and is forced upon them. At one time there used to be a few awkward pupils that were more noticeable in secondary schools. However, they were not allowed to disrupt other pupils or they received punishments that deterred them. Nowadays, we not only see a large increase in sullen, aggressive and highly violent foul-mouthed behaviour in secondary schools, but these modern values are spreading to younger and younger age groups. Many ancient and common wisdoms speak about very young children and how impressionable they can be. Two of these are:

Soft wax will take any impression.

The younger the child, the greater the impression.

One friend of mine who taught seven-year-olds set up some traditional games for his pupils' Christmas party. The headmaster told him that such games were old-fashioned and in this modern age he should have a 'disco', a 'rave'; all junior schools had them now. My friend said he would have nothing to do with it. The headmaster saw to it that these youngsters joined the 'disco'. Pupils imitated their 'pop star idols' such as The Spice Girls and Oasis in their behaviour, dress and dancing. There were many 'movers, shakers, pouters and posers' dancing to such music as, 'Let's Spend The Night Together', 'What's Love Got To Do With It?' and other highly educational offerings. 'Pop stars' are perhaps the most influential gods or idols in Modern Cool Britannia. 'Pop music' is associated with drugs, promiscuous sex, violence and foul-mouthed language which seem to be the modern model for our education system. In a materialistic society where excess individual freedom is praised and rewarded, 'pop stars' are successful and role models to be copied. The fact that many are grossly immoral does not detract from their material success and allure. Indeed, their excessive immorality pays huge dividends in publicity, fame and fortune. Many common wisdoms come to mind here, but we will just mention two sayings:

If you lie down with dogs, you'll get fleas.

If you have immoral gods, you get immoral disciples.

Another teacher reports this anecdote about a class of eight-year-olds. She said to the class, 'Now we are going to make up little stories with the word *charming* in.' Several pupils had made up such little stories as, 'The princess met the prince and she thought he was charming.' The teacher then told the class, 'We are going to make it a little more difficult and try to use the word *charming* twice in the same little story.' One little boy said, 'My thirteen-year-old sister came home very late last night and told my father she was having a baby and my dad said, charming, effing charming.' Humorous though this tale might be, it is a sad reflection on modern childhood, education and society. Molière complained about children growing up too fast in his time. Today his observation is even more relevant:

There are no children nowadays.

Hordes of teachers are seeking early retirement or change of job. Those who hope to remain as teachers are calling for drastic alterations to their lot, so they can do what they want to do – teach effectively. However, being brought up and trained in a materialistic world, too many teachers believe that additional material resources are the main answer. Common sense experience over many years shows that extensive material resources do not make for good schools nor for good examination results. Recently experts rediscovered this obvious and common knowledge. Their own expertise blinded them and some of us to these facts. What is amazing is that experts are ignoring their own evidence and still strain to pour material resources into schools. The real problem in schools is a moral behaviour one, not a materialistic one. As I write this chapter there will be thousands of pupils across the country having their lessons disrupted by badly behaved students. A single anti-social pupil can bring an entire school to a halt, never mind one lesson or one class. Not so long ago who, in their wildest dreams, who would have imagined that the behaviour of one boy about ten could close an entire school? This actually happened when the teachers went on strike because of his disruptive actions. Teachers are very capable of dealing with this pupil, but expert laws prevent them from doing so. Even the children could tell the experts what needs to be done to resolve such a situation, but we know that:

You can tell an expert, but you can't tell him much.

More and more teachers and pupils are being brutally attacked and that includes murder, rape and other atrocities. One headmistress had her house fire-bombed. Indeed, is there any kind of crime that has not been committed in our modern education culture? Teachers are no longer readily willing to supervise pupils during playtimes and lunch breaks. This is not surprising as teachers can be blamed for anything that happens. Even if a child falls over kicking a soccer ball, the teacher is open to legal prosecution for negligent supervision. In our politically correct culture, we no longer have clumsy children, only incompetent teachers. Excess political correctness for children has led to its opposite for teachers, political incorrectness and being called incompetent is an example of it. There are so many expert laws, rules and regulations being brought in about safety that children will soon have to be placed in an airbag to play soccer and other games. Then, if they fall over, they will not hurt themselves. Bullet-proof vests will be a requirement for school uniforms. Some students and teachers in America already wear them. Expert laws are not just leading to a siege mentality, they have created a siege reality. In the not too distant future, teachers and pupils will have to be accompanied to school by 'minders' and lawyers who sit in class with them throughout the day. Schools will become like fortresses with armed guards patrolling inner and outer perimeters. Many common wisdoms apply here. Just two of them are:

Prevention is better than cure.

Safety lies in the middle course.

Excess violence or threat of danger has led to its opposite, excess safety precautions. People do not want expert security systems and laws to protect teachers and children against increasing criminal behaviour and violence. They require the criminal behaviour be dealt with according to common sense laws so there is less of it. Expert laws protect the individual rights of the criminal at the expense of risking the lives of children and teachers. One criminal, about to be released from prison, threatened 'to do a Dunblane' when he left jail. The Dunblane tragedy involved a man shooting sixteen primary school children and a teacher whilst they were at school in Dunblane, Scotland. What the experts did to deal with this threat was to get legal injunctions warning the criminal against going near schools or carrying weapons on the street. In essence the message of experts to parents and schools is, 'Because of expert laws protecting the criminal's individual rights and freedoms, we cannot really do anything until he actually injures or kills someone.' Violent threats, as well as the execution of them, have to be punished. Even if he does kill some children, proving it was an evil act of intention is quite another expert matter. Lawyers would argue that he was driven to do it by some force completely outside his control. There are many children missing or dead where no one has been prosecuted. If someone is found guilty of brutally raping and killing a very young child, the sanctions taken against the killer are inadequate. They fall short of the common sense expectations and will of the majority:

Punishments must fit the crimes.

The threat of violently killing young children is, to the vast majority of people, of the greatest severity and we expect it to be treated as such. Merely issuing expert legal pieces of paper warning the person who has threatened to kill not to go through with the threat is based on rationalisations that criminals and lawyers often use. The criminal issuing the threat of violence was only joking; he was temporarily angry or was merely trying to impress his peers; his girlfriend had run off or he was under stress and so on and so forth, are familiar excuses that experts use all in the name of 'a more humane and progressive society'. Instinctive feelings of the majority reject such reasoning which is detached from common sense and used to rationalise dangerous threats. Amongst other things, everyday experience tells us that verbal threats often act as an introduction to great physical violence. These types of threats are coming more and more from tiny tots, not just from adolescents or adult criminals. One of many examples is a six-year-old boy suspended from school for a spate of violent threats and attacks including giving a teacher a black eye. Also, in recent memory, two boys of eleven brutally murdered an even younger boy:

Evil is defined by the nature of the crime, not by the age of the criminal.

In keeping with common sense laws, it should be made clear at school, as well as at home and elsewhere, that threats of violence are not acceptable and carry deterring sanctions. Repeated warnings, which seem to be the major method of trying to stop threatening behaviour are not enough. Offenders know it is wrong. To keep telling people that threatening and other forms of bad behaviour are wrong, is a waste of time. Actually it encourages the behaviour it is supposed to stop. It is giving constant attention to the offenders which is what they crave and is a major reason they do it in the first place. Attitudes to threats and violence are developed in early childhood and must be dealt with at that time in a fair but firm manner. When the home is not handling bad behaviour in an effective manner, a good school can help compensate and insist on good standards of behaviour. We do know that some children who behave badly at home can be well-behaved at school with teachers who expect and demand good behaviour. The reverse is also true. Some children may be well-behaved at home if the parents demand it and out of control at school in those lessons where some teachers are unable to cope. Unfortunately expert laws do not allow teachers or parents to apply common sense laws in an effective manner including the following one:

He that chastises one amends many.

Government is at present stressing a return to traditional methods of teaching. This means that experts feel that modern methods have failed. What the government does not realise is that any success of traditional methods was due to the fact that it was underpinned with traditional moral values of behaviour. The most powerful effect of expert laws has been to undermine and ban traditional moral discipline. Thus, teaching methods of any kind that are divorced from moral values are bound for failure. Effective teaching cannot take place when there are constant disruptions from anti-social pupils. Over the past few decades, when teachers have used their instinctive feelings for justice in dealing with anti-social pupils, they have been deterred by expert policies, laws and rights. Even highly violent school beginners are quick to recite their expert legal rights when teachers have tried to restrain their brutal behaviour. Such threats as, 'If you lay a finger on me, I'll have the law on you and you'll get sacked.' come from the mouths of tiny tots. Even children who are described as illiterate and antagonistic to learning know their expert legal laws and rights in as much detail as Einstein knew his equations. Anti-social pupils have learned a great deal. The story of *The Lord Of The Flies* illustrates a common knowing:

Children can be very cruel, if given unrestrained freedom
to be so.

When common sense had not been replaced by expert laws and theories, teachers were expected to act at school in place of parents and as good parents would. The majority of teachers did this job very well to the benefit of pupils, parents, education, the community and society at large. The term used for the teacher acting in place of the parents was a part of the wisdom and language of education. In more formal documents and contexts it was expressed in Latin, 'in loco parentis'. Nowadays, expert laws do not allow parents to act as good parents, let alone teachers acting in their place:

Expert laws and theories promote conflict amongst
teachers, parents and pupils.

Expert theories and laws have had some interesting outcomes in education. One young criminal about twenty years old claimed *the reason* he became a criminal was because he was sent to the wrong school. The local education authority paid the young criminal £70,000 without the case going to court. Most people believe it pays to get a good education. With modern expert laws, it seems if you claim you went to the wrong school or had a less than perfect education, it pays also. Some pupils are suing their schools when they fail examinations. If teachers decide to sue pupils for not working hard enough or for creating stress for them, there would not be enough lawyers or courts in the land to deal with the situation. Perhaps this is why Britain is going into Europe. Experts may feel we do not have enough lawyers and courts of our own. Also, every single pupil can sue if they choose to claim that education has made them suffer stress. Who amongst us has not suffered some kind of stress while at school? I know I did:

Expert laws in education teach the price of everything and
the value of nothing.

When I was at school around the time of the Second World War, education as a whole was in far better shape than it is now. Though education was far from ideal in the 1950s, it has gone downhill since then. The fact that some children now are computer 'whizz-kids' is not a measure of a good education. It is more an indication of our lust for modern technology in education and like all lusts or obsessions it will end in tears. Well, this is not strictly true. There are some tears now and all along the way. We may not be near the end though the excess use of technology is pointing to an end for the natural environment and life as we know it. Whereas in times when nature was more respected than it is now, the maxim, 'education for life' was fitting. Today, the opposite is nearer the truth as we are moving toward destruction of nature and 'education for death'. We already possess the technology to vandalise nature and commit planetary suicide:

> Just as death follows life for individuals, death follows life for civilisations and planets.

Technology in education is not as white-hot as some experts would lead us to believe. There are advantages and disadvantages to it as with anything else. Some children spend so much time on their computers at home that to use them a great deal in school as well is like sending coal to Newcastle. The other day I was in a shop and purchased two articles, one at thirty pence and one at thirty two pence. At the cash-out till there was a young lady about seventeen and she started to add up my goods on the computer. After pressing various buttons or keys I said, 'It's sixty two pence.' She said, 'Oh, you can do it faster than me. I can't add up except on a machine.' Then she issued me with a receipt which had on it over twenty lines of writing and figures. It is mainly through a deluge of paper-work that information is passed down from experts to teachers. The information explosion has become a great burden to everyone including teachers. President Franklin D. Roosevelt complained about it in the 1940s and the increase in amount of information since then gives teachers far, far greater cause for alarm. Roosevelt said to a person who delivered masses of memoranda and other documents:

> I hope you don't think I am reading all this paperwork, I can't even lift it.

Increase in sophistication of technology and access to mounds of information should not be confused with high achievement in education. A friend of mine is a professor at a modern university and teaches degree courses in business studies which involves the use of mathematics. He is having to teach students what, a few years ago, was junior school arithmetic. Some cannot convert fractions such as forty three fifty sevenths into a percentage. It is beyond most of them. Not surprisingly, employers are complaining that job applicants at all levels are very poor. They are unable to speak or write simple English, do elementary arithmetic, or interact with any acceptable measure of social skills. This is another indicator how expert theories and laws are making education fail:

Technology and information without wisdom is like a boat without a rudder.

To compensate for the failure of education, some literacy, numeracy and other subjects are being studied in the work place and even in public houses for those in need, and there are many. Britain is near the top of the league for illiteracy in the civilised world. For example, it is reported by experts that we have more than three times the illiteracy rate of, say, Sweden. In what our experts consider uncivilised parts of the world, many who cannot read or write know more about practical mathematics and nature study than some of our top scientific specialists. Expert advisers have told government and the rest of us that leaving two hundred metres between genetically modified crops and ordinary crops will prevent cross contamination or fertilisation. Perhaps our experts are so involved and keen on technology, they have been unable to see the obvious facts. The forces of nature like winds, insects and other animals, including man, are capable of transporting seeds from genetically modified plants for thousands of miles never mind two hundred metres. This is another example of focusing the part at the expense of the whole and using expert knowledge devoid of wisdom:

An ounce of practical experience is worth a ton of theory.

Just after the Second World War when there were far fewer expert laws, rules and regulations, teachers were trusted to get on with their vocation. Compared with today, they did a good job. However, even at that time, academic performance was separated from moral behaviour to some degree. For example, qualifications were academic in nature, not moral ones. The separation was also reflected in end of term reports with a column for academic scores and another one for teachers' comments on attitude or behaviour. Since the war, expert policies and laws have separated academic work from moral behaviour much, much more. The responsibility for moral behaviour has been increasingly taken out of the hands of teachers and parents by politicians and passed into the hands of lawyers and social workers. Now moral behaviour is so low that experts are recommending special lessons in morality such as good race relations. This will make matters worse. Firstly, everyone already knows that we should treat others as we would hope to be treated. Secondly, the extra expert policies, laws, rules and regulations coming into schools to deal with moral issues, like all expert laws that conflict with common sense laws, will fail in dramatic fashion:

More expert laws on morality, less morality.

Splitting morality into smaller bits like sex education and racial discrimination is aping what science does. It is looking at smaller and smaller parts at the expense of seeing the whole. We have to use laws that apply to many situations, to the larger picture – to the whole. Common sense laws do this. Having due regard for one's fellow man applies to all situations and covers race, sex, sport or anything else. I have indicated before that focusing on the part can be useful, but only when the greater whole is borne in mind also. Parts should not just become ever smaller separate, specialised areas. There are all kinds of specialists in the sciences and the arts. Often art is regarded as the opposite of science, but they both seek similar objectives – unity in variety and its opposite, variety in unity. Seeking unity in variety is discovering laws or relationships of nature's parts to its whole. Seeking variety in unity is using nature's holistic laws to find examples of them in nature's parts. A really good science teacher knows much about the arts just as a good arts teacher is familiar with many aspects of science. Both art and science study the same thing – nature. This illustrates common sense laws two of which are:

All things are related.

One thing leads to another.

Immediately after the war morals or good behaviour was a more integrated part of every lesson and every aspect of school life. Good behaviour was expected and demanded. Bad behaviour firmly but fairly discouraged.

Fairness in its real objective sense means that which is agreed to and accepted by the majority of people. Education then, in the 1940s, applied objective common sense laws to moral behaviour. When I was at school my friend and I were regular visitors to snooker halls when they were regarded as dens of iniquity. They were a favourite meeting place for local criminals. One evening we saw our chemistry master enter, so we ran and hid in the toilet. He was not put off and came into the toilet area and knocked on the door of the cubicle in which we were hiding. He said, 'I know you are in there. Firstly, you should not be smoking, it's bad for you and you will write out that message one hundred times by Friday. Secondly, you shouldn't be in a snooker hall, you have an examination tomorrow and you should be revising for that. I shall deal with you both further tomorrow at school. Goodnight boys.' We both held our breath and did not make a sound. The next day at school, he remonstrated with us further and said he had been too generous. For hiding in the toilet and refusing to speak to him, he added a further hour of detention after school in which we had to revise the questions we got wrong in the examination. The point of this story is that teachers were concerned about the whole pupil and his life style. If this same incident happened today, because of expert legislation, individual rights and the separation of school from 'private life', I would be able to sue this teacher for harassment in my private life. This is not to mention the permanent psychological damage that my lawyer could argue it would do to me. Our teachers earned our respect by being concerned about us as people not just as academic machines. This concern and respect for the good can sometimes involve a firm hand and guidance. An ancient wisdom pertinent here is:

He that respects not is not respected.

The headmaster of my school was held in very high esteem by the local community and was both respected and feared by the pupils. However, the fear was associated only with what would happen to you when you did something wrong. The common sense law about this would say that if you did nothing wrong, you had nothing to fear. At school assemblies each morning, the headmaster used to call any boy out who had been involved in some very bad or good activity and punish or reward him accordingly. It was a great deterrent to bad behaviour and an inspiration for good actions. Once a boy of fifteen had bullied another boy. He had punched him and taken some articles from the other boy. The headmaster caned the offender in front of the whole school. After caning the boy the headmaster said, 'Did that hurt Smith?' 'Yes sir,' the boy replied. 'Good, punishment is supposed to hurt. You don't like being hurt do you?' went on the headmaster. 'No sir' answered the youth. 'Well, others don't like to be hurt either. I suggest in future, Smith, you do unto others . . . You have sullied your own reputation, the good name of the community in which you live and also damaged the high standing of the school.' If this happened today, the headmaster would get the sack and be jailed with the recommendation that he received psychiatric counselling to help him overcome his brutal and sadistic behaviours. Expert laws and theories concerning individual freedoms and human rights would ensure the headmaster was expertly sanctioned and sectioned:

Common sense laws judge differently to expert laws.

Around the 1950s there were more shared values in schools that were common to the home, the community and society at large. When I got punished at school, I used to warn my cousin of dire consequences if he told my parents. In those days, parents trusted teachers to act in the best interests of their children, their school, their community and society at large. Expert policies and laws have changed all that. If my mother did find out that I had been hauled over the coals at school, she would support the action of the school because she trusted teachers. She would say if I had been punished at school, 'You bring shame on yourself, your family, the school and the village.' More often than not, she would sanction me further for disgracing the family name.

Most people, with few exceptions, admit that getting caned at school did them more good than harm. Indeed, most say they deserved it. Of the exceptions who say that being caned was harmful, there are some who use it as an excuse. Some, in later life, search for something to rationalise the sad state of their present lives. They can seize upon anything in their past lives which modern experts will accept as being harmful and caning is one of experts' pet causes. This is not to deny that there are some pupils who are physically abused at school as opposed to firm but fair punishment. In a society where physical violence is increasing everywhere, it would be folly to think that it does not apply to some teachers as well. However, to say the great daily provocation they endure, it is to their credit the vast majority have been so restrained. One wisdom that is expressed in numerous ways and has existed in all cultures throughout history is:

Spare the rod and spoil the child.

Good teachers have little need to use the cane, but it should be available for some offences. Good teachers can be inspirational and spell-binding to students of any age and can make topics fascinating. For example, one school I knew of employed a local joiner to teach woodwork. He had passed some written joinery examinations and was allowed to teach as there was a shortage of teachers in this particular school. It was in a rough area. Within a few weeks, the headmaster, other teachers and the pupils acknowledged that this ex-joiner was the best teacher in the school. The headmaster, who I knew, told me that in all his years in the profession, he had never come across a better teacher. After about three years, the headmaster advised the joiner to go to teacher training college and get a professional qualification or he would be held back in his teaching career. By now the joiner had established himself county-wide as a teacher of outstanding ability. He was a man of great common sense. He went for interview to a training college far from his own county *and was turned down* for a place in the college. Other candidates had better academic qualifications. Even behavioural scientific research shows there is no relationship between academic achievement and the ability to teach. Many of us have experience of teachers with high academic qualifications but poor at teaching. Good teaching depends on common sense. You do not have to be an Einstein to teach children the theory of relativity. They, like my cat, already know it. In an earlier chapter I drew attention to the common sense saying or law which states categorically that, 'Things are relative', and that includes time. What Einstein rediscovered was that sometimes an hour can feel like a minute and its opposite, sometimes a minute can feel like an hour. Getting pupils to appreciate these inner knowledges and wisdoms is what makes a good teacher. Two common wisdoms that fit the ex-joiner are:

An ounce of common sense is worth a ton of expert academic knowledge.

Teachers are born not made.

The joiner who was rejected at interview for teacher training college became one of the youngest and most successful headmasters in Great Britain. He was invited to become one of Her Majesty's Inspectors of Schools. Each year he was asked to take up the job, but turned it down as he loved the work he already did. He was headmaster of several schools during his career and was very content to make poor schools into good ones. An ancient wisdom describes this ex-joiner's chosen lot in life:

> Content is the philosopher's stone, that turns all it touches into gold.

This ex-joiner was rejected at interview, so let us examine how reliable interviews are. Interviews, as we all know, are very influential to most people's lives at some time or other. Almost all jobs or positions in society depend on interviews, whether in industry, commerce or education. Experts, along with many other people, think they can pick out the best candidate for a particular job from a group of candidates to be interviewed:

> We believe nothing as strongly as that we want to believe.

It is based on this strong belief precipitated by experts that give existence to interviews. Thousand are conducted daily, some for posts in education. The amount of time and other resources expended on modern interviews, including personnel, is vast. How effective are modern expert interviews? One experiment done to discover how reliable and valid interviews are went something like this. Ten expert interviewers, such as psychologists and other expert scientists who studied different aspects of human behaviour, interviewed ten people for a specific job. The requirements for the job were spelled out and agreed by the interviewers before the interviews took place. Findings showed that the expert interviewers were no more effective than closing their eyes and sticking a pin in the list of candidates to pick someone. Some expert interviewers picked one candidate at the top of their list as the best person for the job. Other experts put the *same* candidate at the bottom of their list as the worst person for the job. Put another way, the experts' selections were no better than chance or random selection. It was exactly like a lottery. Experts' excess efforts to control and predict things such as interviews result in the opposite, random or chance outcomes. We all know that many crucial aspects of our lives happen by chance. How we met our marriage partner is usually one example. Experts think they control chance far more than they do. They ignore an ancient and common wisdom cited by Ovid:

Chance has power everywhere.

At interviews generally, the selection is done by people in high places. Sometimes there is a token layman or ordinary worker present. References for a teaching post are also given by those in high places. The people who really know candidates the best are the people who work alongside them or for them. In the case of a teacher, the students know far better than the director of education who is a good teacher and who is a bad teacher. In schools, expert systems like interviews get too many people in the wrong jobs:

Experts get too many square pegs in round holes.

Good people are not considered or are rejected by experts, like the joiner I have talked about earlier. If people are keen to be a teacher, they should be given a chance in schools. After a few weeks, they will know if they are fitted to it at that time. Of course, if you are hoping to teach Shakespeare, you would be wise to make yourself an enthusiast. Politicians and laws have put education further and further into the hands of experts and technology. They soon will not need teachers at all. Experts can put computer screens in every classroom and run everything from a master computer in the Houses of Parliament. Too much technology is anti-social and works against the expression of the better sides of our nature. Experts are dehumanising education and teachers and trying to make them like machines in the name of efficiency and 'modernising' education. Teachers are increasingly told what to do, how to do it, when to do it, where to do it and why they are doing it:

Experts have faults, but apparently being wrong is not one of them.

Education mirrors modern science in the tradition of separating things. In education the physical, mental and moral are called motor, cognitive and affective domains of behaviour. There are numerous other separations into smaller parts. For example the cognitive or academic domain is split into subjects like mathematics, English, geography, history and the like. These subjects are split into smaller parts still. Mathematics is separated into arithmetic, algebra, geometry and so on. Of late, since there is a growing recognition that knowledge forms an integrated whole, some subjects are being re-combined. Now, we have social studies which integrates such subjects as history and geography. Themes, projects or topics are being revived which use numerous subjects together. Hence, the excess separation of school subjects into smaller and smaller parts has resulted in moves towards its opposite, combination of school subjects. This is an example of the common sense law which states:

Excess in one thing leads to its opposite.

However, the most important separation of the academic from the moral remains. If themes, projects, or topics are not interlaced with morality, they merely give pupils more freedom and opportunity to practise bad behaviours. In our modern materialistic society, experts have made academic qualifications their priority. Not only are experts taking morality out of the hands of teachers and parents, they seem to be abolishing it, as they are doing with the notion of shame. The great emphasis has been on the cognitive or mental aspects of behaviour at the expense of the affective or moral and social domains. This separation of the parts from the whole to specialise in smaller areas of academic endeavour in order to increase its performance has had the opposite effect. It has lowered academic performance and almost made morality or wisdom a thing of the past:

Academic performance separated from moral values is less accurate, less interesting and more dangerous.

Pupils are given so much freedom that they are quick to say they do not like some areas of study and choose not to do them. I did not fancy learning Latin at school, but had to do it. My Latin teacher told such fascinating stories about the life of ancient Romans that I was enthralled. People of all ages love good stories and they are basic to education. Teachers of younger children use this story-telling technique far more often and to better effect than teachers of older students. In education, a myth still exists that good teachers should deal with secondary pupils and poorer ones with younger children. Even experts agree that the earliest years are the most important in education, for it is in these formative stages that attitudes to learning develop. In reality, by the time children start school, most attitudes to learning are pretty much established though they can be changed by some teachers. For a good education, it is important from the earliest of ages at home, children are told stories, read stories and read stories themselves. Parents who fill their homes with books and stories, rather than with modern mechanical toys, need not worry about the child's education. If children are interested in books and reading, a good education will take care of itself, for education is essentially about stories and story-tellers whatever the subject. Some teachers, of course, do more harm than good. One piece of graffiti that contains some essence of truth is, 'Employ those who have never been to school while they still know everything.'

Good teachers are good story-tellers.

Another myth about good teaching is that you have to be professionally trained. Just as we are born learners, we are also the opposite, we are born teachers. Parents teach their children and some are excellent, unhindered by expert training. Children, even very young ones, are first-rate teachers. If you watch them teaching some other children or showing their parents some skill they have discovered or copied, it is obvious they have much teaching ability. Another story springs to mind about this. A teacher was given a 'backward class' where no one could read, write or do even the simplest of arithmetic sums. After two years all could read, write and do good standard arithmetic. Some had a reading age beyond their chrono-logical age. The headmaster was delighted and amazed and brought in one of Her Majesty's Inspectors of Schools. The inspector asked the teacher how he had achieved this minor miracle. The teacher said, 'Well, I spent time teaching one or two to read, write and do sums, then I got these children to teach others, who in turn, taught others and so on.' The headmaster pointed out to the inspector that many parents had been up to school. One comment of the parents was that the teacher had held the children's noses to the grindstone, for he had insisted the pupils took books home to read, but the families were delighted. Many thought that their children would never read. The teaching ability of children is a great resource that is not used enough in schools. By teaching other children, pupils learn much in a more holistic and enjoyable manner. One of the best ways to learn something is to teach it:

> Humans are not just learners by nature they are, by nature, teachers also.

Schools moved more to informality from more regimented systems after the war. The new-found freedom was there to be enjoyed. In the formal approach, pupils used to sit in rows and copied what the teacher said had to be done. With the growing emphasis on individual freedoms, self-expression and creativity became the buzz-words in education. Like most things directed by experts it went to excess. I had cause to visit one school in the 1960s. As I approached a classroom of eight-year-olds, all hell was let loose. Children were shouting, throwing things, wrestling, pulling hair and all manner of things. I wondered where the teacher was. Suddenly, an adult appeared from behind a storeroom door in the classroom. When I dared, I ventured, 'What are these up to then?' She said, quite proudly I thought, 'Oh, this is a creative learning lesson.' To a boy who was wrestling another boy, the teacher screamed, 'Stop that immediately Melvin!' The boy shouted back, 'Certainly Miss, which way did it go?' and carried on with his scrummage. What the children were really doing was practising and reinforcing anti-social behaviour. Genuinely productive, creative activity usually demands great concentration, commitment and peace and quiet:

> A quiet teacher makes a quiet class.

> There must be a balance between formality and informality in teaching.

> Excess familiarity breeds contempt.

The daughter of some friends is training to be a teacher and she was in a school practising her teaching. I asked her how she liked it and she told me, in an amazed tone, that the school was so old-fashioned the pupils still chanted their times tables. 'The teachers at the school just aren't with it when it comes to modern teaching methods,' she told me. We all know that people like to chant things, including children and their times tables. Chanting is heard in choirs, at soccer matches and in numerous other places. Chanting tables gives the opportunity for sharing, for identification and if a child does not know a few of them, he soon learns from the others. It gives a sense of positive community, and we have little of that left now. What would be wrong would be if chanting was the only way multiplication sums were done. This was hardly ever the case. Chanting tables was outlawed by experts. Now, with a failed excess of its opposite, not chanting tables, chanting tables is making a comeback:

If modern teaching methods are 'with it', many pupils would be better off without it.

A range of teaching methods has to be used to achieve effective education. At one end of the range is what we will call *command learning*. One extreme of this is where the teacher spells out the what, how, where, when, who and the why of learning. The opposite extreme is what we will call *discovery learning*. This is where pupils choose the what, how, where, when, who and the why of the learning. There are various degrees of the what, how, where, when, who and why components between command and discovery. For example, the teacher may decide a little, or a medium-sized or even a large-sized part of what the pupils are to do. Combined with this, he may also decide where, who, when and why it is to be done and leave how it is done entirely up to the pupils. On the other hand, the teacher may decide on how something is to be done but let the children decide what they are going to do. Permutating or combining the various degrees of the what, how, where, when, who and why provides a great number of different situations children can experience. Children also like at different times to work as individuals, with a partner and in various-sized groups or teams. When all these situations are permutated or combined, the number of different learning situations in which the teacher can involve the children is extremely extensive. Learning situations demand balance between familiar practices and the opposite, something different. Nothing should be done to excess, for this excludes doing other worthwhile activities:

School work should balance routine with variety.

In a materialistic society the general rule seems to be, '*the bigger, the better*'. This runs counter to common sense laws. There are many instances in modern society which reflect the obsession with large-sized things. Making it big, hitting the big time, big business, big bombs, big superstores, big houses, big roads, big towns, big cities, big money, mega-bucks and so on and so forth are examples. One widespread saying that denies common sense is, 'You can't get too much of a good thing.' We have already shown this to be false. We said that if you ate a bucketful of even your favourite food, it could kill you. In any event, big schools were not a good thing in the first place. Big schools help kill the spirit of community of villages and towns which is essential for a decent society. Schools have to be an integrated part of smaller communities and huge schools do not lend themselves to this. Big schools create the opposite of what they were supposed to achieve. In the main, big schools have been a big failure and have fallen into disrepute:

> The bigger they are, the harder they fall.

Big schools are often at a disadvantage in educating people in the true sense. They create illiteracy, people who cannot do simple arithmetic, pupils with low social skills and an increasing involvement in the expanding drug culture. Big schools are less likely to produce good citizens. They reinforce the deterioration of social values. They contribute more to greed and lust for any kind of power, too often the more immoral the better. Yesterday, a sixteen-year-old schoolboy who had won an award a few years before for being a 'whizz-kid' on computers was interviewed on television. He was projected as a model for other children to be successful and really get on in life. When asked what he hoped to achieve in the future, the boy said he was aiming to become rich and powerful because 'that's what it is all about'. This ambition is regarded by experts as the highest good in our materialistic society. If this is what education stays 'all about', then society has got problems that will not be solved:

> The greedy mouth of covetousness is not filled except by the earth of the grave.

> The more you get, the more you want.

Big schools exist at the expense of many important things including a good education. Anti-social and anti-education pupils can thrive or hide more readily in a large school. Huge schools do not make for fulfilling the needs of the pupils such as acceptable identification, affiliation, spirit of community, peace of mind and the great inborn desire for true learning, to mention some. Unlike big schools, the head teacher of a small school is able to keep his finger on the pulse of all pupils and teachers. He can make many assessments each day concerning standards. Teachers and pupils, too, make scores of assessments every single day about performance. Pupils, never mind teachers, know precisely who in their class is progressing and at what rate. It is the aim of every teacher to progress each pupil each day and they are the last people who need telling who is progressing and by how much. Teachers are making evaluations morning, noon and night. Marking and making comments on pupils' work are examples. There are many *obvious* measures of progress. For example, there are reading books graded in difficulty. If a pupil has got to grade five reader, then his aim and the aim of the teacher is to advance to the grade six reading book and so on. There is no need for experts to dictate and assess standards via the National Curriculum and a legion of expert inspectors and advisers. Teachers need to be allowed to revive common sense laws so they can do a good job. Having interfering experts is an example of:

Too many cooks spoil the broth.

In a secondary school of five hundred, teachers and pupils can just about get to know one another which is necessary for effective community spirit and good education. With seven to eleven-year-olds, the school has to be much, much smaller. For these younger pupils, a population of five hundred can be overwhelming, alienating and counter-productive to enjoyable, educative experiences. Below the age of seven years, the schools have to be even smaller for the same reasons. Small schools based in and integrated with small communities reflect man's nature. He has lived in small tribal units for most of his millions of years of existence. Expert theories and policies in modern education are against man's better nature. The lust for bigness is contributing to the abysmal state of modern education:

Quantity is no substitute for quality.

As well as man being a small tribal animal by nature, another characteristic of his ingrained instincts is to learn. Question asking gives expression to man's most powerful motive – curiosity. The need to explore, to find out or learn is man's most dominant behaviour and it is mainly through questioning that he satisfies this motive. Asking questions is the main tool of science but its questions contain no morality. Question asking is most noticeable in young children. Some parents are driven mad by their children's never ending questions. Asking questions or curiosity then, is extremely important and forms a very large part of human behaviour. As one observer of behaviour puts it:

> If you ain't curious, you ain't alive.

As soon as children go to school, by and large, they are immediately turned from question askers into question answerers. This goes on throughout the infant, junior, secondary schools and on into universities. After gaining a bachelor's or master's degree, experts reverse this and say, 'Ask an important question and deal with it and that is your PhD thesis or study.' Hence, throughout the time spent in education, effective balance is not kept between these opposites – question asking and question answering. Question asking is related to problem seeking. When there seems to be no obvious problem around to solve children and adults try to find some, like crossword puzzles or trivial pursuits. If children cannot locate any, they make them up. Children's imaginative play involves designing problems of their own to be solved. We must capitalise on this desire to design problems or questions in education. This inborn desire and ability can be used in numerous ways. For example, I often hear from experts that mixed ability groups are difficult to teach, particularly in mathematics. One way of dealing with this is for the teacher to say, 'The answer to a problem is three. I want you all to make up as many problems as you can, the answer to which is three. Try to make your problems as tricky or as difficult as you can.' Such a situation would cater for Einstein and every class member including those who were poor at mathematics. It would also cater for school children or university students:

> There is more than one way of cracking an egg.

The excesses of modern society are reflected in the way the parents and teachers respond to children's answers and other performances. How often do we hear for rather average or even poor performances, such terms used as brilliant, excellent, fabulous? Children have been socialised more and more not just to expect immediate gratification, but to expect great excess of it. Teachers have to be very careful how they use praise. When a pupil does something good, if the teacher just says, 'Good', it can close a situation down which might have been extended to better effect. For example, if a student has just learned or achieved an additional skill, say, how to order a meal in French, it would be better for the teacher to say, 'Good, how do you feel about that?' Then an additional question might be added such as, 'How can you build on that?' Asking and getting students to ask clarifying and developmental questions is one of the most crucial things a teacher can do. These questions draw out of the student knowledge and values that are integrated and this is the whole crux and purpose of education. Other examples of these type of questions follow:

Some clarifying questions

What did you do?
How did you do that?
How do you feel about that?
Can you define or tell me what you mean by_____?

Some developmental questions

Were there some other ways of doing that?
What are some advantages and disadvantages to that?
What are some of the consequences of doing that?
How could you carry that idea further?

Asking and getting students to ask clarifying and developmental questions is just as important for PhD students as it is for infant school pupils. They are also applicable to family life, to business or to any other situation where the aim is for people to clarify and express wisdom. Using clarifying and development questions is a strategy in the first-rate book by L.E. Raths, B. Simon and M. Harmin entitled, *Values and Teaching*, 1966 (Merrill Books). Wisdom, as we know, is made up of meaningful knowledges integrated with common sense values:

Without wisdom, education is worthless.

We have been too kind to experts who ignore common sense. Enrico Fermi illustrates this. He says, 'Before I came here I was confused about this subject. Having listened to your lecture, I am still confused, but on a higher level.' The direct use of common sense laws to explore relationships of various knowledges and values is rarely used in schools. It is a powerful method of teaching and learning. Let us choose a law, say, 'One thing leads to another'. There are many ways of using it one of which is to ask for examples of it and go from there. Let us make it a little trickier and select two objects that seem unrelated, say a piece of cheese and a computer. Actually either one of these could lead us everywhere on its own. Cheese could lead us to animals, farming, exports, animal welfare, economics, mathematics, geography and so on ad infinitum. We will make up any little story to include our two chosen objects, cheese and a computer. My ten-year-old relative insists on doing the story. He says, 'A youth is working at his computer late at night, he gets hungry, makes a cheese sandwich and returns to the computer. He gets tired and goes to bed without switching off the computer. A mouse comes for the cheese and has to walk across the computer keys to get the cheese. This computer accidentally hacks into a computer of an American plane setting out to attack Bosnia and changes the plane's instructions. It diverts it to London Heathrow Airport where the pilot lands just in time for tea.' From this piece of cheese and or the computer, we can be led to all the knowledges and values that have existed in the whole universe throughout its entire history:

All thing are related.

Now let us turn to some other little stories that many of you already know. Over the past fifty years the best schools have not been the ones that have had money pumped into them. Modern facilities and expensive sophisti-cated technologies have not improved true education, rather the reverse. Mathematics is better taught and learned using pieces of string, scissors, cardboard and other ordinary objects that surround us. Good schools are small, integrated with the community and with strong moral values. Huge financing can make for bad schools and experts have proved this point so many times one would think they would have learned a lesson. Pupils should help create, and have more responsibility for, their own school environment and not follow modern dogma of being handed too much on a plate:

You can be given too much of anything.

Governments and expert educators stress that the education system must cater for individual differences and abilities. At the same time, political philosophy dictates that people should have equality of opportunity. Thus, the common or comprehensive schools were formed. They were bigger than those they replaced and some comprehensives were combinations of the schools they did replace. Trying to cater for individual differences by making all schools the same is not the best of ideas. Some people will thrive in small schools, but not large ones; some will do well in single-sex schools; some will enjoy success in boarding schools and some will feel more comfortable in all-age schools. The argument by experts, that schools must be composed of both boys and girls because that is the reality of society outside the school, is not a good one. The reality of society outside the school is that sometimes boys and girls want to be together and sometimes they do not. One could argue that there are more than enough distractions by the opposite sex in the outside world, without providing more at school. If, as experts suggest, school must reflect society outside the school walls, then all-age schools would predominate. Not only is there a mixing of the sexes outside school, there is a mixing of age groups in families and elsewhere. All-age schools have some impressive advantages. They avoid the experts' mania for separating things on the grounds of age. Older children not only can escort the younger ones to school, they help them at school with many aspects of their lives. They can also assist with learning and teaching in a more holistic setting. Older and younger children gain experience of getting on with one another and responsibility gets more meaningful. Smaller all-age schools reflect more the nature of man and his need for small tribal units in which he lived and developed for almost all his history. Therefore, for government to opt for its one pet type of school is very much in keeping with their customary arrogance. Concerning type of school:

Variety is the spice of life.

Once I visited a school that, like early man, did not separate work, play, home, community and education. It was a school that focused on 'rural studies' and was an important part of the community as a whole. Basically it was a small farm and market garden with classrooms and other school facilities. Under the guidance of teachers and community helpers, the pupils were responsible for everything. They looked after livestock like hens, ducks, sheep, cows, crops of flowers, vegetables and so forth. They had to plan all the systems, feeding, cleaning out, gathering, planting, accounting, buying, selling and the like. An essential ingredient was the regular design of experiments for testing out ideas. Pupils were involved at weekend and holidays. At these times, members of the local community helped more directly with the influx of visitors. More schools should organise activities for weekends and holidays. The present amount of free time given to students is excessive and works against the better interests of the pupils, education and society at large:

Idle hands make for mischief.

This small rural school encompassed all the subjects of other schools like English, mathematics, geography and so on. Their curriculum included other subjects not on traditional school programmes like horticulture, vehicle maintenance, rural architecture and management of the countryside to mention some. Subject areas and moral values were not seen as separate. They were viewed, by nature, for what they really are – integrated parts of a greater whole. Because the pupils had real responsibilities, they enjoyed school and were high achievers. Not only was their academic performance better than average schools, their social skills, team work and moral standards were of a praiseworthy standard. This was real education in a real setting. Regular new 'initiatives' from experts to improve education would be laughable were they not so dangerous and destructive. Effective methods of learning and teaching have been around and tried and tested since man was man and by a countless number of people of all cultures down the ages. Everyone knows that the basis of good education is discipline balanced with freedom that has responsibility:

**Nothing is really new in the world including
New Labour's failures.**

Successive governments with their expert accomplices have increasingly destroyed much of what was good in education all in the name of what might be described as pop law imperative – modernise or change things. Intrusion of experts is opposed and detrimental to common sense. Pop laws are anti-education too as it is 'uncool'. One example of a new sense pop law gaining power is, 'Criticism of pupils by teachers is an offence.' It is not good for their self esteem; apparently carrying a gun is. Old common sense in education is concerned with leading wisdom out. Expert new sense leads people astray and separates knowledge from morality with its pop laws. Perhaps a new hidden initiative is that government is going to let truancy rates rise until there are no pupils left in schools. This means no further need for teachers, playing fields or any other inconvenient educational baggage. Pupils can be educated, or is it uneducated and dehumanised by computers at home. Fortunately for all of us, the inborn sensing of many children comes out in their behaviour very often. However, they do not express these to the degree they could and should. The same applies to teachers, but expert laws are prohibitive:

Going back to common sense laws is the way forward in education.

Chapter 8

Work as an Unnatural Adversive Activity

Toil is the law of life and its best fruit.

Ancient and Common Wisdom

Much of current work mirrors modern science and political philosophy with their stress on materialism and lack of morality. Experts have conditioned business in industry and commerce to seek material gain or profit above all else. Hence, the organisation of labour and its practices reflect this. Politicians, irrespective of party, and other experts put the economy or material wealth at the top of their agenda. Their belief is that if the economy thrives, personal and social ills will be reduced. Experience and common sense show this to be untrue. Art Buchwald illustrates when he says, 'As the economy gets better, everything else gets worse.' Experts have rejected and reversed the common wisdom which in this context states:

If a society's moral values are healthy, work and the economy will be healthy also.

If financial or material success made for good personal and social values, the USA would be a model for the good society and human behaviour as would 'pop' stars. In reality the USA is one of the most violent, corrupt or immoral cultures the world has ever known. Its very existence is based on torture, genocide, theft on a massive scale and gross suppression. I speak of the treatment of its indigenous people. Material wealth does not make for a healthy, happy, fulfilled moral life or society. Excessive capitalism with its overemphasis on competition has spawned a culture of greed and corruption. This is so even, or particularly, when the economy is doing well. As the economy booms, the financial rewards of corruption and violent crimes can be even higher. Securing great material benefit and becoming rich produces many drawbacks as well as those gains frequently trumpeted by experts. An example of disadvantage of material riches is illustrated by the following common wisdom:

182

He who has the most possessions also has the most to lose.

The constant cry of politicians, businessmen and other experts is, 'We must become more competitive.' The aim of this is to gain a lion's share of the market place. To persuade the ordinary people that being more competitive achieves material wealth, experts label the process with a scientific sounding name. This gives the impression that it is some kind of law of nature and an excellent one at that. Economic experts call it 'The Principle of Market Mechanism'. Such a mechanism does what experts do with such great regularity and disaster. It focuses on one side of two opposites, competition, and loses sight of co-operation. It is true that part of man's nature is to be competitive. However, when emphasised at the expense of its opposite, co-operation, the competitive element is distorted and produces many negative outcomes. Ironically, it is the overemphasis on competition that creates lack of effective competition. Only when associated and in balance with its opposite, co-operation, is competition beneficial. A common wisdom about the nature of man is quite clear on this:

Man seeks co-operation as much as he seeks competition.

Not surprisingly, modern science was embraced in industry and then in commerce. Science dealt with matter and material and viewed the universe as a great machine obeying mechanical laws. Hence, man was viewed as a machine also, a biological one, but nevertheless a machine and an inferior one at that. Science in the work place was given much momentum by Frederick Taylor around the beginning of the 1900s. He is known as 'the father of scientific management' and believed problems could be solved best by the application of science. Work was analysed in term of making the human machine more efficient so that individuals produced more in a given time. Taylor saw the work place as relative virgin territory in which to develop management science. Al Capone was also concerned about efficiency and production when he said, 'Suburban Chicago is virgin territory for whorehouses.' Taylor subjected tasks on such equipment as lathes to time and motion studies. Time and motion are pet areas in science generally as experts see them as being readily open to measurement and observation which are basic requirements. The important elements that make for a good work place and performance, such as team or community spirit, integrity and responsibility are not so readily measured. They contain morality but science, by its own admission, cannot deal with this. Even if it were possible, financial costing of such things as integrity would seem a contradiction in terms. Experts in striving for profit and reducing financial costs neglect much wisdoms. One is:

The best things in life are free.

To the degree that management science has replaced common sense, it has done much harm. Many fallacies exist in addition to viewing man as a machine. The idea that people have to be trained in expert management theories to be good managers is another. Some people are very good managers who know nothing about management science. Those who are good managers and have been on expert management science courses are good, not because of the courses, but in spite of them. All people in their ordinary lives make thousands of informed decisions every single day. They are vastly experienced in managing tasks, people, finance, time and so on and so forth. I have met many people who have been on management science courses and I ask them about their experiences. The conversations go something like this:

Me: What did you learn that you didn't know before?
Other: Oh, lots of things.
Me: Can you give me an example of what you learned?
Other: Well, we did time management.
Me: What did you learn that was new to you?
Other: I learned that I tend to put off decisions and by the time I decide the problem is worse.
Me: Isn't that an example of the common sense saying 'A stitch in time saves nine?'
Other: Um, I suppose it might be, but I did learn a lot of important concepts or buzz terms.
Me: How does knowing buzz words help?
Other: If you do not press the right buttons in this world, you don't get on do you?

Experts create sophisticated language or jargon that separates them from the layman.

I have had similar conversations with scores of people who go on management science courses and also with the expert professors who run the courses. There has not been a single instance when they have produced anything valid or useful that was not already contained in common sense sayings. I have put similar questions to expert economists with exactly the same results. Their meaningful or useful knowledge is not as good as that of the common sense of the layman. Actually, an experiment was done that compared the predictions of expert economists about the economy with those of a group of taxi drivers. The predictions of the taxi drivers were better than those of the economic experts. Expert economists, like expert management scientists, have not produced a single law of their own that improves on, or even comes close to, common sense laws. When they have come up with something that is accurate, meaningful and useful, it has been a rediscovery of ancient wisdom or common sense law. A few management and economic experts have seen the light and recommend in the work place and in the wider world of business to:

Practise and preach common sense.

The vast majority of research and writings in management science and economics also shows that they are a waste of time and effort. Verbal outputs of experts are prolific and support the modern motive of excess and the expert maxim, 'Publish or perish.' The more writings experts produce the less they contain common sense is a good general rule. As W.H. Auden observes, 'A professor is one who talks in someone else's sleep.' As a common sense saying might put it:

Empty vessels make the most sound.

Expert research, theories and writings do not improve on common sense. For example, one experiment in economics used Leon Festinger's 'Theory of Cognitive Dissonance'. This theory suggests some actions promote conflicting thoughts and feelings. With a smoker, he enjoys smoking but is sad because he knows it is bad for his health. These opposing feelings or thoughts create, 'cognitive dissonance'. This is amply covered by the fact that common wisdoms point out that much of our reality is composed of opposites or dissonant thoughts or feelings. What is more, using the term 'cognitive' over-stresses the thoughts rather than the feelings which can be more important. Cognitive Dissonance Theory was used in this particular experiment to analyse 'consumer post-buying behaviour'. The experimenters rediscovered what we already know and summarise their findings as follows:

Bad news travels fast.

Along with professional politicians and lawyers, expert economists and big business men influence modern society the most. No matter how economists may dress up their field of expertise, it is about gaining excess money or profit. Using terms like maximising income, down-sizing, efficiency, supply and demand, perfect competition and the like does not hide this fact. They are promoting the worst aspects of human nature such as greed. Not unexpectedly, in a culture dominated by rationalism and science, work and business are becoming more and more like them. They are materialistic and lacking morality. Almost all the institutions that define our culture promote and reinforce the idea that material success should be man's main concern. This is against the grain of man's better nature and runs counter to common sense laws:

Where profit is, loss is hidden nearby.

What you gain on the swings, you lose on the roundabouts.

Government policies and laws, aided by science and a legion of experts, are prime movers in our culture of greed, lust for power and exploitation. Too many of us are becoming willing accomplices. Any culture which encourages individuals and groups to exploit other individuals, groups and nature is in dire trouble. Such a culture deserves to face the worst excesses of human indulgence and we are increasingly doing just that. Are there any areas of modern life that are not exploited for material gain? Business enterprises exploit plants, animals, children, greed, sex, violence, work and anything else you care to mention. Living the life of the idle rich or a life of luxury is the aim of modern society. This corrupt aim is extolled by politicians and other experts as a *virtue* and is anti-wisdom. Experts mislead and misrepresent the better feelings of the majority:

We are following a muck cart believing it is a wedding.

The excess wealth of one is the poverty of many.

Seeking material gain as a main aim of work or life creates a dilemma [or cognitive dissonance if you like the term] for the common sense majority. Our inner feelings or natural sensings of wisdom make us guilty and uncomfortable. We try to rationalise our involvement in the pursuit of materialism by saying such things as, 'Well everyone else is doing it. It's the way of the modern world. You can't stop progress'. If we do not take on the values of the culture that surrounds us, we can feel isolated or that we do not belong in our own society. Also, we may feel we may be missing something. We rationalise and think that if everyone else is doing something, there must be advantage in it. However, our collective mind or herd instinct, which is common sensing, tells us that a materialistic gain can be a moral loss:

> Honour and profit lie not in one sack.

There have always been immoral business men and workers since business and work began. Politicians and other experts use this fact to rationalise the outcomes of their own policies and laws. They say that what is happening in modern society has always happened. The politicians and other experts are not so much missing the point, they are trying to hide it. Common sense tells us not only are there corrupt businesses today and always were, but there always will be. What is different and of great consequence in modern society is the vast scale and rate of corruption and immorality in business, work and most other aspects of life. This has been particularly noticeable over the past fifty years when each day more people become involved in more immoral behaviours and enterprises. Anti-wisdoms are being used more frequently that illustrate the growing immorality in business and work. Two are:

> Do others before they do you.

> Look after number one.

This is a consequence of the obsession with competition at the expense of its opposite, co-operation. Morality has not only been seeping out of business and work practices for a long time, it is being torn away more rapidly with expert laws. Some well-known sayings confirm the separation of morality and business. When someone does a deal that produces material gain for a person but flies in the face of morality or common sense laws, some rationalisations are: 'Well, business is business' and 'All is fair in love, war and business'. One witty, though cynical anecdote attributed to Lord Grade involves his grandson who asked, 'What do two and two make grandad?' Lord Grade replied, 'It depends whether you are buying or selling.' Many wisdoms exist about money, profit and greed. One that the whole world knows is:

Money is the root of evil.

Far too many experts show by their policies and actions they work on the assumption that man's main motivation for working is money. Experts are making this assumption become a self-fulfilling prophecy. When morality is being made illegal and taken out of their lives by experts, what is left for the workers but materialism? Work is basic to human nature and fulfills man's needs more than any other activity. Though workers want a fair day's pay for a fair day's work, money is only a means to other ends. Work provides the opportunity to satisfy many more powerful motives than money. It provides opportunity to belong, to share, to identify and to affiliate with others. Man seeks relationships with other people in a healthy environment that give purpose and meaning to life. Good work situations achieve this. Too often work is separated from other things as well as morality, such as the local community in which it is located. Work should be integrated with local communities and society at large. In this way, man's physical, psychological, social, environmental and spiritual needs are more readily met. Here is one ancient and common wisdom which some experts have rediscovered after the failure of their earlier ill-informed prediction of a leisure society. The idea of a leisure society is not only undesirable, it is a fools' paradise. Without work, man would not be man. He would not be a balanced whole. Leisure without its opposite, work, would be meaningless:

Work provides the main source of existence and meaning to every man.

For early man, work and play were not separated as they are for modern man. Work and play have become separated and given special times and places for their enactment. Work too, has become increasingly divided into smaller and smaller parts and specialisms. This has created all kinds of problems. Narrow specialisms do not allow the worker to appreciate readily how the specialised task contributes to the larger picture, including the societal one. Many specialisms at work involve repeating the same task over and over again. For example, sitting at a typewriter or computer all day can be boring, anti-social and isolating:

Small specialised tasks make the worker unable to see the wood for the trees.

Today, compensation is paid for repetitive strain injury. This usually applies to the physical body. Being concerned with the body first is to be expected, since our culture primarily stresses the physical or materialistic matters. However, doing the same job over and over again is often described by workers as 'soul destroying'. Repeating the same task day after day is not only destructive to the physical body, it is harmful to mind and spirit also. Organising work in an excessively repetitive fashion is against common sense laws one of which in this context is:

Variety is the spice of life including work tasks.

Man, for nearly all his millions of years of existence, has been involved in virtually *all* his small tribe's work and play activities. This wide involvement with the whole group's tasks and activities is what man wants and needs. It is ingrained in his psyche and nature. To cater for this, man must be involved in as many things as possible at work and not restricted to specialising in narrow repetitive tasks. In this way the worker's need to have social interaction with many of his firm's work-force can be met and is to the firm's advantage also. Workers by nature have a wide general range of good skills with a few at which they excel more. Good bosses know this and make use of this huge, but frequently wasted, resource. Getting people to use and develop their inborn talents is the hallmark of a good boss or manager:

The greatest resources of any firm are the inborn skills and wisdoms of its workers.

The more work caters for employees' and employers' physical, mental, social, moral and environmental needs, the better is the firm's performance.

Not only does a worker need to have a wide range of effective relationships with his fellow workers, he needs to know how his work and that of his fellows contribute to the larger whole of community and society. As workers themselves so often say, they want to 'know the wider or bigger picture'. Narrow specialisms stress separation rather than togetherness. They are often unnecessary and destructive and this part-practice prevents identification with the larger whole, such as the firm, the community and society at large. Workers and employers recognise the importance of good team spirit, yet design practices which separate things, and this procedure goes against team spirit. One saying becoming more common illustrates the excess emphasis on increasing specialisation:

> Specialisation means getting to know more and more about less and less.

Since life and man himself are made up of paradoxes, it is to be expected that opposites or paradoxes make up the world of work. Let us take coal-mining as an example. One paradox is that often miners worked in cold, dark, wet conditions to provide the opposite for us. Coal is for warmth, light and dryness. After the Second World War many people were employed in the coal-mining industry. This work was bone-grinding, choking, very hard and dangerous to life and limb. In spite or because of this awful work situation, miners established great team spirit and felt their efforts were meaningful and contributed to the local community, society and the world at large. They also thought they were under-valued by bosses and experts, but they soldiered on with good grace and humour. Their very lives depended on co-operation with fellow workers, as do our own lives, but we seem to ignore this fact of life. Miners knew that the community and ordinary people in society at large held them in very high esteem. They were known for their common sense, practical judgements and being very honest and trustworthy people. They were famously known as 'lions led by fools'. Miners certainly knew the truth of the following paradox through their own experience:

> There can be no pleasure without pain.

Many were too brave and selfless for their own good and were sacrificed on the altar of increasing materialism and decreasing morality. Meeting huge and dangerous challenges gave them a great sense of achievement and closeness of community. The war had a similar effect on community spirit all over Britain. Miners made great sacrifices for their families and the rest of us. Most swore they would never allow their sons to go down the pit. The work was life-threatening as well as awful and deaths were regular occurrences. Another paradox of miners is that when jobs at the pit were plentiful, they did not want their own sons or those of friends to go into the industry. However, when the mining industry collapsed, they expressed concern that there would be no work in coal-mining for the young people of their communities. This illustrates two further paradoxes of life and work which also example opposites:

> When you've got what you want, you don't want it.

> When you haven't got what you want, you want it.

In too many work places entrepreneurs, bosses and managers are at loggerheads with the workers. They have aims that are opposite. Not only is this a separation of workers and management, it is a very antagonistic one. Bosses and workers being at odds with one another has been a cultural norm of too many places for far too long. The workers want as much pay as possible for as little work as possible. Entrepreneurs want the opposite. They want to pay as little as possible for as much work as possible. Such a state of affairs exists due to the great over-emphasis on material gain and the excessive focus on competition. Demanding regular pay increases is counterproductive and in their heart of hearts the workers know it. Any wage increase in a culture of striving for material gain and competitiveness is passed on to others. Tax payers, customers or other firms, in one way or another, have to pay for the increase. A chain reaction is set up. The tax payers and customers are also workers and in turn they ask for pay rises when prices and taxes go up and so it goes on in a futile and endless chase. We will mention two ancient wisdoms here, although many others also apply:

> One man's pay rise is another man's price increase.

> One thing leads to another.

Antagonism between bosses and workers is reflected in their separate organisations such as the Confederation of British Industries and Workers'

Trade Unions. When businesses do well and make big profits, the unions representing the workers press for a share in these profits by demanding higher wages for their members. One the other hand, when businesses do badly, the workers do not want to share in these losses by having a wage cut. They blame the down-turn in the firm's fortunes on poor management. Workers expect their wages to go on rising year on year whilst the bosses expect the same of their profits. Such expectations are unrealistic as is continual growth or even stability in the national economy. Common wisdoms stress:

There are limits to growth.

There are ups and downs to everything including business income and the economy.

People have to accept that their wages or profits have to go down as well as go up. In a business with which he identifies and where he can fulfill his needs for sharing, belonging and achieving effective social relationships, a worker is more than willing to approve wages that sometimes have to go down. A worker can face great adversity with good grace, increased endeavour and great dignity when he has real responsibility and meaningful partnership in the firm at which he works. If the worker feels he shares in the common wealth of the body, mind and spirit of a living organisation, he is ready to be part of any common sacrifice as well. The process of sharing is a very important part of human nature. If we examine our own feelings and experience, we have a strong need to share with others. This is particularly so with our successes and failures. Sharing is also directly related to justice and is evidenced even in a child's conversations when it says things like, 'Fair shares for all.' We all have an innate sensing for justice, though it has been taken from us by experts and corrupted into legal laws that create injustice. At work as elsewhere:

He who shares in the bad times as well as the good is the just or wise man.

As we have indicated before, businesses and work have become increasingly scientific and science cannot deal with questions of morality which are our main concern. We have management science, economic science and a galaxy of other sciences such as industrial psychology, occupational psychology, sociology of work and so on and so forth. With ever increasing divisions into smaller and smaller specialisms, the list seems endless. By comparison with experts, ordinary people are regarded as rank amateurs. With the ever-growing and self-evident messes created by experts or professionals, the man in the street is raising more and more questions about the role of experts in society. Malcolm Allison, the football manager, echoes our concerns when he says:

Noah was an amateur; the Titanic was built by professionals.

Let us examine a foundation stone that allows scientists to be called 'experts'. At the core of all science is *The Scientific Method*. It is only by the use of this method that management and economic science can lay claim to being a science at all. For many years, I along with many other people around the world thought it was scientists who had invented *The Scientific Method*. This is far from the truth. Any one of us, including my cat, could lay as much claim to inventing it as expert scientists. Let us look at what the scientific method involves.

The Scientific Method

Basically, the scientific method is made up of the following steps:

Statement of the problem

This usually starts as a question. For example, 'I wonder why is there so much aggression in the work place?' When the scientist finally publishes his article in a journal or book, the original question will be made into a statement of the problem. It would read, 'The relationship between aggression and . . .' There is nothing we do not know here. Young children ask scores of questions every day and so does everyone else:

Nothing is new or expert about asking questions or identifying problems. We all do it, by nature.

Review of relevant information

To get some ideas about what makes people aggressive at work, the expert reviews his own feelings about aggression and notes what makes himself aggressive. The expert also recalls the situations where he has seen aggression in others. He remembers discussions about the subject with family, friends or even strangers. The researcher brings to mind articles he has read in newspapers, magazines, or recalls information on aggression he has seen at the cinema or on television. Going to special books or journals on the subject is a further way of reviewing relevant information. Everyone does all these things except, perhaps, read research journals. However, since behavioural science journals are so full of expert jargon and since they never contain better information than common sense, reading them is highly questionable. Books, almost of any kind, usually contain many things about aggression as do films, even about Mickey Mouse. Ordinary people generally have more realistic and meaningful experience and knowledge of aggression than experts who write theories about it:

> Experience is the mother of true knowledge.

The research expert does not want to re-invent the wheel, as it were. Therefore, he assembles the information from the various sources we have mentioned concerning what is already known about aggression, especially that in the work place, which is the problem on which he is focusing. If he finds his question or problem has been satisfactorily answered already by someone else, he may decide not to proceed. On the other hand, he may decide to repeat the experiment that he found some other expert had already done. It is part of the scientific quest to repeat experiments to see if they produce the same results each time. This adds to the reliability, objectivity and validity of the experiment. Also, the particular work place he is studying aggression in might not have quite the same conditions as those studied in other experiments. Thus, even doing the same experiment might produce different results. Alternatively, the expert may modify the experiment to suit any special circumstances he recognises in the particular work place he is studying. Repeating things including experiments or testing things out is common to all of us. For example, we tell the same joke to different groups of people and we may change it a little to suit the circumstances. This is exactly what experts do, including modifying their experiments to suit particular situations:

> Nothing is new or expert about reviewing information to solve problems. We all do it every day, by nature.

Making hypotheses or informed guesses

After reviewing what is known about aggression in the work place, the expert generates or makes some hypotheses. These are informed guesses, speculations or predictions based on the review of relevant information, experience, reasoning, observation and the like. The expert may speculate that frustration leads to aggression in the work place. Formally stated the hypothesis would be:

> **The more frustrated a worker gets in the work place the more aggressive the worker becomes.**

The expert may make several hypotheses which link all kinds of factors to aggression such as overcrowding, suppression of workers' talents, bureaucracy, too few staff and so on. Actually, since one common sense law tells us all things are related, experts could go on hypothesising factors that are related to aggression till the cows come home. One advantage of this for experts is they have an endless task and so are unlikely to be out of work. Ordinary common sayings clearly demonstrate that we all make hypotheses, speculations, informed guesses or predictions every day. Some are:

I bet that _____
What you will find is _____
I think that _____
What will happen will be that _____
I expect that _____
My prediction is _____
An outcome or consequence of that will be _____
My guess would be that _____

> **Nothing is new or expert about making hypotheses.**
>
> **We all make them every day, by nature.**

Definition of terms

Next, the expert defines all the main terms in his problem and hypotheses. In the example we have chosen, the expert would define the terms, worker, work place, aggression and frustration. He has to clarify what he means by the terms. For example, does aggression mean the physical type or verbal kind and is being given the silent treatment or having an unfair amount of work given to you a form of aggression? The researcher has to be as accurate as he can be with defining his terms. Ordinary people define their terms in everyday life and ask others to clarify what they mean by certain words in particular situations. Some examples of common sayings that demand definition of terms are:

Ah, it depends what you mean by _____

Well, tell us what you mean by _____

I don't understand what you mean by _____

What I mean by _____ is _____

There is another meaning to _____ which is _____

You have a funny interpretation of _____

> Nothing is new or expert about defining terms or what we mean. We do it regularly, by nature.

Collection of data or information

Now the expert has to collect data or information to test his hypotheses. He may do this by structured interview, a written questionnaire or some physiological indicators of aggression or all of these, plus other measures he thinks appropriate. We all collect data or information all the time to solve problems and test out our ideas or hypotheses. We may not do it as formally as experts, but formality is no guarantee of good knowledge or wisdom. Formality in scientific experiments means rigidity of approach. If rigid rules are not obeyed, it is not science. The human brain is designed to collect and process information to solve problems. Human nature also contains wisdom and morality which science does not:

> Nothing is new or expert about collecting data or information. We all do it all day, by nature.

Testing hypotheses or speculations

Here the experimenter compares the scores of the workers on the measures of aggression and frustration to see if there is a relationship between the two. Not only is he interested in if there is a relationship, he must assess the *strength of relationship*. For example, he may find that thirty per cent of the people who are aggressive are also frustrated. This would not be such a strong relationship as if eighty per cent of those who are aggressive are frustrated. Even when the expert researcher has gained this knowledge, we can ask him the question, 'How useful is this knowledge in improving the experience of the workers in the work place?' The workers themselves have far more experience of the work place than the expert. An ancient and common Arabic wisdom is relevant here:

> The tongue of experience has most truth.

Interesting though this experiment is to the expert, ordinary workers are usually well aware of who of their fellow workers are aggressive. They also know the degree to which they are aggressive and what usually makes them frustrated or aggressive. In addition, workers are more aware than experts of what makes themselves and even their bosses frustrated and aggressive. Having regular or even daily contact with their fellow employees gives the ordinary worker a vast range of experience that experts cannot gain in the relatively short time they are conducting their experiments. When experts are doing experiments in the work place it becomes a laboratory and a false one at that. The presence of experts affects the behaviour of the work force. Frank Westheimer lampoons expert research when he observes, 'A couple of months in the laboratory can frequently save a couple of hours in the library.' An ancient wisdom that is fitting here is:

> That which proves too much proves nothing.

A large part of everyday life is made up of testing out our hypotheses or ideas. Ordinary workers test their own ideas, speculations, predictions or hypotheses regularly. For example, a worker may feel that if he tries to be more friendly or cheerful to, say, customers or work colleagues, he may get a better response from them. This is the kind of hypothesis most of us have tested at some time or other and quite often. However, we may not put the results into practice as much as we feel we should. There are lots of everyday sayings which show quite clearly that all of us test hypotheses or predictions. Some are:

My prediction is _____
I bet that _____
What you will find is _____
I would expect that _____
My guess would be _____
I reckon that _____

The whole of the future tense of the many hundreds of verbs in the English language are concerned with prediction and hypothesis-making in one way or another. This is not to mention the future tense of verbs in foreign languages:

Nothing is new or expert in testing hypotheses.

All of us test hypotheses daily, by nature.

Findings or results

In this section, the researcher states whether he finds enough evidence to support the hypotheses or not. For example, in the case of the hypothesis we have used as an illustration, the finding might be stated by the expert as follows;

The hypothesis that the more frustrated a worker gets in the work place the more aggressive the worker becomes, is supported.

The expert then goes into details of his facts and figures, in relation to his measuring instruments, to show the numbers add up to what he is claiming as success for his hypothesis:

Numbers and measurement are crucial to the scientific game.

Though the expert's hypothesis may gain support, it can leave more problems than it solves. For example, when people say why they are aggressive they may not necessarily really know. However, they come up with some kind of explanation because they are expected to do so by the powers that be. If they do not provide an explanation, they know they could be regarded as mental cases. Others just enjoy being aggressive. It gives them status and much attention, but not many in the work place are likely to admit that they enjoy being aggressive for the sheer hell of it. Also, one could ask, how is aggression different from anger? Even if frustration does cause aggression, there are hundreds of situations that cause frustration. Particular situations that cause frustration and aggression in some people do not have the same effect on other people and so on and so forth. Mark Twain lampoons the efforts of expert researchers when he says:

> Researchers have already cast much darkness on this subject and if they continue their investigations we shall soon know nothing at all about it.

We all state findings, results or outcomes of our own predictions, speculations or hypotheses. Everyday language illustrates this:

You know how I predicted he would get the sack, well, he did.
The arguments I put forward about John getting promoted, turned out
    to be accurate.
Told you I'd get a pay rise and I did.
I expected to get Tim's job, but Mary got it.
My guess about the research department was spot on.

> Nothing is new or expert about stating results of testing hypotheses. We do it by nature.

Discussion and recommendations

In this final section of the scientific method, the expert analyses the various aspects of the experiment he has done to highlight strengths and weaknesses. He may point out that some workers were unco-operative whilst others treated the experiment as a joke. The expert may also recommend some refinements to his measuring instruments which could make a subsequent experiment more effective. He may discuss further avenues of research that have been highlighted by his experience in the present experiment. Based on his findings, he may recommend attention be given to areas of work that cause frustration – as if the workers did not know these areas already. It is the workers who told the expert what the problems were and how to solve them. Now the expert can make what the workers already know official and acceptable to experts. Unlike many scientific experts, workers can discuss problems and can make common sense recommendations on how to solve them based on real experience, if allowed to do so:

> Nothing is new or expert in discussion or recommendation concerning problems or other elements of the scientific method.

Scientists then, took a list of operations that everyone uses every day, stripped it of its morality and called it *The Scientific Method*. Expert scientists explained that the reason for detaching these operations from morality was to get *pure knowledge*. People use all the operations of science, but they apply them to moral problems that are integrated with knowledge. That is, the operations for ordinary people form an intrinsic web threaded through natural wisdom that does not falsely separate knowledge and morality. As well as people using a moral version of the scientific method, animals including insects use it too. They are problem solvers, collectors and processors of data or information, testers of hypotheses and so on. Even some experts admit to this obvious observation. Scientists and expert rationalists may argue that animals, unlike themselves, are unable to communicate the findings of their experiments to others. Even this is not true. Bees, for example, tell other bees exactly where to find nectar. In addition, some animals make far more accurate predictions about the future than experts. The common lady-bird knows when there is a bad winter ahead and buries more deeply into leaf mould. Scientific experts envy such skill. Scientists probably copied their scientific method by watching cats or some other animals. Scientists will not sing the following refrain at expert conventions, though it is true:

> Birds do it, bees do it, even educated fleas do it . . . the scientific method, that is.

Hypothesis testing is a main tool of the scientific venture so experts have created the myth that animals are incapable of doing it. If experts did not create myths, they would not be regarded as extraordinary or superior. One myth concerns attitude to change. How often do we hear bosses and experts say, 'People are resistant to change'? What this means is that bosses and experts are not resistant to change, but ordinary workers are. We all actively seek change and are rewarded by it for its own sake. Sometimes we seek change that we know is harmful rather than doing the same old things. It is when people have change thrust upon them instead of involving them from the very outset that makes for resistance. Quite sensibly, people can resist change when they see it being harmful and imposed on them. Not all change is for the better. However, people can stand any amount of change which they feel is for the better. The notion too, that people will accept change, but only slowly, is again wide of the mark. If you asked many people in our materialistic society when they would like to change their lives by winning millions on the lottery would they say, in ten years, in one year, or yesterday? People would accept the change to a vast reduction in crime and many other changes they saw for the better, in a flash. Common sense laws have much to say about change. The best known two are:

Change is as good as a rest.

The only constant in life is change.

Another mistaken idea of too many bosses, managers and other experts is that workers have to be driven to increase production. As a result businesses can become far too authoritarian. Such a view is based on the false assumption that people really do not want to work and when they do, it is only for money. Being an excessively driving authoritarian boss or manager results in the opposite of what it is supposed to achieve. Being bossy creates antagonism and low performance or production. This does not mean there should not be high standards of behaviour and discipline; these should be a norm for the firm. Overly authoritarian leaders can take advice from many common sense laws, two of which are:

He who lives by the sword shall die by the sword.

Do unto others.

Shared power and responsibility are the hallmarks of a good firm. To achieve this, it is important for individual workers to have meaningful contact with as many other people in the firm as possible. By involving workers in a wide range of decisions, they become more aware of the social implications, responsibilities and problems of the business as well as their impact on the local community and the wider culture. Workers in these circumstances realise that individuals, experts and governments cannot solve social problems including those of work. They will become more aware that businesses in large part must take on the responsibility of solving social problems by the application of common sense laws. It is no use having solidarity of workers as separate from solidarity of managers or entrepreneurs. Workers and bosses are dependent on one another. Entrepreneurs only have existence and meaning in relation to workers. The opposite is also true. Business men have a moral obligation to keep workers on in bad times as well as good, just as workers must stand by entrepreneurs in bad times as well as good. Workers and bosses must act together, as one. If sacrifices are mutual, both benefit including enhancing identification and trust:

> **Adversity and success make good companions.**

> **United we stand, divided we fall.**

Too many entrepreneurs and bosses believe that increasing production as much as possible is the main aim of business. Excessive production has resulted in having mountains of butter and grain as well as thousands of cars stacked up without demand for them. Paradoxically, many in our global village are starving. Production and demand must be more in balance. Excessive consumerism should not be encouraged as it is by almost all our institutions and advertisements. I heard on television recently an advertisement which, in effect, said, 'If you've shopped until you drop, and still want more, ring this number.' Excessive production or consumption destroys quality of life. We ignore common sense laws at our peril:

> **A *little* of what you want can do you good.**

With most of society's systems geared to greed, overproduction and over-consumption, it is not surprising there are constant wage demands. Pay should be regarded as business profit not wages. All workers should be involved, at a particular firm, in deciding who gets what. In a moral organisation, fair financial reward looks after itself. Some business men regard paying wages as a loss from their personal profit. Robert Bosch makes an interesting point by using opposites when he says:

> **I don't pay good wages because I've got a lot of money,**
> **I have a lot of money because I pay good wages.**

There have been good and bad entrepreneurs, leaders, managers and workers since work was work. In modern society, due to the number of expert theories, laws, rules and regulations, even good bosses and workers are unable to function as they would like. Some entrepreneurs have tried to counteract the cult of excess materialism and competition by giving co-operation and other aspects of human nature the opportunity to flourish. The John Lewis Partnership is one example. The word 'partnership' is highly significant, because this is what Lewis sought with his workers, the community and the world at large. Effective relationship or partnership gives existence and meaning to life including work. Lewis was very successful in his mission. In his books, *Partnership for All* and *Fair Shares*, he stresses that his guiding light is *common sense*. Lewis readily appreciates excessive competition and materialism are anti-social and destructive to body, mind, spirit and to communities as well as society at large. Stressing competition at the expense of co-operation also produces low performance and profit. In this context a common wisdom would read:

> Excess competition produces the opposite of what it is supposed to achieve.

Lewis knew a basic component of human nature is justice. When he was twenty three years old, Lewis discovered something about his father's business that offended his sense of justice. He found out that he, together with his father and brother, took a profit which was greater than the total wages of the workers put together. After years of planning and changing the business, Lewis made the entire capital of the firm the property of the partnership in the form of shares. More important to Lewis was the social structure and interaction of his workers and business relationships. He knew full well that:

> Man does not live by bread alone.

In the John Lewis Partnership, not only do workers share in the profits, they share in everything else like knowledge, decisions, power and responsibility. Workers want to be involved as much as possible and the John Lewis Partnership gives opportunity and encouragement for wide ranging involvement. When moral and social issues are at stake, and they usually are, all members are equally responsible for decisions. The spirit of fairness or justice is paramount for workers and customers. An example of this is that if anything can be purchased cheaper elsewhere, Lewis's department stores will refund the difference immediately. All common wisdoms speak about justice in one way or another. Two are:

> Right wrongs no man.

> Share and share alike.

There are a few other businesses which have put morality that is contained in common sense laws at the centre of their operations. These too have enjoyed success. One example is the Scott Bader plastic business in Wollaston in England, though Ernest Bader is Swiss whereas John Lewis is English. Around 1950, Bader's company transferred its capital to what was called The Scott Bader Commonwealth. The term commonwealth is also meaningful as the wealth was to be common to all. If the moral values are healthy so are the finances or economics:

> Common sense brings common wealth.

The profits from the Scott Bader firm go to The Commonwealth which is managed by its members. Bader also stresses the spiritual side of man's nature as well as his social needs. He considers it essential that some of the business profits should be used for cultural purposes in the locality. Amongst other things, this fulfills the needs of the workers to be involved with the community and to see how businesses are integral and very important parts of the community and society at large. Shared culture, power, knowledge and everything in general are seen as essential as it is in the John Lewis Partnership. These businesses encourage co-operation to counter-balance the general ethos of excessive competition which is anti-wisdom. Both Lewis and Bader brought some real democracy into the world of work:

> Applying common sense laws in the work place makes labour more truly democratic.

I have talked quite a bit about work places being integrated with the community. Perhaps I have been too general about it, so let me give a more specific example. One of the powerful links work should have with the community is education. Apart from work of some kind being available to workers throughout life, students should spend more time in the work place. Even some thirteen-year-olds could benefit by having a proper job for which they are paid. Education and work for them should be fully integrated. One option would be to spend a year or two in the work place where there should be some educational and training facilities. Coupled with this, the youngster should go back to school in the community at times to use educational resources not available at work. The opposite should happen too. Workers should be able to use the school to extend their education and training. Students and workers could help each other to develop skills, knowledges and values that are embedded in wisdom. Such a programme would ensure that employers, workers, pupils, employment, education and the community were as one:

Learning and education go on throughout life.

A task shared is a task halved.

I have asked numerous highly rated workers how they became so well regarded. What the answers boiled down to was being interested in people, engaging in a wide variety of activities, leading a balanced life and taking a pride in what you do. For example, one canteen lady told me she loved reading poetry and classical literature. She told me that there was more sensible psychology in plays and novels than in any psychology book. A lady of over eighty was still cleaning toilets after forty years at a mansion open to the public. She was asked what she thought about her job. The old lady replied, 'I really love it. It is very crucial work. Nothing is more important than having clean toilets is there?' Dignity of labour can be found in all kinds of work. There are many brain surgeons and others in high status jobs who are not as happy with their work or as satisfied with life as this old lady. She certainly knows the meaning of the wisdoms:

Count your blessings.

Satisfaction depends on your will.

Expert theories are so imbalanced by focusing one end of opposites like competition and so lacking in morality that criticism is mounting. Even some expert economists are abandoning ship and setting up alternative groups, cultures, conferences, meetings, organisations and the like. Rejecting the theories and practices in which they were schooled and qualified is hard for some experts. We must give credit where it is due and praise their conscience. Sadly, the main power still lies with the majority of dangerous experts including economists whose theories foster immorality in increasing excesses. There has always been criticism of expert economics since it became an academic and recognised area of study and operation. For example, Sir Peter Middleton, a civil servant says:

> It would be a dreadful mistake to equate economics
> with real life.

P. Ekins, M. Hilman and R. Hutchison, in their 1992 book called *Wealth Beyond Measure*, reject the usual expert economic theories that focus on money at the expense of morality. These authors recommend a holistic approach that brings together what experts have increasingly separated, namely, state, market, community, family and individual. Similarly, E.J. Schumacher demonstrates he is a holistic thinker by blending spiritual health with material well-being. In his book of 1973, entitled, *Small is Beautiful: A Study of Economics As if People Mattered*, Schumacher uses much common sense. Not surprisingly, experts described his book as controversial and revolutionary. His book became quite famous and it is interesting to note that the title of his book contains an ancient and common wisdom:

> Small is beautiful.

Schumacher highlights economies of scale and points out that smaller countries prosper more than large ones. He says, 'that with industries and firms, just as with nations, there is irresistible trend, dictated by modern technology, for units to become ever bigger.' Any so-called achievements of big organisations like General Motors is really a federation of smaller sized firms. Big businesses like superstores force small shops to close down with a chain of other consequences such as deterioration of local communities. In their thirst for profit and power, big businesses affect all aspects of our lives in one way or another. Seeing how big business impacts on our lives is an interesting exercise for anyone to do, including pupils at school. Is there any area of our lives that is unaffected by big business? Small businesses, like small schools, reflect man's nature and long history of life in small tribal units. Wisdoms related to size of scale are varied in their expression. Two examples are:

The best gifts come in small packages.

Quantity is no substitute for quality.

One attempt to escape expert theories, laws and practices has been for people to set up their own small businesses. Even government does not deny that small businesses are very important to the economy and the society generally. However, according to one report, the New Labour Government has been instrumental in imposing an extra *two thousand* laws, rules and regulations on small businesses in less than two years. Hence, it seems impossible to get away from expert theories and laws in the way we would like without ridding ourselves of experts themselves. In this context a common sense law reads:

More business laws, less business justice.

There are many other indicators of the upset of ordinary people over experts and their theories about work, management and economics. One is the network of common workers who are attempting to cut out experts and develop their own local economic systems. They are trying to take the economy that affects their lives into their own hands. An example is the Japanese housewife who started to buy milk in bulk in 1965 to save money. From this beginning, the Seikatsu Club Consumers' Co-op was developed. It pursues 'green' economic policies and practices. The club has grown into a worthwhile economic system distributing around four hundred products all according to strict ecological and social or common sense laws. In other words, this is economics integrated with morality. There are some *twenty thousand local groups of about eight member families each*. The club has more than twenty five million pounds in member investment. If suppliers do not live up to its high moral standards, the club produces its own goods:

Where there's a will there's a way.

Ordinary people, especially housewives, have more meaningful knowledge and experience of work, management and economics than experts. They have to rely more on common sense than expert theories. If they could lift the massive expert books on economics and read them, they would have no time to be sensible. Housewives are planners, psychologists, decision-makers, budgeters, financial advisers, nurses, accountants, negotiators, team leaders, leisure officers, catering managers, to mention a few of their roles. They can be called upon to perform all these jobs in a single day. Housewives keep many balls in the air at the same time and juggle them in a very effective fashion. Are there any male executives, even the most highly paid ones in the world, who can perform this feat? Wives and mothers, unskilled in expert theories and practices, are generally excellent managers and economists. Even expert economists criticise expert econom-ists. Unfortunately, very few act on these criticisms. However, they do act on the next quotation by breeding their own kind at an alarming rate. J.K. Galbraith, a famous economist, admits:

> Economics is extremely useful as a form of employment for economists.

Some people seek to have more secure jobs by joining the information handling sector of the work-force. This is seen as a good career move as the British industrial base gets smaller and crumbles away. As technology develops further, those in the information society, who spend their time pushing information around to one another, could well be made redundant. However, the capacity for people to make work for themselves should not be underrated. Where one of our great dangers may lie is in letting our manufacturing industries disappear. Another drawback of the information society is that the present excess of it conflicts with man's nature. Just because we can generate an almost limitless supply of information and transmit it in the blinking of an eye, does not mean that the information can be digested. Man's ability to process information has not changed for millions of years. The human brain has remained much the same as it was when he lived in caves. Even if man could process all the information that is thrown at him, most of it is useless anyway compared to his common sense. Actually, the fact that expert information is generally useless helps many to survive as they can file much of it in the waste-paper basket. Such a procedure is to the benefit of the organisation for which the people work. If they dealt with all the paper work or information in the way experts expect them to do, they would have no time to do any other tasks. The expert assumption that the more information people are supplied with, the better the decisions and performance, is false. If amount of information was helpful, things should be getting better at a phenomenal rate. The opposite is true, important things to life and survival are getting worse. Andrew Brown puts the information society and excess use of technology into perspective:

> The Internet is so big, so powerful and so pointless that for
> some people it is a complete substitute for life.

Modern expert theories and laws have created too many negative attitudes towards work. Having poor feelings about work shows the damage experts have done. Man, by nature, is a worker. Without work, he could not have evolved at all. Work was necessary to get food and keep body and soul together. It is in the very fibre of his being to be involved in work with his fellow men. Some people, when they retire, do not know what to do with themselves and can get very sorry about their plight. Often, they will create work to occupy themselves or they will try to get back into the work-force. People should not be forced to retire if they wish to carry on working. Their experience and wisdom should not be thrown on the scrap heap on the whim of expert theory and law. There are many ancient and common wisdoms in every culture and language that bear testimony to man's desire and need to work. Two examples follow and the second one is from the Bible, New Testament, Thessalonians:

> Labour is the foundation of all.
>
> If any would not work, neither should he eat.

One attitude to work is demonstrated by a nineteen-year-old girl who talked about the government's attempt to get single parents into jobs. She has never worked and has two children by different fathers. She lives on welfare benefits. This young mother said of the scheme to get her into work, 'Oh, I would never take a job that I did not really enjoy'. In one way she has a point. Work should contain enjoyment. However, the modern aim of wanting to be happy all the time is not in touch with reality or common sense laws. Unless there are times of unhappiness at work, its opposite, happiness, would be meaningless. It would be an interesting calculation to compare the long term financial and social costs of this girl and her children with some 'fat cats'. One story in the media tells of a boss who sacked seven hundred and fifty workers, lost his own job and walked away with seventeen million pounds. A second boss has just acquired a ninety million wage package in a firm where they are making workers redundant, according to another report. The young mother takes it as a right that the tax payer should support her and her children. The fat cats take it as a right to receive vast amounts of money while workers are sacked. This is the level of morality or wisdom of modern labour and it is enshrined in expert theories, policies and laws:

He that has no shame, has no conscience.

There are other indicators that show experts are having an increasingly negative effect on people's feelings about modern day work. Lots of workers are seeking early retirement or change of job. Also, some workers such as firemen, I believe, can retire at forty if they have an injury. By the time we are forty, most of us have some kind of injury and can use it to play the expert system. One person I know got injured in rugby, but convinced the powers that be that he had sustained the injury at work. Hence, as well as his normal pension, he received a disability pension also. More and more people are taking advantage of expert laws and employment rights:

Expert laws always have loopholes.

To get out of the 'rat race' people are forsaking modern occupations and going back to those that are closer to nature. One example is the high-salaried city financier who gave up his post to become a blacksmith in a country village at a fraction of his former earnings. When interviewed, the ex-financier said becoming a blacksmith was the best move he had ever made. A friend of mine is a dentist and was always complaining about how much he disliked his job. At forty, he gave it up, trained as a landscape gardener and says he loves his new work. He also said, 'I used to hate getting out of bed in the morning when I was a dentist. Now I can't wait to get up and go to my work.' There is an ancient and common wisdom which says that sometimes you have to go a few paces back before you can go forward again. To fit the situation of the ex-financier and ex-dentist the ancient and common wisdom would read:

Sometimes we have to go backwards in finance to go forward in spirit.

The sorry state of work is evidenced by the number and outcomes of official bodies trying to put right the things that are wrong with employment. So many people are employed in these schemes attempting to right wrongs in the labour market, there will soon be no one left to do any proper work. In addition to a ministry for employment, there are committees, think-tanks, focus groups, special units, job centres, conferences, regional initiatives, local schemes, pilot studies, new deals, counselling experts, industrial tribunals and so forth. This is the usual expert way of dealing with matters. There are so many parts that the problem as a whole is missed or denied. *Work is a moral problem.* In their heart of hearts, the majority of people know that to deal with the problem as a whole requires the application of common sense laws:

> In employment experts cannot see the wood for the trees.

Let us examine one of these expert bodies a little closer. Industrial tribunals are made up of members of the judiciary along with trade union representation. Trade union officials are often as bad as other experts like those of the legal profession. They soon become pseudo-experts in politics and employment law which they themselves helped create. Some of the awards made by industrial tribunals defy almost any common sense law you can bring to mind. No wonder some usually sensible people are tempted to try their luck at getting money for things they take in their stride in their normal work-a-day lives. As some ordinary people have said, 'It's money for old rope'. If anyone in the work place thinks he or she deserves compensation for a grievance, the rest of the workers in the firm should decide what it is to be. Should the grievance not be settled amicably within the firm, temporary randomly selected Justices of The Peace from the local community should decide. Experts from the judiciary and trade unions should not enter the equation:

> The common sense of the layman contains truth and justice.

One case that got to an industrial tribunal was a young woman who applied to a firm where the work required some heavy lifting. Obeying 'the equal opportunity laws', the employer took her on to his staff. After a short time, the girl told her employer that she was pregnant. Not wanting a pregnant girl lifting heavy weights, the employer dispensed with her services. She took the employer to an industrial tribunal and the employer had to pay her compensation for unfair dismissal. Another compensation case presently in the melting pot involves two policewomen. They were sent to the primary school in Dunblane where sixteen children and a teacher were slain. They claim they did not receive adequate counselling afterwards. The two female police officers are claiming £400,000 each. One little girl saw her friends butchered at the Dunblane school and suffered a shattered foot and damaged sciatic nerve. She was compensated with the much smaller sum of £4,500. The two police officers would have been well-advised to note the wisdom:

> A good name is rather to be chosen than great riches.

Police can claim compensation for seeing crime; firemen for seeing fires; doctors and nurses for dealing with car accident victims; pupils for failing examinations; builders for catching cold on chilly buildings sites and so on. The majority of common sense people have always believed that police were supposed to see crime and its outcomes just as firemen are supposed to see fires. All occupations and activities have consequences or outcomes and not all of them are pleasant. Expert theories policies and laws have created our compensation culture. The majority of workers know and agree with wisdoms that relate to work which also apply to life in general. One well-known saying is:

> You have to take the rough with the smooth.

More expert laws are on the way which will do more harm than good. I read in the newspaper the other day that laws are being prepared to ensure workers do not get told off at work as it stresses them. Another right is to come on the legal statutes that ensures workers can go home in an emergency. Some lady I know read this last proposal and said, 'It depends on what you mean by an emergency. I regard it as a family emergency when I haven't enough ice in the house to put in my gin and tonic. Moreover, my five year old son views the loss of his teddy-bear as a more serious emergency than if I broke both my legs.' She was being humorous, but she does make a serious point. We shall probably have expert national, regional and local bodies set up to deliver a stack of 'independent inquiry' reports to inform us all what constitutes an emergency. What we do know from experience is that no matter how many expert laws are put out about going home in an emergency, a few will feign illness to watch a football match. Expert laws penalise the innocent and do not prevent those bent on cheating the system doing so. Indeed, expert laws create mistrust of good citizens and in turn they mistrust others. A lot of the increase in paper-work in businesses is about mistrust rather than the stated aim of providing useful information. Materialism and greed create mistrust rather than it opposite, trust, which flourishes when wisdom or common sense is not suppressed. The vast majority of ordinary people are trustworthy if they are trusted. One wisdom is:

In trust is truth.

One more index of growing opposition to expert theories and laws is the rediscovery of writing and books that contain ancient wisdoms or common sense. One such volume is by Dale Carnegie. He is an American and his book, *How to Win Friends and Influence People*, was first published in 1936. It became an overnight success and was printed abroad in a dozen or more different languages. Carnegie's book is crammed with ancient wisdoms or common sense laws. He applies them to business, work, social interaction, family relationships and most other aspects of life. What follows are a few of the many wisdom he uses:

Be a good listener.

Show respect for the other man's opinions.

Appeal to the nobler motives.

Ask questions instead of giving direct orders.

Be courteous.

Give the other person a fine reputation to live up to.

He who treads softly goes far.

Although experts find it difficult to disprove the common sense laws recommended by Carnegie, his book is regarded as 'unscientific'. It does not contain mathematical formulae, statistics, measurement, calculations, graphs and expert language that science requires. Eddie George, governor of the Bank of England makes an interesting comment on measurement and calculations. He says, 'There are three kinds of economists: Those who can count and those who can't.' Actually, Carnegie did an excellent piece of research to produce his book. It was obvious, ordinary and common-sensical, all of which are opposite to the ideas of being an expert, a specialist or a scientist. Carnegie interviewed many successful people in all walks of life and listed their recommendations for good achievements. He then identified the sayings on which all these people agreed. This inter-judge agreement showed that it was common sense laws that were identified and valued; that is, they were *objective*. Agreement between people about something is how even experts define objectivity. Experts, to protect their minority views and well-rewarded academic citadels, do not have sufficient regard for this common sense saying in respect of Dale Carnegie:

Give credit where it is due.

In the 1930s and 1940s expert science was continuing its relentless advance with increasing momentum as it does today. Experts continue to produce and emphasise their own theories and jargon in an endless number of books and academic courses on management, business, economics and the like. Carnegie's book had little or no influence on academic experts. They considered it beneath them to read it and many viewed the title as laughable. Such is the power of experts that Carnegie's book became a music-hall joke. Today there is a little more respect for Carnegie's writings and a few experts are now advising their students to read his works. Unlike expert books, Carnegie's work has been read by many ordinary people for over sixty years now. Experts would do well to heed common wisdoms, two of which are:

He who laughs last, laughs longer.

Only wisdom stands the test of time.

Though there is mounting criticism of experts, it is not being translated into as much action as it deserves. Experts still hang on to their power by hook or by crook. Colleges like Henley and Harvard Business School have boomed over the last decades in producing business, economic and other experts. Expert seats of learning pay lip-service to common sense laws, but are being forced to give a little more attention to them recently. In practice, the extra attention turns out to be an increase in lip-service. Unless they have changed drastically over the past few years, colleges such as Henley still give students books of around 800 pages to read and memorise in economics and other subjects. Then the students are expected to regurgitate them in term papers or examinations. Experts at such colleges would claim, of course, that their programmes and books do contain common sense. This is so because it is unavoidable rather than being embraced as the best knowledge and guide for action we have got. In college examinations or term papers, if a student stresses common sense laws at the expense or exclusion of expert pet theories and language, he or she is marked down or fails. Edmund Burke's observation on experts has substance and is depressing. His use of the term 'sophisters' for experts is fitting for it means, 'fallacious reasoners or quibblers'. Things have got far worse since Burke wrote:

> But the age of chivalry is gone. That of sophisters, economists, and calculators, has succeeded; and the glory of Europe is extinguished forever.

Experts in management science and economics, like other experts, focus too much on one end of opposites and try to resolve paradoxes. This is an unwise pursuit as opposites or paradoxes are facts of life. Economic experts speak of 'perfect competition' when common sense law says, 'Nothing in this world is perfect'. Economists do not appreciate the importance of opposites enough. Mathematics is a central component to economics. Opposites define the reality of mathematics and statistics. We have addition and subtraction, multiplication and division and differentiation and integration in mathematics. The basis of statistics is to calculate similarities and differences, which are opposites also. Perhaps the example of the common sense law of opposites in mathematics and statistics, which are the regular diet of economists, are too obvious to see. Obvious things are often difficult to see, especially for experts. Their whole existence is geared to dealing with things that are clever and not obvious. Though experts are forced to use some examples of the law of opposites, they do not appreciate the great number of situations to which this law applies. It is all-powerful, yet their own expertise has blinded them to the obvious. In fact, is not doing the obvious the opposite of what experts do? Experts do not recognise the great significance of common wisdoms, two of which are:

In the obvious lies the truth.

Common wisdoms including opposites define our reality in business as elsewhere.

Sadly experts of all kinds have made much work an increasingly unnatural and aversive activity. All types of governments have contributed to this state of affairs as well as other power brokers such as big businesses and other members of the celebrity elite. Thus it would have been surprising had New Labour not continued this slide into moral oblivion. You will be able to cite, from your own personal experience of work and common sensing, many examples of the growing stress of workers. One recent illustration is that not so long ago we used to have one of the best pension systems and now we are heading for having the worst. Gordon Brown our 'prudent' Chancellor of the Exchequer plundered pensions and financed every other disastrous adventure his government embarked upon such as five wars in seven years including Iraq. Common sense told us that the work given to the soldiers in Iraq would be virtually impossible. Many people predicted that after a brief success because of superior technology, the American and British troops would, as an old man I know forecast, '. . . be shot like fish in a barrel because the enemy could fade in and out of local communities unseen at will'. No war is 'prudent' but New Labour's excursions have been mind boggling – especially Iraq. It was agreed by some and, with foresight not hindsight, that Tony Blair, along with the likes of Iran and North Korea, were greater enemies to the safety of Britain and its people than was Iraq. One law of war and life is:

Know thine enemy.

Ronald Reagan had a rather generous view of politicians as workers – well, he would wouldn't he? He said, 'Politics is not a bad profession. If you succeed there are many rewards. If you disgrace yourself you can always write a book.' One could point out to Ronnie that there are many rewards for work in politics even if you are a failure – ask Tony Blair, Peter Mandelson and many others.

Work or action came before and created language, that is why work or action speak louder than words.

In the modern world almost everyone wants to be a celebrity and become a pop star in music, fashion, the media or entertainment or anything else that gives fame and fortune. Tony Blair, always wanted to be a pop star. He tried music first and failed:

> There is too much image and not enough substance or common sense in the modern world of work.

CHAPTER 9

Politics: The New Honour is Dishonour

Too much power corrupts.

Ancient and Common Wisdom

Political values and common sense values

One definition of politics that many people would agree with is, 'gaining power and ends by whatever means'. The words 'by whatever means' are very significant for they do not exclude highly immoral behaviour of any kind. Great acts of folly can be rationalised, all in the name of the public interest. The majority is not fooled and politicians have become a dangerous joke throughout the world. J Quintan points to the futility of expert politicians. He says, 'Politicians are people who, when they see a light at the end of a tunnel, order more tunnel.' Professional politicians in Britain and elsewhere have led their people into increasing danger and corruption. Professional politicians not only blithely misrepresent the values of the majority, they often never have the votes of the majority even when they are elected to be the government. For example, when the New Labour Party was elected to power in 1997, it only received 43.2 per cent of the votes. Since only 71.5 per cent of the total electorate voted, it shows that just about 31 per cent of the whole electorate voted for New Labour. This means that around 69 per cent of the electorate did not vote for the government ruling it. This is nowhere near representing the majority. Letting expert politicians govern us is an example of this old wisdom:

To put the fate of the many into the hands of the few
is folly.

It would not be so bad if the political candidates were wise men, but they are obviously not. They are excessively ambitious people who have been selected by a tiny minority of 'experts' from the political party's central office. The vast majority of people know full well, when they vote, that the person thrust upon them does not represent their views. Many feel it their duty to vote for someone, but it's basically Hobson's choice. Candidates who do represent the views of the majority are almost non-existent. Where they do exist, they are regarded as the opposite of slick modern political operators. Often they are ostracised by senior members of all political parties. They are labelled 'not progressive', 'not with it', 'old-fashioned' and such like. Politicians do not act as if they know that:

Common sense or wisdom is never out of date.

Values of professional politicians are often in conflict with common wisdoms. Politicians try to improve on common sense laws. This is illustrated by the never ending production of expert legal laws. It is one of our biggest and most polluting manufacturing industries. Being motivated to improve on laws of nature, contained in common sense wisdoms, is both arrogant and ignorant. George Bernard Shaw highlights this when he says, 'He knows nothing; and thinks he knows everything. That points clearly to a political career.' Politicians constantly speak of minimising corruption and tell us how moral they are, particularly when they have done something wrong or suspicious. After one dubious transaction by government, The Prime Minister came on television to stress to the nation that he was, 'a pretty straight sort of a guy'. Though many of us feel Tony Blair might be a nice neighbour as would John Major before him, the Prime Minister ignores numerous common sense laws in respect of politicians, himself included. Two are:

Self-praise is no recommendation.

Too much power corrupts.

There is no evidence that professional politicians are more fitted to govern than any group of ordinary people selected at random. The opposite is the case. Thomas Jefferson stresses the importance of common or ordinary folk when he says, 'The people are the only sure reliance for the preservation of our liberty.' Politics is regarded throughout almost the entire world as one of the dirtiest of professions. Is there any wonder that many people say that they are not interested in politics? This is very understandable as the layman wishes to distance himself from the corrupt activities of the experts. Even many who vote are voting against something rather than for something. Politicians say that politics is about values and justice and we have allowed them to corner the market. Since we are all interested in values and justice, as they give purpose or meaning to our lives, we are all equipped to say how society should be run. Virtually all people have views on this. That is, we are interested in politics, but in a much better form than the professionals or 'experts'. Aristotle recognises this common desire when he says:

Man is by nature a political animal.

As politicians made what they do a more and more separate, specialised and expert activity, mistrust of them has grown accordingly. People rightly have always suspected the motives of those individuals who seek great power over many others. It is no coincidence that, as political law-makers and their conspirators – lawyers, became more expert in replacing common sense laws with expert legal laws, they were more disliked by the people. Throughout recorded history there has been a great aversion to professional politicians and lawyers. Their laws have ensured that we have to be party to their expert rationalisations. We feel guilty about allowing them to make us prisoners in the systems they have created. Some common people are resigned to what they consider an unchangeable fate, but others are seeking ways to escape the expert trap:

Doing nothing when a wrong is done by others is doing a wrong also.

It is ironic that those professing expertise in human values and justice, such as politicians and lawyers, are viewed as the ones most lacking in good values and justice. Criticism of professional politicians has been quite consistent over of years, though it is growing in momentum in more modern times. Cicero, who lived from 100 to 43BC, has this to say, 'A most wretched custom is our electioneering and scrambling for office.' In 1753, Benjamin Wichcote highlights the hypocrisy of politicians when he points out, 'Among politicians the esteem of religion is profitable; the principles of it are troublesome.' More recently in 1977, Ronald Reagan has this to say, 'Politics is supposed to be the second oldest profession. I have come to realise that it bears a very close resemblance to the first.' Politicians do get in touch with the truth at times and there are many statements similar to that of President Reagan by numerous other political figures. The comparison of politics with prostitution does prostitutes an injustice. Many are far more honest than politicians:

Politicians know that politics is the use of public affairs
for private gain.

Politicians and their advisers increased their power, expertise and special-isms when science entered the political arena. True to the tradition of modern science, more separation of the whole into smaller parts gained its expression in politics. We now have an academic subject called political science which has been separated into more and more subdivisions. In the late 19th century science was starting to be applied to politics and reached its peak in the 1950s and 1960s. Long ago philosophy embraced most subjects as a whole and then chunks were split off to give rise to more specialist areas such as history, logic, mathematics, politics and so on. Political science divided into smaller specialist subjects such as the psychology and sociology of politics. Then these parts were separated still further. For example, a sub-division of social psychology of politics is political socialisation. Since the 1960s some experts say that science in politics has waned somewhat. Be that as it may, science still has a tremendous influence on politics as it does in most other areas of our lives. One more up-to-date approach in politics is called 'political economy' which reflects some other modern theories also. If you do not know what the 'political economy' theory focuses, you will not be surprised at what it emphasises. This expert theory deals with, *rationally self-interested behaviour*. Could there be a better description of politicians' behaviour? Rationally self-interested behaviour fits them like a glove and so it should; it has been made to measure. Various wisdoms and common sense sayings spring to mind. Two are:

Rationality and self-interest are refuge to the unwise.

If the cap fits, wear it.

Though politicians claim they do not wish to interfere with personal morality, their vast production of laws has greatly influenced our morality. Expert laws have created the opposite of morality in almost every aspect of our lives; they have promoted, encouraged and legalised immorality. One example is that political policies and laws have resulted in over-production of food whilst allowing people to die of starvation. Any laws that do not coincide with common sense laws increase immorality. Replacing common sense laws with expert legal laws is immoral in itself and people of virtually all cultures recognise the immorality of professional politicians. One of an extensive number of examples is that of H.L. Menken who says, 'A good politician is quite as unthinkable as an honest burglar.' Lloyd George also admits to the immorality of politics when he says:

> If you want to succeed in politics you must keep your
> conscience well under control.

With few exceptions, the immoral practices of governments stretch far back in the history of political systems. In more recent times, any random selection of the behaviour of national leaders would produce a catalogue of shame. Figures such as Josef Stalin, Idi Amin, Slobodan Milosevic and Robert Mugabe have been responsible for a variety of crimes. One of the consequences of modern mass communication technology is the increased visibility of politicians' activities including those of immorality and incompetence. Politicians are well aware of the importance of morality even when they are instruments of its demise. Truth is a relative stranger to many politicians, though they pay much lip-service to it. Lip-service is the main stock in trade of politicians. An old saying is particularly well-suited to politicians:

> Half the truth is often a whole lie.

The New Labour Party exploited morality to secure power in Britain in the 1997 election and ran an 'anti-sleaze' campaign. Instances of the Conservative Government's acts of corruption were repeatedly brought to the attention of the electorate. Though the majority of people agreed with the criticism about the sleaze of the Conservative Government, they did not expect a cleaner than clean government, as promised, should New Labour get to power. A bus conductor was talking to a lady on a bus I had boarded. He said, 'All political parties are corrupt and are as bad as one another. Look at local Labour Councils; they have been involved in more swindles than I've had hot dinners. Expecting politicians to tell the truth is like expecting Pavorotti to win the pole-vault in the Olympic Games.' The lady replied, 'I couldn't agree with you more. If people expect New Labour to be less sleazy than the Conservatives, they've got another think coming. Anyway, I think I'll vote Labour to give them a crack of the whip and see what they can do. They can't do much worse than the last lot, can they?' With the reputation that politicians have plus the increase in corruption in modern society, only a Labour Party zealot would believe its leaders would be exceptions to unworthy deeds. A vote does not mean the voter believes the politician's 'manifesto', even though candidates think they have winning ways:

> You can fool some of the people all of the time and all of the people some of the time, but not all of the people all of the time.

As I write this page the New Labour Government has been in power less than two years. Its Members of Parliament have already been involved in more sleaze than is enough for a lifetime.

> Point not at the spots of others with a foul finger.

The Prime Minister appointed one Geoffrey Robinson to the Treasury Ministry. He started to devise systems to plug loopholes in the tax laws. It appears he had millions stashed away using the loopholes that he was plugging. Some may regard this as noble sacrifice and repentance. Before entering politics, the same minister is reported to have had a financially beneficial association with Robert Maxwell the newspaper tycoon who made £400,000,000 disappear. Some of this cash was the pension money of ordinary people that was entrusted to Maxwell who was a former Member of Parliament. It is interesting to speculate about why people should allow an ex-politician to look after pension funds when politicians have such a poor reputation for honesty:

> Who trusts to rotten boughs, may fall.

Peter Mandelson, who was viewed as the main spin-doctor responsible for getting the New Labour Government elected to power, was the Prime Minister's close adviser. Mandelson was given the major credit for re-packaging the Labour Party and creating a modern image which was to be *New Labour*. Ordinary people are well aware that spin-doctors make things appear to be what they are not. They know the term spin-doctor is a politically correct term for legalised deceivers or professional cheats. Mandelson's department was charged with investigating Geoffrey Robinson's department due to some 'irregularities'. Mandelson failed to disclose that he had borrowed well over £300,000 from the minister whose department his own department was investigating. He said he had done no wrong and there was no conflict of interests. After pressure grew from many quarters Robinson resigned. Not long after Mandelson followed suit. Some time later, Mandelson is quoted as changing his mind and admitting that it was wrong to do what he had done:

Hasty climbers have sudden falls.

When Mandelson maintained he had done no wrong the Prime Minister gave his full backing. Indeed, Tony Blair made it seem that his favourite spin-doctor was being self-sacrificing for the sake of the New Government when Mandelson resigned. Tony Blair made it appear that the sleazy act of his most valued spin-doctor was noble and typical of Mandelson. In this and numerous other similar instances, Tony Blair shows us that he himself is no mean spin-doctor. It is a basic requirement for all politicians. Though Mandelson was forced into an admission of wrong-doing by pressure from the media and public opinion, the best that might be said of him was that he resigned. Many wonder, 'Is this supreme spin-doctor spinning repentance?' Ordinary people as well as many experts suspect that his admission and resignation was the only way left open for him to return to power quickly. The Prime Minister predicted a come-back for his main adviser and he seems to be encouraging a rapid one. Hence, politicians can make some of their predictions come true. In respect of Mandelson and other politicians:

It is difficult for a leopard to change its spots.

Numerous other sleazy incidents have occurred that we know about now. The likelihood is there are others we do not know of yet. One solid hypothesis we can make, based on our experience of politicians, is that there are many other sleazy occurrences yet to happen. One Member of Parliament was forced to quit the political scene due to queries about expenses. Another MP nearing old-age pensioner status was caught in a house specialising in naked body-to-body massage and baths with young females. Amongst other things the house was associated with illegal immigration. When the police raided the house, the old MP refused to assist the police with their enquiries. He said he had done nothing wrong. We suspect his wife would not agree. In expert legal terms, this MP exercised his right to silence. He is a politician known for often taking the moral high ground:

> Talking a good moral game but playing a bad one is the hallmark of many professional politicians.

Even politicians are squeamish about this so they make expert laws that legalise more and more immoral acts. They have a vested interest in immorality. A few MPs do stress morality and seem to practise what they preach more than others, but we all have good and bad within us. One female MP gave up her baby according to one report, such was her ambition. She has justifiably criticised fashion models for baring their bodies for media photographs and worse. This MP is reckoned to be a plain-speaking, down-to-earth person who speaks a lot of common sense and has risen to a ministerial post. Everyone has some skeletons in their cupboards, so let us give this MP credit for speaking the truth more than some of her colleagues. However, I did hear one young woman who is a model say of this MP, 'I would never dream of giving up my baby to further my career. It seems that in politics, if you can fake sincerity, you've got it made.'

> No one is perfect and politicians provide one the best examples of this.

Many sleazy interludes of MPs in the New Labour Government have been described by the Prime Minister as 'trivia'. We can predict that the wives, husbands and families of those involved in adulterous relationships do not regard the incidents as 'trivia'. One male minister 'befriended' a total stranger in an area infamous for picking up homosexual partners. He claimed, after agreeing to go to the stranger's house for a meal, the stranger introduced him to some friends and he was mugged. Although the police traced the stranger and his friends, there was no court or prosecution. Ordinary people wonder why. Some have repeated an old adage in respect of this government and its ministers:

There is one law for the rich and powerful and another for
the poor and powerless.

The Prime Minister's decision to support the sleazy behaviour of his Foreign Secretary, his favourite spin-doctor and others, may be one he lives to regret. He was a strong critic of the former Conservative Government's sleaze. Will Rogers pointed out, 'The more you read and observe about this Politics thing, you got to admit that each party is worse than the other.' Since Members of Parliament are our leaders and supposedly support honesty and other basic values, in theory at least, they ignore most common wisdoms including:

Good leaders lead by example.

A man is best judged by his deeds not his words.

The Prime Minister and many other politicians maintain that private and public lives should be kept separate. Ordinary people are correctly sceptical of those who are immoral in their private lives but claim they can still be men of honour in their public lives and duties. We do not take kindly to Jekyll and Hyde personalities. The idea that private lives do not affect work lives runs counter to our own experience. We all know that our personal lives affect our work lives and that the opposite is also true, our work lives affect our private lives. As we have seen, separating things is what experts do. Therefore, it comes as no surprise that professional politicians try to separate private and public life. It is just as harmful as the experts' separation of the whole person into body, mind and spirit. 'All things are related' is a common sense law and applies to politics as it does elsewhere. Perhaps the Prime Minister believes politicians are an exception to this rule. However, you do have to question the judgment of a man in these matters who described Bill Clinton as a man of 'integrity'.

To condone immorality is to be immoral.

Another great moral issue is crime and punishment or law and order. This is the main concern of people, not money or the economy. People would sooner have less money in a society of low crime than high wages in a culture of high and expanding crime. However, it is not an either one or the other situation. The reality is that with far less crime there would be more material resources and money available to everyone. Crime and anti-social behaviour is the greatest burden on the public purse. Is there any area of our lives that is not affected by crime or antisocial behaviour? Worse than the financial costs of crime is the incalculable drain on the bodies, minds and spirits of our citizens:

The amount and type of crime in a society reflects the health or sickness of that society.

Modern expert law, designed by politicians and practised by expert specialist lawyers, decrees there shall be no physical punishment. This leaves the experts with mind or psychological punishments at their disposal. To punish the mind and not the body reflects the one-sided approach to opposites that has become the norm for experts in science and almost every other field of human endeavour. Experts will admit that punishing the mind can be more cruel than punishing the body, yet they forbid punishment of the body as they regard it as cruel, barbaric and uncivilised. Let us bring opposites such as pain and pleasure and punishment and reward to bear on this matter. To remove physical pain from punishment is like removing physical pleasure from reward. This is a highly imbalanced and counter-productive approach. For crimes of physical violence, the chastisement should include physical punishment. The refusal of experts to use appropriate punishments contained in common sense laws is the greatest source of concern to the majority in modern society at the present time:

Punishments must fit the crimes.

Another bone of contention between experts and ordinary people is about prisons. Reports and images in the media as well as visits to prisons present an alarming state of affairs. Prisoners have access to drugs, sex, alcohol and almost anything else you believed was the last things you would associate with jail. Even paedophiles have been reported to have had children made available to them. Terrorists, murderers and other criminals are dressed in designer-labelled clothes and can send out for almost anything that takes their fancy. One prison had a riot after a crack-down on drugs. One warder said that you had to have the co-operation of the prisoners to be able to run the jail. In some prisons, staff have to ask the criminals' permission to search their cells. Guns and other weapons have been found in the hands of inmates. One criminal jailed for stalking is reported to have regular access to a telephone and continued threatening the person he had been jailed for stalking. Some criminals still run criminal empires from prison. Prison officers are complaining more and more that the inmates are running the prisons. The jobs of prison staff are being made impossible to perform. Politicians have created these situations and ordinary people wonder why. Maybe the description of politicians by Richard Harris can give a clue:

> Probably the most distinctive characteristic of the successful politician is selective cowardice.

Just recently paedophiles, who were associated with the murder of some children in satisfying their lust, have been released from prison. Even experts say they are likely to rape and kill again and are regarded as the most dangerous men in Britain. The headline in the newspaper about their release announced 'The Home Secretary Is Powerless To Do Anything'. What makes it that the Home Secretary, police and prison staff have their hands tied so they are unable to do anything about these dangerous practices? It is due to expert laws and theories that politicians themselves have created. The Home Secretary is one of the most powerful law agents in the land so if he is powerless, what hope is there for the man in the street? Politicians have replaced common sense laws with an endless brand of their own 'expert' laws and ordinary people have to bear the consequences. Politicians are worse than criminals; they specialise more in paying lip-service to common wisdoms including the following one:

> You have to accept responsibility for the consequences of your own actions.

Prisoners are given free food, heating, accommodation, electricity, clothes, dental and medical treatment, leisure facilities and other commodities that ordinary people cannot afford. Even some prisoners have described modern jails as being like holiday camps. There are no long waiting lists for medical treatment in prison. Unlike ordinary people, inmates have no trouble finding a National Health dentist to deal with them. Prisons have dieticians and one prisoner was considering suing the system because his breakfast was not on time. Other prisoners can have sex change operations when people on the outside have long waits for crucial health treatment. Some brutal killers are back out on the streets within two years because of political expediency and expert theories. One Hebrew proverb reflects the same sentiments of the many wisdoms of other cultures. You will notice it contains opposites:

> He who starts by being merciful to the cruel will end up being cruel to the merciful.

Experts argue, of course, that the real punishment of prisons is the denial of freedom of association and of movement to travel or choice of where to live. We have news for experts. There are many ordinary people who do not have freedom of associating with others they choose or going where they want. They cannot afford it, or when they can, they are afraid to leave their homes due to the dangerous ethos that experts' laws have fostered in our society. Ordinary people would be very pleased to have all the facilities and resources that are freely available to criminals in their protected environment. In terms of freedom of association, people often choose others of their own kind. Prisoners are associating with those who have similar values. Prison are not deterring criminals from re-offending and they are not rehabilitating inmates to lead a better life. In fact:

> Modern prison systems in Britain have the opposite effect to their purpose.

The aims of all political parties and those of ordinary people are almost identical. Everyone wants better systems of health, education, transport and so on and so forth including prisons. Though the aims of politicians and ordinary people are the same, it is the theories and laws created by experts that guarantee failure of the systems. Their theories and methods are at odds with nature and common sense laws. Let us look at some ancient wisdoms and practices in relation to helping to cleanse bodies, minds and spirits which is the true basic aim in the treatment of prisoners. One ancient and common sense is to be found in every culture and language throughout history. You all know it and we have used it earlier in this book. The French version of it is, 'Reculer pour mieux sauter'. It means basically:

> Sometimes we have to go backwards in order to go
> forwards better.

One powerful method associated with this law to help purify bodies, minds and spirits has been passed down the ages and is still in use today in some places. In times of trouble or of experiencing problems the practice was to go to an isolated place where there was peace and quiet and to meditate, reflect and fast. This can be applied to criminals in prison to aid cleansing of body, mind and spirit and is a way forward to better the lot of prisoners and society at large. In practical terms it would mean that:

1. Prisoners would be kept alone in their own small, peaceful, quiet sound-proof room with the bare minimum of furnishings.
2. Prisoners would have no visitors and prison staff would not be seen or heard.
3. Simple and small amounts of food and water would be available at times but not at others. Food and water would be delivered but not by human contact.
4. Length of prison sentences would be drastically reduced. After a time this regime would be gradually modified.
5. Prisoners would be allowed reading material for an hour a day. This would be initially recommended by Justices of The Peace.
6. Later prisoners would go, initially for a day per week, to firms requiring help and could include on the job training, where help was required locally with environmental or other community projects, prisoners would be involved.
7. Temporary randomly selected Justices of The Peace would decide on the length and variation in the regime depending on the crime.

Many wisdoms tell of the healing powers of peace and quiet or silence and tranquility. A Babylonian Thalmud gives us:

> Silence is healing for all ailments.

This regime of silence, solitude, simplicity, sacrifice, hard work and community involvement would apply to all prisoners including murderers. Capital punishment with appropriate chemicals can be achieved in such a way that it is as painless as falling asleep. Hence some say it is not a punishment at all and a waste of life. Like the majority, I am not against capital punishment when I believe it is a potent deterrent but the system I have suggested combines punishment with in-built chances of repentance and redemption that are beneficial to society both materially and spiritually:

> Ordinary people accepted the end of capital punishment on the basis of rigorous punishment and effective rehabilitation.

Experts promised these rigorous regimes and then produced prisons that were dens of iniquity. Expert laws and political correctness have made prison warders the same as police. They can be present at the scene of violent crimes, but the compulsory risk assessment of personal injury and the possibility of being sued or sacked for abuse render them useless spectators. The common sense system I highlight would not only help prisoners and the general population in body, mind and spirit, it would improve the whole economy. Some expert rationalists would no doubt say that isolation of this kind could drive some prisoners mad or to death and suicide. Suicide prisoners would be exceptions to the rule but, as we have stressed before, exceptions do not make the use of the rule invalid. In any case, mental imbalance, suicide and murder is growing in modern prisons. The ancient mode of purifying body, mind and spirit could do no worse than the present expert system which is producing ever-increasing mental imbalance, violence and deaths inside and outside prison. Our own experience and that of the long history of man indicates that peace and quiet lend themselves to less violent behaviour after a time of reflection, fasting and meditation. There are many wisdoms that apply:

> Peace that tames the savage breast.

> In quietness is to be found your strength.

Quite often small misdemeanours and small anti-social acts are ignored so time is not wasted catching more serious criminals. However, an increasing number of serious crimes go unpunished, so complex, technical and extensive are expert laws. Too many cases referred to the Crown Prosecution Service end in farce or immoral actions. The Crown Prosecution Service decides which cases go forward depending on whether or not the experts think they have good evidence for a prosecution. Often so many cases go to the Crown Prosecution Service that the lawyers do not have time to read the briefs let alone digest, understand and use them. Lawyers know that hardened or professional criminals with their smart lawyers are difficult to prosecute so easier cases of the more innocent go forward. The general result is that the more innocent are being made more criminal whilst the more criminal are being made more innocent. One really old lady who would not pay her community tax bill was sent to jail and at the same time known murderers and other known criminals are allowed to walk freely amongst us. Locally selected Justices of The Peace using common sense laws have no need of experts in the Crown Prosecution Service, so it should be disbanded immediately. Ignoring small instances of anti-social behaviour to focus on bigger crimes is a mistake. Big crimes normally start with small crimes which must be dealt with before they develop into large offences. Common sense laws are clear on this point:

Bad behaviour must be nipped in the bud.

A stitch in time saves nine.

These wisdoms are being revived in some places with a consequent reduction in crime. In modern language the equivalent of these wisdoms is called 'zero tolerance'. This means police deal with any small occurrences of anti-social actions before they grow into more serious crimes. A police officer should live in and be an integral part of the local community. She or he would be seen walking the beat as the main part of the job and would deal with anti-social behaviour of any kind. This would include such behaviour as throwing bits of rubbish down in the street. On the spot fines would be at the police officers' discretion. Officers would also have the power to make persons who litter the street with rubbish spend time cleaning up a section of the street. If children were to be seen on the streets during school time, the officer would query and deal with the absence from school. For more serious offences, the officers would make an arrest and bring the offender before local Justices of The Peace within hours or days, not weeks, months or even longer. Any complaints about the police would also be dealt with by local Justices of The Peace. Police officers would not do hours of paper-work and fill in scores of expert forms as is the case now. The officer, offender and victim would tell their stories in simple language to Justices of The Peace. One way experts make a farce of even their own expert laws, never mind common sense laws, is highlighted by W.S. Landor:

Delay in justice is injustice.

Officers would not have to submit their evidence to an ever-increasing hierarchy of superiors, various individual experts and legal agencies. They would present evidence directly to Justices of The Peace. These would decide on innocence or guilt and if guilty, choose sanctions which would begin without the customary expert delay. The length of time it takes expert law systems to grind to a conclusion has little to do with justice and some cases go on for years. Indeed some cases never actually end. Ordinary people, using the laws of common sense or wisdoms, would cut through the colossal and very harmful red-tape, bureaucracy and officialdom. As a result, there would be much more justice. J.A. Froude gives one example of an ancient wisdom that fits here:

Justice without wisdom is impossible.

Everyday conversations show the increasing concern about the state of justice and violence in our modern society. One survey made public today indicates that over 60 per cent of parents are afraid to let their children out to play. They stay indoors and, ironically, live on a diet of increasingly violent television programmes and computer games. If there were less demand for violent reading, viewing and killing games, there would be less supply from exploitative and immoral commercial enterprises. We must all shoulder our share of the responsibility for the present state of our so-called 'progressive' and liberated culture. Instinctively, the majority deplores the commercial exploitation of violence even though some may become part of it. It is difficult to avoid in this day and age. Common sense laws do warn us however, especially about excessive consumerism. One of a host of laws is:

There are more foolish buyers than foolish sellers.

Ordinary people have an opposite view to politicians and other experts about brutal violence. The vast majority of the population, including a minority of politicians, never wanted capital punishment banned. Experts rationalise their position by saying that no civilised nation executes its murderers as it is barbaric. What this means is that experts consider themselves civilised and not barbaric. It also means that experts consider the vast majority of the British people to be uncivilised and barbaric, for most agree with a death penalty. After guiding our society to the present highly violent and brutal state, the sheer arrogance of experts is breathtaking. What an insult to ordinary people they are supposed to represent! The majority who believe in capital punishment is labelled by minorities, such as government, as 'the hang 'em and flog 'em brigade' or as 'right-wing fascists'. To their faces, of course, politicians tell ordinary people that they are wise and the salt of the earth. Politicians are masters of deception. Winston Churchill said:

> The typical British MP stands for election, sits in the House
> and lies just about all the time.

When the majority want brutal killers put to death, it is uncivilised and barbaric. When the government wants to execute people like Slobodam Milosevic and Serbian soldiers, it is noble and just even though innocent people are bound to get killed in the process. If the British government had been around at the time of Christ, it would not have allowed Christ to 'die and save us all'. The foundation stone of Christianity is the capital punishment of Jesus Christ. Political religious leaders crucified a very moral being which was highly inappropriate or wrong. Even Christ was not against appropriate punishment. He threw the money-lenders out of the temple, if I remember my junior school bible stories correctly:

> If the capital punishment of Christ saved us all, it is not
> without advantage.

In the modern Western World, much of the argument about capital punishment hinges on two opposites, 'Thou shalt not kill' and 'An eye for an eye and a tooth for a tooth'. 'Thou shalt not kill' is a good rule to live by, but like most rules, it has exceptions. Though brutal killers may be considered exceptions to rules for moral living, not all exceptions are bad. In terms of man's behaviour, Jesus was an exception, for he was an unusually good or moral being. By supporting capital punishment, I am not recommending, 'An eye for an eye and a tooth for a tooth'. Let me give an example which might illustrate. In the last year or so, a woman in the USA was finally executed for killing another woman a decade earlier. The way she had killed was horrific. She had persistently struck the head of the other woman with an ice-pick until the victim screamed and pleaded to be put out of her misery quickly. The murderess boasted that she had an orgasm whilst she was repeatedly plunging the ice-pick into her victim's head. When she was executed years after the crime, the lethal injection that was used to end her life does not compare with the way she killed her victim. One placard outside the prison showed that some of the assembled crowd wanted 'An eye for an eye and a tooth for a tooth'. At least one placard read, 'Forget the lethal injection, use the ice-pick.' The majority's demand for the death penalty only pertains to exceptionally horrific crimes not to all killings and:

> Punishment should fit the crime, but not be the same
> as the crime.

Some experts argue that in some places in America where capital punishment is used, the number of slayings does not go down. However, this is due to the system experts have created. Let me illustrate a little further. In states where capital punishment was used, as in Texas, killers knew that, with the lengthy processes of expert laws, trials, petitions and appeals, they would not die for ten, perhaps twenty years or more. Where the law and the capital punishment processes were speeded up in the USA, there was a substantial fall in the number of murders. For a killer, there is a great deal of difference between being executed relatively quickly after he or she has committed murder and being executed years and years later. The time gap between the crime and capital punishment is still too long. Nevertheless, there is a growing recognition by experts that time between crime and punishment is an important factor in the effectiveness of the punishment. Even criminals in their more truthful moods state that capital punishment does deter. A few experts are taking more notice of the odd one or two ancient wisdoms that deal with crime and punishment. Two obvious ones are:

> Long on law, short on justice.

> Survival is basic to human nature.

Experts have other objections to capital punishment. They say capital punishment should not exist because someone who is innocent could be executed. Though expert laws seem to be increasing in number and type by the month, expert laws have been replacing common sense laws for several thousand years. These expert laws have been responsible for executing many innocent people directly and indirectly. Expert law that dispensed with capital punishment has been responsible for terrorist killers and murderers executing many innocent people including tiny children. Also, it would be extremely difficult for common sense laws applied by randomly selected Justices of The Peace to do worse than expert laws and lawyers. Expert laws have given the right to murderers to kill again and bind innocent people in chains of fear. Tacitus refers to an old wisdom that guides us in breaking these chains:

> The supremacy of the people tends to liberty.

Because one common sense law says that nothing is perfect, means that even when common wisdoms are used, some innocents will die. However, not as many will die as using expert laws which produce more bodies and horrors almost every month. Experts also use the rationalisation that the act of execution of the murderer is the same and as bad as the act of the murder itself. These who maintain there is no difference between the crime and the punishment express a minority view, but it is the law. Alfieri cites an ancient wisdom that applies to this situation:

> Disgrace does not consist in the punishment but in the crime.

Politicians justify their great production of expert legal laws to maintain law and order in society. Expert laws have resulted in the opposite – law and disorder. Most other expert systems devised by politicians turn out the opposite of what was intended. The Welfare Benefit System has suffered reversal in what it is supposed to achieve as a consequence of expert laws. One example of the vast array of counter-productive expert laws is in a volume of 1994 entitled *Income Related Benefits: The Legislation*, when the Conservative Government was in power. There are around 800 pages in this huge production. Imagine the lot of ordinary women and men in benefit offices and job centres who are supposed to read, understand and administrate such incomprehensible expert creations. This book is only one very small part of the whole welfare system's paper work or reading requirement. Without being familiar with expert policies, reports and laws, benefit office and job centre personnel cannot do their jobs. Since staff cannot possibly know all of these expert laws, their jobs are impossible especially when confronted with an increasingly enraged public. Two common sense laws are:

Excess benefit laws lead to poor benefit systems.

Simplicity is usually the best answer to problems.

In addition to income related benefits, there are housing benefits, invalidity benefits, child benefits, family benefits, sickness benefits and jobseekers' allowance to mention a few. Welfare benefit areas are being split into smaller and smaller parts. Is there any area that can be exempt from welfare benefit? Could there be a 'being-thin' or 'being-fat' and a 'small-bust' or 'big-nose' allowance as sub-divisions of disability benefit or 'image allowance' benefit? Perhaps I am already behind our progressive times and these allowances already exist in one form or another. There is an International Obesity Task Force as if people did not know that common sense eating is what is required:

Politicians cannot see sense for being blinded by their own nonsense.

When the Conservative Government was in power, it was not keen for the tax payer to foot the welfare bill. It looked to private enterprise and the free market to finance and operate the welfare systems. Now it is not in power, it seems rather keen on the tax payer being responsible for the cost of the welfare state. Even politicians are critical of their own profession and other politicians. When the ex-Prime Minister Stanley Baldwin died, Winston Churchill said, 'The candle in that great turnip has gone out.' Benjamin Disraeli, in his era, stated in The House of Commons:

Mr Speaker, I withdraw my statement that half the cabinet are asses. Half the cabinet are not asses.

The Welfare State was designed to help those who had fallen upon hard times through no fault of their own. Being out of work, sick or homeless was to qualify people for assistance until such time as they got on their feet and could once again fend for their families and themselves. Welfare support was to provide temporary aid, not a way of life that could be *chosen* by the lazy, the fickle, the promiscuous or other anti-social elements. Expert systems have socialised people from an early age into a culture of dependency. One little boy of eight was asked by a visitor to his primary school what he wanted to do when he left school. The child replied, quite solemnly, that he was looking forward to the day when he could receive his 'giro', which is a welfare benefit payment. The Welfare State was originally based on common sense laws such as:

Do unto others as you would hope they would do unto you.

We must help others who cannot help themselves.

The welfare of one is the welfare of us all.

Without obeying these and other common sense laws, we cannot have a good and just society. Through a succession of governments with their expert laws, rules, regulations, guidelines, codes of practice, individual rights and charters, welfare handouts have become an expected, nay, a demanded lifestyle for far too many people. It is legally their right, but it does not sit easily with common sense people, even though they may claim what is entitled to them by law. Some feel guilty and immoral in their inner being. My sister and her husband said they felt awful about collecting child benefit although they had worked hard all their lives for very low wages. They were poor by many standards. I pointed out that if they felt so bad about receiving the child benefit, they need not have it. 'We were tempted to do this, but we felt that if we did not take the money, it would probably go to some causes or people who were less deserving than our own children. You know what politicians are. Some of our neighbours are hardly ever at work. They are in the pub whenever it's open, smoke like chimneys and neglect their children dreadfully. They receive support from the government in benefits and the taxes we pay, so, why should we subsidise them? If the government could be trusted to put the money to better use, we would not collect the child benefit. However, we do feel it is wrong for the general tax payer to help support the children we chose to have:'

People know that what is legally right is often morally wrong.

Governments, since the time my sister had children, have put forth many more laws that favour 'alternative relationships' at the expense of common sense families and their values. This includes the tax system, which is loaded against sensible people to the benefit of others. Some commentators suggest that a contributory factor to the destruction of the traditional family with wife, husband and children, is that a disproportionate number of government ministers are in 'alternative relationships'. However, at the lip-service level, politicians say they support traditional families and their values. Tony Blair enjoys popularity and one reason for this is that he appears to be a traditional family man in his own domestic life. Nevertheless too many do not follow his lead in this matter:

Politicians want to have their cake and eat it and too many people are following their lead.

Everyday there are countless thousands cheating the welfare system. One report suggests that government officials at Whitehall admit there is £800,000,000 being swindled each year out of housing benefit alone. Since governments play down their own mismanagement, this figure is probably a conservative estimate. As the expert system lends itself so well to corruption, many ordinary people have been quite honest in not taking more advantage of welfare. Some do take full advantage of what is on offer and though it is legal by expert laws, it is highly immoral. One news story was of a man about thirty years old who does not work. He has fathered a string of children by numerous girls many of whom are around fifteen years old. Not only does this father, along with his mistresses and assorted children, receive all kinds of welfare benefits, he receives a disability pension. I seem to recall that he had a 'bad back' or was it a bad part of his front? The sum of moral, spiritual, social and financial costs of this tribe of people is huge. In fact the long term, when these mistresses and their children have more children, the costs will be incalculable. The disabled father and any new or old 'girlfriends' still have the political and legal right to go on producing more children for the tax payer to support:

Irresponsibility breeds irresponsibility.

Rights are not best given or assumed, they are earned.

The majority does not agree with people receiving money for not working. When some people are temporarily unemployed, they should do some kind of work for their benefit money. There is much to be done on environmental projects and local firms can often welcome temporary labour at times. In addition there are always community projects crying out for help. Assisting old or disabled people with household tasks such as shopping, decorating or mowing the lawn and so on are examples. No one should be allowed to be idle; the rich would be expected to do work that benefits the community and society at large. When people have been forced to work for their benefit money, it has given balance and more purpose to their lives. Some involved in this 'workfare' said that although they were reluctant at the start, they became involved, for it gave meaning to their lives and made them feel an integral part of the community. They became more acceptable and valued members of the community as well as developing new skills, work opportunities and more friends.

Most things that are worthwhile are earned.

Work is the basis of everything.

Lack of work, poverty and crime are connected. Tony Blair reckons, according to one news story, that he is going to eliminate child poverty in the next twenty years. Let us use a common sense law to make a hypothesis or prediction. One common sense law is, 'Things are relative'. This applies to poverty as it does to other things. Some people and children in India and Africa consider themselves well-off if they can get a little food and clean water on a daily basis. In twenty years time poverty will still be relative, so our hypothesis or speculation would be:

Tony Blair's government or any other will not eliminate poverty in the next twenty years.

If, today, we re-distributed wealth and gave everyone say, a million pounds, within a short time some would have lost it all and others would have doubled or trebled their money. Some people will always have less than others and will be at the bottom of the pile. If there is a top, there has to be a bottom. Some people in Britain, presently described as poor, have a surprising amount of modern technology and other consumer 'gear'. Poverty is an attitude of mind, not just possession of money. There are those who consider themselves rich in body, mind and spirit, but who have minimal material possessions. Such people are far more balanced and happy than many monied persons we could mention. Hence, Tony Blair's claim that he is going to eliminate poverty is surprising. Well, maybe not. He is a politician and as Nikita Khrushchev, former Russian Head of State admitted:

> Politicians will promise bridges even when there
> are no rivers.

Politicians of course would claim success by saying, 'We made it perfectly clear that poverty was to be defined as not having a personalised moon vehicle. Since every child now has one of these space cars by the age of fifteen years, we have fulfilled the government promise. The fact that one hundred of these vehicles crash every day with a most unfortune loss of life does not detract from the government's achievement. We are developing the most comprehensive legislation to deal with these terrible accidents, but not until we have the report from the independent enquiry which the Prime Minister so wisely initiated. The Welfare State is safe in our hands and we are developing more laws to make it even better. In any case, we are able to clone replicas of children killed in these exciting space vehicles if we can locate even one cell of their corpses. I can say with some pride that one mother who received such a replica of her daughter can hardly tell the difference. She says the third arm is more than useful when they play that old-fashioned game called washing the dishes. Better still, it is a real eye-catcher as a fashion item and an extra free sex aid.'

> You can have too much of anything.

In respect of the Welfare State, many politicians know what must be done, but they do not have the courage to grasp the nettle. The present welfare system must be abolished. As one wisdom tells us, 'Sometimes you have to be cruel to be kind'. The tax system would obey another common sense law and would be simplified. There would be no income-tax. Funds would be raised by putting a tax on all consumer goods and services. Such a system would provide the necessary money to help those in real need. It would mean those who were greedy consumers paid more for their material life-style. Those who consumed little would pay little. This would reduce the excesses of our consumer society. To get rid of the present unholy mess in the welfare system, people would be told that within a few months all benefits would be stopped. Families would look after their own and pay for their mistakes themselves just as they take credit for their successes. Consequences of irresponsible behaviour would not immediately be thrown on to the tax payer as it is now. Anyone thinking he or she is deserving of temporary support would put the case to locally randomly selected temporary Justices of The Peace who would decide. For those who have become too dependent on the state, necessity would become the mother of invention in respect of developing self-reliance. Common sense laws would be the order of the day especially the one that justly and wisely informs us:

Charity must begin at home.

Politicians have also ignored the will and common sense of the majority concerning immigration. Since the end of The Second World War, there have been too many immigrants to Britain. We are over-populated so taking in immigrants, white, black or any other colour, is adding to the main problem of government rewarding people for having children, especially those who cannot support them. What was the figure for immigrants or asylum seekers entering Britain in one year around 1998 – 63,000? More expert theories are being floated to make it legal for anyone in the world who suffers political or sexual discrimination to come and have sanctuary in Britain. This can take in most of the population of the world. Almost everyone could make a case for being discriminated against politically or sexually. Girls could complain that some men they took a shine to discriminated against females by going out with males only. Asylum seekers could claim they came from a political system where laws allow discrimination against heterosexuals, homosexuals, small people, large people, manual workers, animals and so on ad infinitum. With fewer people we could have less cars, fewer roads, fewer houses, less pollution, less rage and so forth. Many common sense laws from every culture throughout history warn of over-crowding or excess population:

Too many apples split the bag.

Too many grains of sand sink the ship.

Too many cooks spoil the broth.

The increase in number of laws about discrimination and the existence of the Council for Racial Equality have added fuel to the fire as have courses on 'racial awareness'. The murder of black teenager Stephen Lawrence by white youths made the majority of Britons ashamed to be British and white. The police action in this case was beyond belief. A high ranking police officer, who had much evidence to make arrests almost immediately, did not do so for some considerable time. Basically, he claimed he did not know the rules of arrest. Some witnesses were not used and other evidence was ignored or mishandled. We did not realise that when police officers or big business men committed crimes, they could escape fitting punishment by resigning, bad as expert laws are. I will let you make some hypotheses or speculations about this shocking racial incident. We do not need special expert laws about discrimination. Common sense laws do the job far, far better. This one alone is worth any number of expert laws and would have dealt with the incident with more justice:

Do unto others as you hope they would do unto you.

Most of us in Britain are immigrants. Many of our forefathers were Roman, Saxon, Viking, Norman or other. The idea that we are racially pure, as it were, is bunkum or rationalisation detached from wisdom and experience. H.A.L. Fisher in his 1935 work entitled *A History of Europe*, illustrates when he says, 'Purity of race does not exist. Europe is a continent of energetic mongrels.' It is a minority of whites who discriminate unfairly against coloured people just as it is a minority of coloured people who discriminate against whites. What our everyday experience tells us is that whites would much sooner have common sense black neighbours than anti-social whites. The opposite is also true. Black brothers though they may be, they would also prefer good white neighbours to anti-social people of their own colour. The majority of Britons want immigration stopped. If truth be known, the majority probably wants recent immigration reversed, no matter what the colour, so crowded is this island. Even some recent immigrants want immigration ended. Though much publicity seems to be given to figures like 80 per cent of muggings in some parts of London are attributed to black youths, less consideration is given to the fact that some of our best citizens are black also:

People are basically more alike than they are different.

Racial discrimination is relative. Immigrants still prefer to come to Britain compared with some other places where discrimination is worse. Because of expert laws, the anti-social minorities who are violently racist are growing. In 1999 one estimate of the racist groups in America was put at 500. The great experiment of the melting pot of different races in the United States of America leaves a great deal to be desired. It is one of the most violent cultures on earth as well as the most ethnically diverse. Though some mixing is desirable, anything that goes to excess creates more disadvantages than advantages. Those who say that coloured people are inferior and bad are literally speaking uncommon nonsense. It is uncommon because it is a minority view, but as usual, a minority with disproportionate power. It is nonsense because it defies all common sense laws, not least of which is:

There is good and bad in all of us.

One area where we have been too willing accomplices with experts is in our obsession with technology, but often we dislike ourselves for our excesses. Some of the consequences of galloping technology I have already mentioned, but there is worse to come. New technology starts with a few having it, then it becomes available to more and more people until almost everyone can get it. For example, bows and arrows were first available to the few and then to the many. As a killing machine on the streets, by the time the archer had killed one person, he could be overpowered before he could re-load. With a machine gun, this is not the case. With the right technology, one anti-social individual could kill many, many people in the same time as an archer can kill one person with his bow and arrow. In terms of technology improving the quality of our lives and speeding things up to make living more 'convenient', excess has caused more problems than it has solved. It is a case of:

More haste, less speed.

As technology develops and gives people the capability to kill more people faster, the number of bodies at murder scenes will increase proportionately. Couple the relentless sophistication of technology with increasing rage and the Dunblane body count will seem relatively small with the passage of time. In modern times, how to make and use nuclear devices is common knowledge to first year physics students at university. Probably there are already some school children with this knowledge. I do get behind the times. Thus, apart from mad dictators, terrorist groups and mad politicians, we have to worry about any individual anti-social neighbour or stranger. Sooner or later, he or she can get access to the technology of weapons of mass murder and destruction. The time will come when countless individuals could blow up the planet if they so wished:

It only takes one bad apple to spoil the whole barrel.

Paradoxically, experts look to technology and more laws to solve the problems created by technology and expert laws. What we do not need is additional experts imposing on us more of their rules, regulation and laws. There will be no prizes for guessing my views on Britain joining The European Union. As if we did not have enough expert laws of our own, politicians have made us import more from Brussels. European laws have already dictated the size and shape of fruits and vegetables we must grow, how we should bring up our families and how we should run our businesses and other institutions. What aspect of British life is going to escape this added European source of production of more expert laws? Hitler must be kicking himself in hell and thinking, 'Germany has got a major say in the running of Europe and without a single bullet being fired and with willing expert followers to boot.' So immoral are the European Commissioners in their financial dealing that auditors refused to sign their accounts. In 1999 a report on the Commission's activities was so damning that all twenty Commissioners resigned. The whole culture was described as one that fostered ignorance, corruption and mismanagement. This motley crew is not even an elected body. We should not be surprised about their behaviour as they were appointed by politicians. It is typical of politicians to lead us further into their immoral cesspool. Is there a single common wisdom that politicians do not defile? We certainly know they do not:

Lead by example.

After the condemning report some rationalisations used by our pro-European members of government and the commissioners themselves, Groucho Marx would have admired. They said that the report gave them a better opportunity to improve the European Commission and Union.

Joining the European Union has already brought more disadvantages than advantages. The bigger the trough the more snouts it can accommodate. Though our politicians are probably as bad as their European counterparts in this corrupt system, it is a case of:

Better the devil you know than the one you don't.

As well as Europe, Ireland is a problem. The British government, in collusion with the Irish leaders, allows brutal murders and beating to occur after releasing killers to stop violence . . . all in the name of the Peace Process. Governments in England and Ireland know who the main terrorist offenders are, but expert law and lack of political will prevent the killers being restrained. The terrorists have been allowed to hold great power and resources and live like celebrities. They have killed and maimed pregnant women and innocent children and have been set free due to political expediency. Effective peace is unlikely to come about when expert rationalists like Ian Paisley and Jerry Adams lead negotiations. A series of ordinary citizens selected at random should be given the opportunity to deal with the situation. The leaders in Ireland, like most leaders, are ambitious predators for power. One old wisdom is:

It is a foolish sheep that makes a wolf its confessor.

Because our type of democracy is seen as superior to various other countries does not mean it could not be far better. Political systems and performance are relative as is any system or performance. For example, one medical student friend of mine received an assessment of his performance from his professor. It read, 'A tremendous improvement Mr Smith, but still atrocious.' Our politicians have not made an improvement even as far as the stage of being atrocious. Tony Blair has appointed friends or 'associates' to positions of power. They are known as 'Tony's Cronies'. The Lord Chancellor is one, and he is known to be arrogant, which does not sit well with true justice. The main government spin-doctor, Mandelson, is known as 'The Prince of Darkness'. Politicians of most modern parties descend to lower and lower depths with the passage of time:

Politicians are the disease for which they pretend
to be the cure.

There are various changes that could be made to better our political system. Having ordinary people select their representatives themselves rather than them being selected by some national or local government body would be a start. Better still is dispensing with professional politicians altogether. Ordinary people have the same aims that all political parties, irrespective of ideology, claim they have. We all want better justice, better family life, better education, better health, better environment and better anything else. You do not have to be an expert or modern to know this. What is more, New Labour policy is getting like Old Conservative policy and the Conservatives are getting more like Old Labour:

What goes around comes around.

Since common sense laws give guidance on what is good and how to achieve it, we have no need for professional politicians. Ordinary people are more than competent to represent themselves. One method would be randomly to select representatives from a locality. Alternatively, ordinary people could select a spokesman to speak for the group selected at random when required for a short temporary period. No one would become a long term representative as this is specialism or professionalism, which is to be avoided. Another way is to make a more democratic use of technology. Such is our present technology, that on any given issue, the feelings of all the people could be obtained at the press of buttons. True democracy requires practical decision-making from as many people as possible on all issues all of the time:

Professional politicians do not represent the common sense and will of the people.

Politicians use power for their own pleasure rather than for the welfare of the people as they claim. They cling to office and stay in power for far too long and, as a consequence, become increasingly corrupt. Randomly selected representatives would be changed every few weeks. Expert rationalists would argue that regular change would destroy continuity or consistency. This is fallacious. Common sense laws would provide the continuity and consistency much more so than experts and their laws. In any event, there is no virtue in being consistent if you are consistently

wrong, as many experts are. Patrick Murray draws attention to the necessity
of replacing politicians frequently. He says:

> Politicians are like nappies. They should be changed
> regularly and for the same reason.

Our government is prepared to bomb Serbia, but is unprepared to deal with
similar atrocities in Ireland and dictators in Africa. Some regimes in Africa
such as that of Robert Mugabe are extremely corrupt, violent, suppressive
and infringe as many human rights as President Milosevic. When some of
these unscrupulous leaders come to Britain, politicians legitimise their
immorality by involving the Queen. Politicians schedule some kind of royal
social event for these power-mad African moguls. The Queen has to grin
and bear meeting with these unholy scoundrels:

> Politicians, when it suits them, use the monarchy in an
> attempt to dignify their own incompetence.

Governments take to the moral high ground when it is to their advantage
and play the individual rights or freedom card when caught out in immoral
acts. Tony Blair justifies the bombing of Serbia and killing of its citizens by
using high sounding moral language. Moral right, fairness, honour and
humanity is on our side Tony Blair tells us. He informs the armed forces
they can be proud of obeying the call of their country in the name of the
greater good and in the interest of justice. The Prime Minister promises to
stop the atrocities of rape, murder, pillage, terrorism and mugging on the
streets of Bosnia. He has not stopped rape, murder and mugging on his own
doorstep in London let alone in England and the rest of the United
Kingdom:

> People in glass houses should not throw bombs.

Experts would argue that ordinary people making the decisions would not
work in times of war. Certainly, ordinary people would be reticent about
going to war. However, they would have the same advice available to them
from the armed forces that politicians have. What is more, in any war, it is
the ordinary people who fight and die, not expert politicians. Further, we
cannot believe by any stretch of the imagination that Tony Blair or the

present Minister of Defence, George Robertson, have more meaningful knowledge or wisdom about aggression or war than the ordinary man in the street. Also, random selection of decision makers would ensure women would have much say in the running of the country, as they should. With the involvement of females, we would get more common sense applied to aggressive acts including war:

**In war, professional politicians lead from behind,
a long way behind.**

One model for a good society from which modern politicians could learn much is that of the indigenous Americans. The tribes were at one with nature and their whole environment. They realised that the health of their surroundings was the same as their own health. They would no sooner pollute a river than they would pollute their own blood stream. They were well aware that the water from the river became their blood stream by drinking it. The tribes did not separate physical punishment from their sanctions against anti-social behaviour. They knew, that at times, corporal and capital punishment of the few were necessary to preserve the safety and integrity of the many. Only enough buffalo were hunted for their needs and they honoured these and other life forms. Nothing was done to excess that would unbalance nature which they viewed as a whole with themselves as a part, but not a dominant or exploitative one. Their chiefs were truly servants of the people and they were meticulous about honesty. Their honesty became known worldwide. Even children and adults in England, when they wish to emphasise their honesty, still say, 'Honest Injun'. As an increasing number of scientists have found to their amazement, many of these knew relativity and quantum theory. These so-called primitive people took the experts theories in physics for granted. It was common knowledge to them:

Nothing in this world is really new.

Another blue-print that expert politicians could use to transform and improve their mode of operations would be to read the columns of journalist, Lynda Lee-Potter. Though some other writers pen much common sense, Linda Lee-Potter's writings are jammed full of common sense laws. What is more, she applies them to all areas of life. Linda

Lee-Potter has carried the innate wisdoms, that are within us all if we care to use them, into the modern era:

Common sense laws are the touch-stones of life,
including politics.

Over the past several thousands of years, politics has developed into a specialised area and profession. We have allowed politicians to monopolise and direct our values and morality. Politics is about values and morality and politicians have led them away from the expression of the better side of humanity. Since ordinary people have been effectively side-lined, they appear to be disinterested in politics. Such a dirty game is politics that the majority of people give the impression of, 'Let the politicians get on with it and let me get on with my ordinary everyday life'. Experts have conditioned people to believe that politics is a specialised profession separate from and beyond the common herd's abilities. With a system that encouraged or allowed everyone to participate, as in regular random selection of ordinary people to perform political duties, their true inner feelings and desires for involvement would be evidenced:

You can't always tell a book from its cover.

The constant cry of government to, 'Modernise, modernise, modernise', is the direct opposite of what ancient and common wisdoms are. They are not modern. Common sense laws are old, very old. Experts have made a mockery of common sense laws. Cyril Smith was a Member of Parliament for The Liberal Party who was known for his down-to-earth common sense approach. He spoke more common sense than many other politicians put together. The next saying is attributed to him. After that is a common saying that contains much substance also:

Parliament is the longest running farce in the West End.

There is many a true word spoken in jest.

Because I am recommending power be put in the hands of ordinary people, I am not a supporter of communism. In practice, communism is the same as fascism. Communist leaders are rank capitalists at heart. They live like the worst kind of kings or czars with Saville Row suits, country mansions and millions of dollars stashed away in foreign banks. They are given to more excesses than our Western leaders and, worse than our politicians, they stay in office until they are senile and die. Communism is highly dangerous. Communism, like other political systems, has the power in the hands of the few at the expense of the many:

> Experience and history show that political ideologies in the hands of experts are very dangerous.

Shortly after Tony Blair was elected to power as Prime Minister, he said to his New Labour Government, 'We are the servants of the people.' Quite rightly, this statement reflects the essence of a true democracy. Almost everyone in the country suspected that it was pure lip-service. Now one wonders if the new government had any intention whatsoever of representing the will of the people on crime and punishment, on traditional family values, on immigration, and on other issues crucial to a good society. To misquote a saying from the bible:

> Consider the politicians in their field, they toil not but oh how they spin.

CHAPTER 10

Modern Culture and New Sense Pop Laws

> Fame to infamy is a well trodden path.
>
> Ancient and Common Wisdom

There has been a fall in common wisdom and a pop rise in anti-wisdom. The modern 'cool' generation abbreviates those parts of popular culture with which it identifies and calls them 'pop'. Abbreviation or speeding things up is a main characteristic of modern culture. Has there ever been a time when so many young people want to become pop stars and indeed have the opportunity to fulfill their ambition quickly? We are increasingly known as 'Cool Britannia'. Pop culture is associated with drugs, sex, rock and roll, violence and bad language. Rock and roll was used as a politically correct term for sex as far back as 1926 by Afro-Americans and others. Some people can become famous overnight and very rich at the same time. This is not to mention fouling up their lives, health or even being involved in death not too long afterwards. The pop culture reflects and is reflected by our modern society of 'having it all and having it now'. Speed and 'blowing your mind' are of the essence. Like many things in our progressive era, seeking celebrity status has become more widespread and the pace of it has quickened. Modern romantic relationships reflect modern technology, which, by the time you get it home, is out of date in half an hour or less and you want a different model. Living in the fast lane is where we find the pop idols and where a generation of 'wannabes' want to be:

Speed isn't everything, it can kill.

The grass is not always greener in others' gardens.

Technology is the potent instrument of change. The invention of moving images and sound on films together with the development of recording systems such as discs and tapes gave a powerful boost that shot the modern show business and celebrity industry into orbit. Our lives, habits and values were changed in an accelerating and dramatic fashion. Now, for example, are there any aspects of our lives not influenced by television and pop culture? Are eating habits, grooming, courting, working, health, education, crime, leisure, friendships, marriage and so on ad infinitum, free from influences of television or pop culture? This is yet another example of the common sense law:

All things are related.

Experts have taken man's innate desire to play, split it into smaller specialisms, commercialised them and created professional performers in music, theatre, sport and so forth. Man, like many other animals, plays as well as works. The opposites of work and play exist together and give meaning to one another. For early man, play and entertainment were integral threads of the whole that bound together bodies, minds, spirits and habitats into living meaningful experiences. As indicated previously, ancient man did not separate work and play in his mind or in time and place as much as modern man. Even today the separation of work from play can be blurred and ancient undertones come to the fore. Some play activities of ordinary people, such as sports or amateur dramatics, can be regarded as a form of work by professional actors or players. Nevertheless, the performers can retain the play state of mind even when the activities are paid jobs. Play, like work, is defined by attitude of mind rather than by the name of the activity:

Some people work at play and others play at work.

Some ancient activities that were necessary for survival, such as getting food, are now modern sport, leisure or play forms. Throwing spears and other objects along with chasing or running and jumping were necessary skills for man to hunt and sustain life. Now their equivalents are to be found in sports such as the Olympic Games. There are more modern reflections of earlier work or survival forms being used as leisure activities. Some people go for a holiday on a farm and do farm work as a leisure activity. More people are going back to what became work activities and using them for hobbies, play and fun:

Play and work are opposite sides of the same coin.

Experts are making modern work and play dysfunctional. The numbers of sick-notes are indicative of work malaise and violence, greed and corruption in sport are examples of malfunctions in play activities. With the passage of time, play has become not only separated from work and other areas of life like family, religion and education, it has been divided into smaller specialist categories. For example, there is playacting, music, dance and games of chance, strategy and physical skill. Bingo is a modern example of games of chance while chess is a game of strategy and soccer would fall into the games of physical skill category. Play and games were split into further smaller parts and we have various types of drama, sport, art, comedy and so on. The divisions still proliferate and we now have gymnastics and dance in water and throwing the Wellington boot, the haggis or even midgets. Art has its own specialist areas or genres. There is fine art, like painting and sculpture, representational art, impressionism, cubism, graphic design, ceramics, pop art and so on. Films have their special differentiations also. We have period dramas, action movies, psychological thrillers, musicals, soft porn, hard porn, science fiction, comedies and so forth. We also get combinations or integration of play forms like a historical, comedy-mystery, drama on ice with sports stars making guest appearances:

> **Differentiation and integration characterise life at biological, psychological, social and cosmic levels.**

Experts differentiated music into parts such as classical, jazz, folk, rock and roll, punk, heavy-metal and focused parts at the expense of the whole of music. Pop music has been the part over-stressed at the expense of the whole of music and for the wrong reasons like money, greed and celebrity. When integrations have been attempted, many have been faulty and prompted by exploitation. To try to integrate younger and younger children into the world of 'pop' is immoral. Experts such as businessmen, politicians, lawyers and too many parents are involved in trying to integrate 'precocious' children into the pop culture when they smell the scent of celebrity and money. These excessive and faulty differentiations and integrations happen in various other parts of show business like sport, fashion, modelling and the like. Faulty differentiations and integrations occur at all levels of life and organisms. Cancer is an example at the level of cells in the human body. At the political-social level Britain's entry into Europe could provide another example of faulty integration and differenti-ation:

Common sense laws balance differentiation and integration far more effectively than expert theories and laws.

Man is not only a performer, he is a spectator. Some evidence indicates that man is less of a performer now and is more of a spectator. If time spent on television viewing is anything to go by, some do not have much time left for actually doing other activities. In that about 98 or 99 per cent of the British population watch television, it is a very popular cultural activity. Peter De Vries examples one who does not watch. He says, 'My father hated radio and could not wait for television to be invented so he could hate that too.' Over-use of televisions or computers can fracture families and separate members from one another. Some children have televisions in their bedrooms and this can lead to less family sharing or interaction. Another factor that must be borne in mind also is that:

Quantity of spectators is not the same as quality or goodness of the spectacle.

The political performances of Hitler were popular spectacles with the masses in Germany. He received more votes in a free election than other German Chancellors who succeeded him like Konrad Adenauer and Helmut Kohl. Nero, the Roman Emperor, who was the epitome of evil and a show-off, enjoyed much popularity also. Rulers and political figures have always realised that people are fascinated by spectacle, image or display. Politics, as a specialised activity, has been developing for several thousand years which is a part of the modern era compared with the time man first roamed the earth. Politics has always been a form of show business. Paul Begala reckons that, 'Politics is show business for ugly people.' With modern technology, spectacle and image can be spread and imitated more widely and rapidly. Indeed, so important has become image that we shall not have Emperors with no clothes, we shall have the clothes but no Emperors. Well perhaps not, flesh is too important to modern image-makers. We all seem to be increasingly involved in the image industry or 'show-off' business. In Shakespeare's *As You Like It*, he observes, 'All the world's a stage. And all the men and women merely players.' Modern 'stars' or 'celebrities' are no *mere* players. To quote a modern expression, pop stars and celebrities are 'big wheels' in our material and technological age. Their appearance, behaviour and values dominate our culture:

Image is more important in modern society than substance and the trend is growing.

All men are animals of pretence or illusion. It is part of our nature. We tell jokes and play the clown. What is of concern in modern times is that images are being used far too much to hide reality. Spin–doctors are creators of images that deliberately mislead. This week a pop celebrity is in desperate circumstance in hospital and the 'star's' public relations officer created the image that the celebrity was just 'tired'. Jokes have become reality and realities have become jokes. This is an old joke. A girl went to university and after the first term she came home and told her parents that she was pregnant. 'Who did it?' asked her father. The girl said, 'Well, it's one of two.' Her father asked, 'Which two?' The girl answered, 'It's either the basketball team or the soccer team.' Some people in the pop culture have sex with more people than this in a shorter time and that is no joke. Old jokes have become modern realities. What goes on in Parliament, in courts of law and in the show-business industry is no longer a sick joke, it is sick reality. A growing part of the entertainment industry, especially pop culture, exploits the worst side of man's desire to play or have fun. Is the following what might be called a truism?

Modern values are the opposite of old values.

Image and substance are regarded as opposites. Much of the reality of play, like most other things, is defined by opposites. Apart from the opposites of work and play, we also have other opposites such as imitation and 'being different' or 'doing one's own thing', reality and illusion, tragedy and comedy and in fashion and out of fashion. What are regarded as opposite emotions like laughter and crying have reflections or connections at biological, psychological, social and environmental levels of existence. We may laugh so much, it makes us cry. Entertainment that is supposed to provide good fun and happiness, because of its nasty excesses, has produced far too much pain and suffering, even death. These are more examples of the powerful common sense law that:

Excess in one thing leads to its opposite.

A major aspect of image-creation is language and modern language has become disturbing to the majority. There has been a growing focus on smaller restrictive and offensive parts of language at the expense of better forms of expression and greater wholes. The wholeness of nature is reflected in language. Letters that are parts of words are relatively meaningless on their own. When they become connected with other letters to form words, they have more meaningful existence. Words gain further meaningful existence when they are connected or related in sentences and so on into paragraphs and stories. Words written on a page are in straight lines, but when taken all together, they become a circle – a whole. For example, if we take one word and look up its meaning in the dictionary, we get some other words to define that word. If we take one of these new words that define the first word and look up the meaning of that, we get other words. If we continue looking up new words in the chain linked to the first word, we shall eventually go through all the words in the dictionary and come back to the first word where we started. We shall have completed the circle – the whole. Letters and words are like particles in sub-atomic or quantum physics. They only have existence and meaning in their relationships with the larger whole. That is, the same common sense laws or wisdoms apply to people, to sub-atomic particles or quantum physics and to words:

No man is an island.

No particle is an island.

No word is an island.

There is good language and its opposite, bad language. Modern society and, in particular, the pop culture are using more and more bad language. The language of pop culture is to be found almost everywhere. It is on tee-shirts, in the names of pop groups and the lyrics of their songs, in films, advertisements, television shows and most other places. For example, we have Killing Machine, The Stranglers, The Sex Pistols, Garbage, Death Row, Cradle of Filth, Skitzo, Gangsta Rap and a growing list of titles, words and lyrics advocating violence and other excesses. Indeed, one pop group was called 'INXS' until the main 'star' ended up dead. The language and actions of pop groups and modern show business at large glorify drugs, violence, killing, rape, sadistic sex, promiscuity and any other activity that could shock and so provide publicity, celebrity and easy money. Show business 'stars' are copied role models by increasingly younger fans and it shows. We have far too many violent and foul-mouthed infants not to mention adolescents and adults. Experts, especially politicians, call all this extreme hate behaviour by politically correct titles such as, Progressive Era, Freedom of Choice, Adult Entertainment, Modern Values, New Age, Individual Rights or The New Morality:

> New Morality is a politically correct term for the opposite of what it is, Old Immorality.

Some rationalists say that swearing is 'only words'. This is another example of reasoning devoid of wisdom and a denial of experience. We all know that bad language, apart from being aggressive and abusive itself, can often be an introduction to greater violent behaviour. Another point is that the words swearers use are the most vulgar, aggressive and abusive ones they can lay their tongues to. If there were fouler expressions, they would use them. Saying swear words are 'only words' is giving equal weight to all words. If swearers consider all words of equal status, why do they use this restricted small part of language and specialise in it at the expense of the greater whole? Is it because it is language that is the most shocking and attention-getting they can find? Films, television and pop concerts suggest that:

> Foul language that was an exception to the rule is in danger of becoming the rule in show business.

It is common knowledge that show business people are extremely self-centred and desperate for attention. Some actors boast that when they were very young children, they would do anything to be the centre of attention and they have not changed with age. Marlon Brando says, 'An actor's a guy who, if you ain't talking about him, ain't listening.' Being extremely self-centred, foul-mouthed and immoral are modern require-ments for stardom in the pop world. One girls' pop group was asked by an interviewer, 'Why is it that your group has the best singing voices and yet did not have as much success as really poor singing groups?' The leader of the group replied, 'We were too clean and we recognised it, so we began boasting about our sexual escapades and publicised that we could swear with the best or worst of them. Once we did this, we began to take off.' Another girls' group just starting out was asked on television why they thought they would make the 'big-time' when there were so many other girl bands about. They chanted in unison, 'Because we've got attitude':

Having attitude is a politically correct term meaning being aggressive and foul-mouthed.

Excesses of pop culture, especially those associated with its music, are based on the experts view of 'yoof' culture or adolescence. Youth culture has been allowed to greatly influence almost every aspect of modern life and it is against the will of the majority. It has increasing expert and political backing. Tony Blair has reinforced and extended the image of Britain as a youthful, trendy, cool, modern, pop society. The characteristics, treatment and behaviour of adolescents are based upon modern science. Experts have created a myth about teenagers. Adolescents are rebellious, experts tell us, because the science of physiology shows there are hormonal changes associated with the development of sex organs and spurts in growth make for awkwardness. All manner of experts like politicians, physiologists, behavioural scientists and educationalists, to mention a few, subscribe to this view. Experts agree on this great upheaval and conflict theory of adolescence, so it has become an 'objective scientific fact' of life. Like much of modern science and other expert knowledge, it is an inaccurate picture of reality. The major contribution to the creation of modern youth or the adolescent cult is more concerned with greed, commercialism and exploitation than it is with physiological change:

Experts focus on the part called adolescence or youth at the expense of the whole life span and society.

The publicity and scientific support given to the expert notion that adolescence is a very special stage of traumas and conflict due to physiological changes in the body, ignore obvious facts. One of the most dramatic changes in life's stages is when a child is born. Apart from the effects on the mother, the child is pushed from the warm, dark, cosy world of the womb into a world with variable temperatures, flashing lights, great noise and other shocking sensations. These traumas are greater than those of adolescence. Teenagers or adolescents know, because experts and everyone and their grandmothers have told them so, that they are expected to be rebellious due to their hormones. Obviously, experts have ignored everyday experience which shows that very young children can be far more rebellious than teenagers. When infants are rebellious it is called by other names such as tantrums. Rebelliousness is a special term reserved by experts for adolescence to support their theories and it has been glamorised in writings, songs, films and elsewhere. It is accepted in families, education, work and much of the entertainment industry is built on the false foundation of experts' theories of adolescence:

Youth culture is more a product of expert theories than a result of physiological or hormonal changes.

Middle age or menopausal time is as traumatic or dramatic as puberty and adolescence. It is a time when children leave the nest, a time when relationships have broken, a time of parents being ill or dying and the period when career and other prospects diminish. All these have impact upon the whole person including his or her physiology. Middle-age crisis is not an uncommon term. Old age too, is a more disturbing stage than adolescence when there are things to look forward to, unlike the old who face imminent death. The departure of friends, partners and relatives are regular occurrences. Experts have created a system where old people have been made to feel useless and a burden. Old people can be more rebellious than adolescents and with more just cause. In old age experts, along with the rest of us, use a less romantic word than rebellious; it is cantankerous. Old age is when physiological, anatomical, psychological and social systems break down and golden age of youth is just a memory. The great excesses of pop stars give some meaning to the following saying:

Youth is wasted on the young.

In a common sense society with the appropriate family life, education, activities and rites of passage, adolescence need not be the problem it is now. The separation of life's stages is based on more experts' thirst for power than on biology. In a scientific society that focuses material and physical bodies, it is not surprising that youth and the physical aspects of sex dominate our culture. Adolescence is a time when teenagers become sexually active and their actions become more noticeable and news-worthy. If a three-year-old punches and kicks its mother it does not gain as much publicity as a teenager doing the same thing. In modern society, is there any group of people, objects or events that have not been 'made sexy' or violated in a manner that glorifies sex and violence? Advertisements use sex to sell anything and everything. John Lahr notes, 'Society drives people crazy with lust and calls it advertising.' George Orwell tells us what we all know, 'Advertising is the rattling of a stick in a swill bucket.' Pop culture with its excesses has increasingly invaded family life, education and all our institutions including the church. We have raves in the nave and Jesus Christ has been given the pop culture treatment. He has been elevated to a 'superstar'. I say 'elevated' because some pop stars have rightly said they are more popular than Jesus Christ. Exploitation, particularly that of sex, is central to the pop star cult. It is to the credit of the majority of young people that they show as much good judgment as they do. With the constant bombardment and glorification of the sleazy and violent side of sex and life by experts, teenagers can still exhibit much common sense especially as:

Money is the root of youth culture.

Some older people immerse themselves in the image of Cool Britannia and parallel the promiscuous side of youth culture and pop star values. In a recent edition of *The Times*, a lady of about fifty years old in sunglasses is reported as talking about, 'the sex lives we barely believe we deserve with beautiful, eager creatures old enough to be our sons . . . We find ourselves on the dance floor of dark sweaty clubs at 4 a.m., surrounded by muscled young men punching along to the beat.' If such modern 'ladies' were the mothers of pop stars, we could make some interesting predictions or hypotheses about what their children would say. Some teenagers are disgusted by the thought of their mothers having sex with their husbands let alone 'toy boys'. Also, there are markets that provide young girls, such as those from Thailand, for geriatric romeos. I wonder if these 'hip' females who provide fodder for 'grab-a-granny night' and old male Casanovas would pay lip-service to traditional advice and tell their children or grandchildren:

Don't do anything your parents would be ashamed of.

Another newspaper, the *Daily Mail*, reports in one article about the author Wendy Leigh. She is quoted as saying, 'For the past 23 years I've lived in

America. But after reading Candace Bushnell's investigation of Englishmen and the London sex scene, I suddenly realised just what I've been missing. I originally moved to America to research three books on love, sex and relationships – *What Makes A Woman Good In Bed*, *What Makes A Man Good In Bed* and *The Infidelity Report* . . . I discovered quickly that American men expect every woman to instantly fall into bed with them.' The author relates the sexual self-confidence of American men, who are more confident than the English, to 'growing up in a country where the pursuit of happiness is part of the Declaration of Independence'. American men know their political rights. With specialist research like this, there can be no denying this lady is an expert. Compared with many other writers on sex, Wendy Leigh is relatively demure and old-fashioned by some modern standards. I did not realise that sex was done much in bed in modern times; in aeroplanes and on office desk-tops, yes, but bed! To have 'Bed' in the title of sex books seems a little traditional. Joan Rivers echoes more modern attitudes to sex in her questions, 'After lovemaking, do you, [a] go to sleep? [b] light a cigarette? [c] return to the front of the bus?' In the future, as the pace of life speeds up, 'a one night stand' will be regarded as slow-track sex. If Wendy Leigh goes all the way, with her research, she may re-discover old sayings, if she has not done so already, about man:

Early to bed, early to rise . . .

Over-familiarity breeds contempt.

As indicated previously, the whole person has been split by experts into body, mind and spirit. The body was split into more parts and its sexual aspects focused to gross or vulgar extremes. Sex is also being split off from other emotions such as love, honesty, friendship, kindness, sharing, belonging, and other dimensions of morality. It has been further divided into smaller parts like straight sex, gay sex, oral sex, pre-marital sex, married sex, adulterous sex, and group sex, to list some of the differentiations. In addition, we have developed, publicised and exhibited more parts by increasing the number of sexual positions and actions than in *The Karma Sutra*. Of course, we have specialists in these increasing number of differentiated parts of sex. We have 'Deep Throat' experts to mention one of many examples. Do we not already have a modern term for experts on sex, namely, 'Sexperts'? Not only do we have separations or differentiations of sex into smaller and smaller parts, we have the opposite – integrations. Experts have integrated sex with anything and everything. Sex is exploited and integrated into the sale of crisps, cornflakes, cars, clothing, diet, religion – you name it and sex is used to market it. Like excess differentiation or separation, excess integration has resulted in great corruption and immorality. Amongst the many anti-wisdoms that have developed in the pop culture is:

With sex, nothing succeeds like excess.

Modern values have reversed common sense laws. Much behaviour is the opposite of wisdom; it is *anti-wisdom*. It is to be found in ever-growing profusion in show-business and is reflected in all walks of life. Anti-wisdoms, for example, are to be found in education. Any sensible hard-working, well-spoken kind, good-mannered pupil can be violated and even hounded to death because of his or her values. Anything less than outrageous, violent and foul-mouthed behaviour can be vilified and classified as 'weird, nerdish or geekish' by too many members of the New Britannia generation. The modern anti-wisdom is:

To err is human, to be a slob is divine.

The anti-hero has come into prominence in our language and culture over the past few decades now and the excesses of the anti-heroes are continuing to expand. A modern rule or imperative seems to be publicity and celebrity at all costs. Today, immoral acts gain far more publicity, celebrity and reward than moral behaviour. Gaining attention by whatever means as the path to fame and fortune is becoming the modern philosophy in popular culture. Murderers, rapists and crooks of all kinds not only become celebrities, they can get huge sums of money from the media for their stories. One anti-wisdom that more and more people use to rationalise their immoral acts is:

There is no such thing as bad publicity.

Attention-seeking has been carried to great and immoral excesses. Some few days ago I saw a little boy of no more than six years old walking by himself in a crowded city centre. Emblazoned on the chest of his black tee-shirt were huge white letters which said, 'F . . . YOU'. Two weeks before this, in the same town, I saw a seventeen-year-old youth with a similar tee-shirt on the back of which it announced in bold letters, 'DON'T F . . . WITH ME MATE'. A television performer, receiving an award for a vulgar situation comedy, was reported to have used the F-word in his thank-you speech. When criticised, the news article claims, the actor said that the word would soon be in common use by children as young as five. He is correct, of course. What he might be more reticent to accept is that his own behaviour contributes to the foul-mouth language and actions of tiny tots. One doctor I know was bandaging the arm of an injured five-year-old and the child complained, 'Hey, that effing hurts.' The doctor told him that such language was not acceptable to which the child replied, 'Well they say F . . . on the television all the time.' Television stars are models or heroes children and others copy. These performers also provide rationalisations for bad language and immoral behaviour. Another anti-wisdom of many stars of popular culture is:

Where there's moral muck, there's money and fame.

Ordinary people have long known from experience and common sense that television or films have much influence on people. Experts have been telling us for years that the influence of television or film was not a *proven* factor in anti-social behaviour or crime. They argue that children and adults know full well that films are 'pretend' or entertainment and not real life. This is largely true. However, those who watch films also know that much of the violence portrayed in films actually exists in real life. Even if it did not, the make-believe violence could still be imitated. Experts who deny a relationship between television or film violence and real life defied even their own logic. They readily believe that films can be used for educational purposes to help people learn knowledges and skills. That is, experts accept that films change people's behaviour. Therefore, for experts to conveniently assume that people just learn good habits or values from films and not bad ones is illogical, not to mention devious. Here, once more experts fly in the face of what almost everyone knows and a whole host of common sense laws. The following law has been in the psyche and experience of man since time immemorial:

Life mimics art and art mimics life.

What experts failed to accept, like most scientists where observations do not fit their theories, were views of ordinary people. In addition, they ignored the obvious everyday experience of their own ears and eyes. Is there anyone who has not witnessed children imitating stars of stage, screen, radio, sport or literature? Not all people imitate the bad aspects of their idols and not all people imitate the good, but there is a growing band of modern immoral gods. When I was young and went to the Saturday 'rushes' at the cinema, imitating the stars was a main play activity. I believe it was Michael Parkinson the television interviewer and journalist who claimed that he strained at being like his idol Robert Mitchum the film star. He even went to the length of wearing a plaster on his face to develop the dimpled chin of his hero. There were many who used to practise walking like John Wayne or looking mean and moody as if they were James Dean. Elvis Presley was a much imitated pop star. Now we have even infants who ape The Spice Girls, Oasis and numerous other modern stars:

Imitation is the sincerest form of flattery.

The widespread imitation, flattery and worship of modern pop gods does not augur well for a better future. Even some of the experts' own experiments rediscovered what ordinary folk have known for years – that children are affected by these gods and what they portray in films and other media. For example, two matching groups of children were shown films and their behaviour observed after seeing the films. One group was shown a violent film and the other group a non-violent film. After watching the films the behaviour of the group watching the violent film was more aggressive than the group viewing the non-violent film. In 1999, after four or five decades, the American Psychological Association has reversed its views. It now believes that violent television programmes and movies do contribute to violence in society at large. Tom Phipps cites an observation that defines experts and their long-standing rejection of the influence of film violence on audiences:

An expert is a man who never makes small mistakes.

The pop music and celebrity culture has gone beyond the culture of science which claims it can have no morality. As we have already noted science cannot say what is good or bad. The dominant part of show business culture does not just lack morality like science, it specifically develops immorality and *boasts* about it. We have stars who delight in informing us how 'macho' they are. Males take great pride in their image of being in a violent and criminal gang when they were youths. They relate tales of their crimes and can 'look after themselves' and are 'street-wise'. Men get much publicity and its attendant celebrity status by boasting about being a 'super-stud' and 'hell-raiser'. Female stars do similar things and to demonstrate how desirable they are, they relate lurid stories of their sexual and brawling experiences with a string of famous 'lovers'. Girls are 'into' physical violence more. Physical violence used to be an almost entirely male preserve. It looks like some girls really, really want equality and to be exactly like boys. '*Vive la différence*', may soon be a thing of the past. These show-business values are to be found in more and more sections of the general population. For example, stories of office girls and other workers or unemployed people selling their escapades to the media are becoming more common. Some girls have returned from holidays and made money and gained instant celebrity status by claiming they slept with eight or more different men whilst on vacation. To add spice to their tales, some report group sex activities or orgies. They appear like professional models in smiling or sultry 'sexy' poses in photographs of national and international newspapers or magazines. For a brief period, they can have more publicity than their idols. One of my professors once said of promiscuous sex that girls were often surprised by the huge amount of interest they got on such a small deposit:

> Values in show-business and those in society reflect and
> influence one another.

Experts argue that those who do not wish to be involved in the culture of violence, drugs, sex, foul language and other excesses, like noise, can avoid them. For example, they say you can switch the television off. It is a matter of individual freedom and choice, experts smugly advise us. They go on to claim, proudly, that they provide a wide range of programmes and it is up to the individual to make his or her own informed choices depending on taste. What a gross and useless rationalisation this is. Even if we avoid the foul programmes by choosing good programmes, we are confronted by modern vulgar and violent pop culture *wherever we go*. In our normal everyday life we cannot escape the excesses of bad language, violence, sex, greed or almost any other evil. It surrounds us. We may avoid the sickness of modern culture for a short time, but these periods of respite are getting, like mini-skirts and tempers, shorter. The destruction of peace, like some other things in our progressive times, is being speeded up:

> Peace of mind and balance are the roots of good popular culture, a better life and a better society.

There are small sanctuaries of temporary peace that reflect the better side of man's nature. The Last Night of The Proms is an example of the better aspects of play, entertainment and good fun. This event, which can be witnessed on television, is supported by an audience that is happy, involved, non-violent, drug-free and good-humoured, where foul language and vulgar sexual display are frowned upon. Some people I know attended the Proms and, on their way home, they witnessed more violent, foul-mouthed, sexually promiscuous, drug-ridden and ear-piercing behaviour than can be experienced watching even the worst aspects of television. We do not want people to have to be 'street-wise', we want safe streets:

> Margaret Thatcher's chances of becoming President of USA are greater than ordinary people avoiding pop excesses.

I have some friends who went to see an Oasis Concert and it was a very different atmosphere to that at classical concerts such as the Last Night of The Proms. Here, the cultural norm was not just recommending and being involved in anti-social behaviour, it was boasted about and glorified. Many of the audience were fuelled by drugs, alcohol and were proudly violent, including being crudely sexual and foul-mouthed. My friends commented that the Oasis spectacle did not make you glad to be human let alone British:

> If pop music is part of 'the best of Britain' as The Prime Minister implies, he lacks wisdom.

People are well aware that classical musicians and singers can be foul-mouthed and violent on occasions. Even pop stars who are associated with more gentle, romantic and wholesome ballads like Barbra Streisand are reportedly rude at times. Her sweet songs such as 'The Way We Were' can hide a 'bitchy' personality. However, one important difference between classical music performers and pop stars like Oasis is that classical stars do not use foul-mouth language in their acts, nor do they recommend or glorify the use of drugs, violence and other forms of depraved and destructive behaviours. This is true of singers in the Streisand mode. However, she does publicly seem to condone some immorality for professional politicians if the reports are true. One claim is that she defended President Clinton's abuse of power by saying something like, 'We appointed a President, not a Pope.' The majority also knows that many ordinary people swear and are immoral at times, but it is the scale and viciousness of pop language and violent exhibitionism that is frightening. Even when people get involved in bad behaviours, they do not feel happy to glorify them which seems a fundamental law or requirement of modern pop culture:

> There is a time and place for everything.

There are other differences between classical musicians and singers and modern pop groups. Classical performers have to practise on their instruments and with their voices for years to acquire high skill. Pop groups can get by, nay, become icons overnight with little or no instrumental skill or quality of voice. With modern technology, pop groups can become stars by being able to play a few chords whilst snarling and screaming or simpering and moaning as if they had been offered a proper job. Often, the lyrics are so obscene or trite that it is perhaps fortunate that they are somewhat obscured by the ear-splitting, head-pounding noise that passes for music. All this is coupled with bodily gestures and gyrations that give the impression that the performers are undergoing brain surgery whilst simulating sado-masochistic sexual activity. The technology of flashing lights, canned sound and periods of darkness hide the lack of talent of these gross poseurs:

> Quantity of noise is no substitute for quality of music
> or singing.

It is possible to select people from the street at random and produce better singers than many in modern pop groups. Perhaps pop groups replaced individual crooners because image and numbers can hide deficiencies. When listening to The Beatles singing as individuals, you can appreciate why they sang as a group. Some musical commentator on John Lennon's solos observed that his main talent was singing by ear through his nose. Classical music has stood the test of time, that is why it is called classical. By comparison modern pop groups are often just a flash in the pan which are replaced by an even worse crop. Some of The Beatles' musical scores are already acclaimed as classics. It is only with the passage of more time that this judgement can be confirmed with any meaningful degree of reliability, objectivity and validity. This pertains to all modern music written in the classical mode or any other genre also. With the passage of time, some of The Beatles' music, unlike much of modern pop, may last longer than yesterday. Compared with today's pop music, the music and songs of 'The Fab Four' are wholesome culture. Real classical music performers have to work much harder at their art than the artless forms of many modern pop stars. What follows is first a modern day anti-wisdom and then, an ancient wisdom:

What you lack in talent, make up for it by immorality, noise, violence and shocking images.

Empty vessels make the most sound.

Since John Lennon has been mentioned, let us examine his philosophy a little further for it reflects the values of some other celebrities or personalities in show business. Through his songs and conversations, he was recognised as an advocate of peace. Abandoning his wife would not do much for her peace of mind. More important is the principle that is central to peace and its opposite, war or aggression. John Lennon was verbally aggressive, and engaged in wars of words, but this not the only concern. The major reason for going to war is because some people want to exert great control over others. They want to be top dog or 'number one'. This is precisely what John Lennon wanted to be. He wanted to be number one in the hit parade as often as possible. It is the same kind of excessive motivation or urge to control, which John Lennon had, that is the root of political manipulation and other anti-social acts including war. An ancient wisdom applies here and it reflects pop star status:

War is the sport of kings and pop stars act like kings.

Some pop stars, who can earn millions of dollars in a short time, try to make peace with their consciences by doing charity work. It has been known for some celebrities to attend charity events and voice deep concern over starving children and underprivileged wretches. Immediately afterwards, they have flown on a plane from England to New York to feast on their favourite pizza or fulfil some other whim. Celebrities, even Princess Diana, often have as much need of the charities as the charities have need of them:

> Fame and fortune give existence and meaning to their opposites – the unknown and the poor.

The Spice Girls acquired much fame and fortune in the second half of the 1990s. This pop group had a special sound bite which was a reflection from the political movement of women's rights; it was 'Girl Power'. What this actually turned out to be was flashing scantily dressed bodies, breasts and knickers at the audiences while telling them what they 'really, really want'. This act, coupled with foul-mouthed language and pinching the bottom of Prince Charles in public, made a spectacle of these girls and revived one the oldest profession's images of 'Girl Power'.

> Egotism – usually a case of mistaken nonentity.

The Spice Girls are mentioned as an example. There are many groups and show-business performers who are far worse in displaying and recommending degrading behaviour. Some performers associated with crude, vulgar, selfish behaviour become respectable and 'find God' or some other form of spirituality. Pop groups and others in show-business strive to be 'different' and to produce creative acts or images that will get them noticed. This obsessive ambition to be different or creative ends up being the opposite. Many pop stars are alike and conform to a norm of being crude, vulgar, and loud in their performances, dress and behaviour. Einstein along with many other experts have rediscovered an ancient wisdom that applies to the act of creating something different. It is another example of the common sense law of opposites. Einstein, whether he was aware of it or not, was citing an ancient common sense law when he observed:

> In every act of destruction there is an act of creation.

The opposite of this law is also true, 'In every act of creation there is an act of destruction.' When politicians and other experts including pop stars create different freedoms, acts or images, there are as a consequence, acts of destruction. 'Being at the centre of Europe', which is the 'creative act or aim' of the Prime Minister and other politicians of all parties, has already been achieved in some ways. We are top of the hit parade in unwanted teenage pregnancies, abortions, drug-taking and sexual diseases in the European league. We are the pop centre of Europe and perhaps number one in the world. We are riding high or low depending on your moral view-point. Anti-wisdoms are being taken to heart by even tiny tots who dress, act and twist and shout like pop stars and 'fashion' role models. There is no wonder there is an increase in paedophilia and other acts of gross misconduct. Magazines and other media have 'sexualised' the images and the bodies, minds and spirits of even young children. One anti-wisdom supported by the government, other experts and the pop or entertainment culture is:

If you've got it, flaunt it.

Pop stars, as we have already seen, reflect expert theories which focus one end of opposites and produce a society of extremes. One more example is the expert theory that it is good for the self to express emotions such as anger freely. This provides an expert rationalisation for violent and other forms of anti-social behaviour as if we needed any encouragement in this respect. When someone expresses anger, others are on the receiving end. Experts are re-discovering that their theories, which place excessive emphasis on the freedom of expressing emotions of the individual or self, produce destructive behaviour. Common sense and experience tell us that one of the best ways to deal with anger is to do something calming. Expressing anger should be done calmly. Much pop music does the very opposite of this. Scientists are now demonstrating that classical music is far more soothing and beneficial to body, mind and spirit than modern pop music. Another aspect of expressing selfish emotions has led to the notion of 'sexual freedom' or 'exploring individual sexuality'. This has contributed to Britain becoming one of the sleaze capitals of the world. An anti-wisdom of modern ideology seems to be:

The greater the immorality and vulgar exhibitionism. the greater the fame and fortune.

A few decades ago, Gypsy Rose Lee said of some female, 'She's descended from a long line her mother listened to.' Today Rose Lee would have to change this to, 'She's descended from a fast line her mother listened to.' Expert theories have made for a demand of speeding up of physical sensations. They have produced a 'quickie', 'touchy-feely' generation and have contributed to us becoming a nation of 'emotional junkies or addicts'. Experts have outlawed such words as 'fornication'. Now we have addictions. Stars of popular culture and their disciples claim to be sex addicts. So pervasive is this attitude of requiring immediate gratification and emotional exhibitionism, that some people demanded the Queen 'emote' publicly when Princess Diana was killed. Not only this, we had a pop star singing at her funeral. When the Queen's father died, she was admired for her dignity, control of her emotions and stiff-upper-lip attitude. When Diana died, the Queen was vilified for this same virtue. This modern fashion flies in the face of many common wisdoms one of which in this context is:

More emotional exhibitionism, less sincere feeling.

To believe that because the Queen does not make a public spectacle of her emotions, as demanded by pop culture, she is cold and uncaring is a misconception. It is rather like believing that because some pop celebrities appear on chat shows telling us how wonderful their lives are, they are happy. Often, a few days later, we read they are in hospital and cannot face life any longer. We need more of the Queen's spirit. She grits her teeth in the face of adversity and gets on with doing the best job she can. At the slightest obstacle or difficulty too many of us act like pop stars; we whine and demand a comforter. Elizabeth II has more than paid her dues and a high price in heart-ache for doing her duty in a splendid manner. However, she will experience less traumas than pop stars whose immorality comes with a high price to pay sooner or later. Pop stars want to be kings and queens, but without the responsibility that goes with these roles. For the British Government to lecture the Queen on how to modernise herself is like getting Bill Clinton to be moral adviser to the Pope. The Queen has more common sense than a whole 'sleaze' of politicians and other experts. Common sense laws are old-fashioned and cannot be modernised. They are long-lasting and transcend time and fashions. The Queen has been badly assessed by expert theories and pop minorities:

Don't judge a jewel by its casket.

The monarchy has always been part of popular culture from sports such as horse-racing to being patrons of the arts, music, and theatre. Ceremonies, rituals and activities that make up popular culture were often popularised or even initiated by royal court circles. Royalty itself is synonymous with the highest form of celebrity and attracts media and public attention. The Charles and Diana saga probably rivalled the television programme *Coronation Street* as popular culture for a time. Prince Philip, according to which journalist you read, had from a bit part to a major villain role in this royal soap opera. Because of his unique celebrity status, Prince Philip has always been considered fair game for media stories and speculation. However, he has not been given a fair deal by the press and many British people. In respect of the stories about Prince Philip, the observation of James Bennett is fitting:

Many a newspaper story has been ruined by over verification.

For over forty years Prince Philip has been a cornerstone of the British Monarchy and an unflagging supporter of his wife Elizabeth II. In all that time he has been damned by many for a handful of politically incorrect comments, some of which were twisted out of their true meaning. In the time of Princess Diana's trials and tribulations with Charles, Philip apparently wrote kind, loving letters to her. This was the opposite to some press reports which portrayed him as an unfeeling martinet. After all the harm 'Fergie', the Duchess of York, has done to the monarchy, Philip's only public comment on her was that he found her 'odd'. He has been a tireless worker in his official role and has gone beyond the call of duty. Long ago he set up The Duke of Edinburgh's Award Scheme to help young people and it has been successful. Prince Philip is a highly practical man and has followed common sense laws more than the vast majority of people in the world. With a track record like his, he would be justified in feeling he has been treated shabbily by experts and far too many of the British people:

Where evil is worshipped, goodness is condemned.

Prince Charles is one of the most famous celebrities in the world. His marriage to Diana conferred immediate world-wide celebrity status upon her also. In terms of popular culture, amongst other things, she became a media star and fashion icon whose images were publicised and copied by many fans or admirers throughout the world. So much a part of modern popular culture was Diana that it was almost inevitable that the major blame for her marriage break-up would be placed upon Prince Charles. Like everyone else, Charles has his faults. For example, he was guilty of suggesting his parents were to blame for some of his shortcomings. In addition, he allowed himself to be dragged into the pop culture practice of discussing his relationship with Diana on television. This was to counter-balance Diana's appearance on television where she blamed Charles for their separation. His appearance on television for such a purpose was against all his normal characteristics and instincts, for he has always been very private and reticent in such matters. However, when Prince Charles' attributes are compared to his failings, he still comes out as a man of much honour, honesty, courage and with a great commitment to duty and the British people. He has been criticised by religious leaders and others as being unfit to be king due to his relationship with Camilla Parker-Bowles. This is the height of hypocrisy when you look at what goes on in the Church. Charles, even on the issue of infidelity, is one of the most sexually moral princes in the whole history of monarchies. Modern church leaders have presided over a great decline in morality during the last 50 years, yet they criticise one of the most moral of men for being less than perfect. Give an inch to church leaders and they want to break a potentially good royal ruler. An anti-wisdom of modern society which is reflected in religion, expert law and elsewhere is:

> If you can't prosecute the guilty, prosecute the innocent to justify your existence.

Charles is a lover of the countryside, country pursuits, painting, classical music and traditional values and art forms. Diana, in their courtship, gave the impression that she had similar tastes, values and interests. In practice, she was, by and large, interested in the opposite pastimes to Charles and these differences became more obvious with the passage of time. Diana loved the city, shopping, fashion, pop music and her values were less traditional or old-fashioned than Charles. Thus, she had various character-istics in common with pop stars. She was often described as an ideal princess for the modern 'with it' society. Diana was a pop star princess.

However, she had some characteristics that are the opposite of pop star culture. She was shy, modest and worked hard to help others. Like many others around the world, I still find it difficult to believe she died in such dreadful circumstances. Diana was too modern and popular for her own good and identified to great excess with trendy values of people living in the fast lane.

Some false stories were circulated about the marriage of Charles and Diana. One was that it was a loveless union of convenience. Princess Diana encouraged this view when it suited her. However, she did admit shortly before her death that she and Charles had been in love with each other. Charles, like Diana and the rest of us hoped marriage would last forever. Much was made of his comment when asked if they were in love as they became engaged. Charles replied, 'It depends what you mean by love.' This was merely a diplomatic way of telling the questioner not to poke his or her nose any further into their private lives. In addition, the fact that Charles is not 'touchy-feely' with his sons in public does not mean he is a cold distant father as some experts would lead us to believe. It is obvious that Charles loves his sons in spite of him not making a public exhibition or spectacle of it. Many ancient wisdoms are relevant here, two of which are:

Appearances can be deceptive.

It is not the gay cloak that makes the gentleman.

Prince Charles is ridiculed for his belief in ancient wisdoms and his views on the interrelatedness or wholeness of all things. He speaks with much common sense on architecture, culture, morality, the environment, religion and all manner of issues that reflect the wholeness of man, his natural habitat, the planet and the cosmos. The question is, will he survive the anti-wisdoms that dominate our culture and which may separate the parts to the extent that the whole disintegrates? If we go on as we are doing there will be little left worth having a king to rule over. Charles is well aware that:

Modern, expert pop values are destroying Britain.

The royals who have done great damage to the monarchy are the ones who indulged in the sleazy aspects of the celebrity status and were modern pop stars of their time. Edward VIII, formerly the Prince of Wales, Princess Margaret and Sarah Ferguson, the Duchess of York, have been in their time examples of the celebrity cult. Rather than sniping and snipping at the traditions of the Queen to modernise her, the government could do it at one fell swoop. Politicians could appoint one of the pop stars they recommend for our young people to copy as models. The Queen could be replaced by Sir Elton John or Mel B better known as Scary Spice. Both are icons of the New Cool Britannia and have the correct qualifications and experience. They would probably claim they represent Great Britain in a far more modern way than the present old-fashioned incumbent. Appointing pop monarchs regularly would really, really bring royalty up to date and it does have advantages. Such a move would achieve the government's agenda and its pledge to 'modernise, modernise, modernise'.

> Politicians do not have the courage of their own derelictions.

The Queen, the Queen Mother, together with Prince Charles and Prince Philip still represent the best standards of British culture though they are being tarred with the 'modernising' brush. Not so long ago, the British Broadcasting Corporation was regarded as 'royalty' in respect of reflecting the best of British values in popular culture. In the 'progressive' era, John Birt, a main BBC director, has presided over the greatest 'dumbing down' of programmes in its world-wide illustrious history. This, coupled with giving great impetus to violence and sleaze all in the name of modernising programmes, has earned him a knighthood. Other television stations can be worse. Michael Grade who is in charge of another channel has sometimes been called 'the porno king':

> Modernising is a politically correct term for vulgarising, dumbing down and use of high techno-pop.

So common is the sleaze and so desensitised have people become to mindless violence that the search for increasingly evil things to do in films accelerates. The Mecca of the film-making world is Hollywood which has always been a major centre of immorality. Wilson Mizner defines this Unholy Grail as follows:

> Hollywood: A trip through a sewer in a glass-bottomed boat.

Michael Winner is famous for making violent films. Many of his films celebrate highly offensive acts of violence. This is cynical, exploitative, anti-social film making. Of course, Winner argues that film violence is not related to violence in society at large. Judging the suitability of films for public consumption should be taken out of the hands of 'expert' censors and put into the hands of temporary, randomly selected Justices of The Peace. The British Board of Film Certification or Classification is like many other experts such as lawyers – extremely dangerous to public welfare. Winner is not the only anti-social person involved. Actors, distributors and those members of the public who go to watch his films are amongst those who must share the responsibility for Winner's sick productions.

Some famous actors and actresses who have contributed to violence and sleaze in modern society are trying to escape the consequences of their own creations. We read of violent American movie stars wanting to move to Britain with their children because they say the USA is 'too violent'. Some television presenters and film stars are getting out of their jobs due to the evasiveness of their sleazy industry. One report informs us that Liam Neeson of *Schindler's List* fame is quitting the film business in disgust. He is quoted as saying that he cannot even bear to watch films, especially his own and adds, 'Having children takes you out of that me, me, me syndrome.' Compared with many other stars, Neeson seems quite gentlemanly. Egotism is rampant in show business and is illustrated by the following, or similar, much-quoted anecdote:

> Fan: You were superb in Romeo and Juliet.
> Actor: I bet you say that to everyone who is superb.

Excessively self-centred, immoral or aggressive behaviour of modern popular culture is often blamed on a deprived childhood. Bad behaviour is not a necessary consequence of a poor childhood. We all know people who had dreadful family backgrounds but who turned out to be good citizens. Conversely, we are also familiar with people from good families who developed into very anti-social teenagers and adults. More recently immoral behaviours of all kinds have been given even greater justification by scientific experts. Now we can blame any anti-social action on our genes. Experts lawyers could seize upon this and re-define a client's violent sexual attack in politically correct terms, perhaps as follows:

Rape is merely an assault with a friendly weapon.

Egotistical or very selfish behaviour is anti-social. Its extreme forms, which show-business people increasingly exhibit, are gaining greater expression in society at large. In the 1976 edition book entitled *The Selfish Gene*, Richard Dawkins explains why we are so selfish. He writes, 'We are survival machines – robot vehicles blindly programmed to preserve the selfish molecules known as genes.' Society, he suggests, is based on 'the gene's law of universal selfishness'. Dawkins goes on to tell us that we are not necessarily compelled to obey our genes and advises, 'Let us try to *teach* generosity and altruism, because we are born selfish.' Dawkins's theory is in the true traditions of modern science. Man is viewed as a machine or robot. The part [selfish gene] is separated and stressed as if it had no opposite. However, books written by Dawkins are highly readable. Nevertheless, his inaccurate scientific theory on the selfish gene helps justify immorality in modern society and is against the ancient wisdom regarding opposites:

Common sense law insists that if there is a selfish gene
there is also an unselfish gene.

People with modern pop values are also guilty of trying to rationalise their gross behaviour by reference to common wisdoms. For example, in a bar I heard a teenager called Kevin tell his friends, 'I'm honest and open about my feelings. If I fancy a girl, I just walk up to her and ask her if she f---s.' Kevin's friend said, 'Right on mate. You have to go for it and sort it right away. Life's too short to p--- around. You can't beat being up front and honest can you pal?' This claim to honesty, if taken at face value appears to be true. However, if someone went up to Kevin with a knife and said, 'I must be honest with you mate, I hate your guts and so I'm going to stab you to death,' Kevin would not find the knifeman's honesty acceptable. If all people acted without any restriction on their immediate feelings or impulses, there would be a lot more dead bodies around. In fact the number of corpses, maimed bodies, minds and spirits is growing in modern society due to excess freedom of expression and action that are enshrined in expert legal rights. Why Kevin's brand of honesty is hypocritical or meaningless is that he does not accept the same brand of honesty in others – like that of the knifeman. Like many with pop culture values, he wants to be special or different and be 'noticed'. Kevin's behaviour clashes with many common sense sayings which can be expressed in ancient or modern form. For example:

> One man's freedom is often the bondage of many.

> If you can't take it, don't dish it out.

Drug-taking has become popular culture. It is considered 'cool', just as carrying a gun or knife is viewed as a fashion accessory for some youngsters. Such is the social pressure that those who do not take drugs have to pretend they do just as virgins are forced to claim they are having sex. Drugs and sex are 'what is going down', or 'where it's all happening'. Sleaze is not just an information highway, it is 'where the real action is'. It is the modern way to 'getting a life'. Going to 'raves' is 'where it's at'. 'Clubbing', too, is an expanding popular sleaze culture. 'Lap-dancing' and worse are socially acceptable:

> Images of drugs, sex and violence are used as a norm in advertising, entertainment and life at large.

As with sex, to hear some youngsters talk, you would think they had invented drug-taking. Various forms of drug-taking have been around down the ages. Plants such as coca and poppies have been used to alter states of body, mind and spirit. What is different in the modern era is the excess of drug use and the early age at which it occurs. Drug-abuse is destructive and highlights the inadequacy of the expert theory of 'Survival of the fittest'. This notion of Darwin's implies self-preservation at all costs, but does not address the opposite appropriately. Common sense law says that 'fittest' only gains existence and meaning in relation to its opposite – 'unfittest' and that:

> There is both a desire for self-preservation and its opposite, self-destruction.

Excess drug-taking is an example of that part of our nature associated with self-destructive behaviour. The state of modern society is so separated from nature that there is good cause to engage in self-destructive activities. Expert theories have created a state of increasing alienation and hopelessness. Escaping a mechanistic world by taking more and more drugs is a telling indictment of experts and their theories. Politicians choose to associate with known drug-takers while saying they want to erase drug abuse. The Prime Minister appointed a drug 'czar' to deal with the massive drug problem that confronts Britain. At the same time, he invited a pop star, infamous for his glorification of drug-taking, violence and foul language, to a social evening at Number 10 Downing Street. A newspaper photograph showed Tony Blair smiling and shaking hands with this modern anti-hero. It seems publicising drug-taking is fine with politicians so long as pop musicians continue to be money-spinners for the national economy. One piece of American graffito advises against taking drugs and at the same time identifies those who bear a major responsibility for the spread of abuse:

> The only dope you should shoot is a politician.

Producing expert laws on drug-taking is counter-productive. As soon as you ban something, it becomes more desirable. In many cases, the expert laws cannot be applied to any good effect so the authorities turn a blind eye. Expert laws on drugs should be dispensed with immediately as should the drug-awareness programmes. Any fool throughout history has known that taking in some substances can be harmful. We do not have laws telling people not to drink bleach or hot lead. In these cases we rely on common sense and do not replace it with expert laws. There are no special hot lead or bleach therapy or rehabilitation programmes – not yet anyway. Is there any common sense person who does not know that taking some substances, including drugs like ecstasy, can kill or injure them? Kevin Rooney states what most people know about excess use of cannabis. 'Pot is like a gang of Mexican bandits in your brain. They wait for thoughts to come down the road, then they tie them up and trash them.' Expert laws and theories are destroying the common sense law that:

> If you play with fire you can get burned.

Isolation with no drugs is the best therapy for prevention and cure of a drug habit. Experts argue that without counselling, methadone and the like some drug users may die. This is true, but the spectre of 'cold turkey' adds to the preventative effect and, in any case, people die with expert treatment and guidance. With isolation and immediate withdrawal of drugs, the dead body count and number of drug-abusers would soon be far less than with modern expert scientific systems. Any crime committed under the influence of drugs, like any other crime, would be dealt with by randomly selected temporary Justices of The Peace. They could prescribe isolation and withdrawal treatment for any bothersome drug-users if they saw fit to do so. Similarly, expert laws should be abolished in respect of prostitution which is popular culture for a growing minority. If, in particular areas, complaints are made about soliciting and client presence, Justices of The Peace would issue sanctions. Expert laws have not diminished prostitution:

Prostitution may be the oldest profession but politics or law is the most immoral.

Sexual promiscuity has become a growing pop culture activity even with youngsters who are still children themselves. Sleazy sexual images bombard us from all quarters. We have 'It' girls, 'Babes', 'Hunks' and people who are sought after because they are 'crazy' or 'way out man'. Pop stars and show-business people produce more than their share of single-parent and dysfunctional families in their selfish wake and their immorality is being reflected in the modern 'wannabe' generations. Furthermore, it is the silent common sense majority who are made legally bound to pay for these gross excesses. Homosexuality is now a 'chic' activity in pop culture values. One of the advantages of homosexuality is that it does not contribute directly to the population bomb. For years comedians have said things like, 'I knew there was a disproportionate number of homosexuals before I entered show-business, but I didn't realise it was compulsory.'

In terms of procreation of the species, homosexuality is an abnormal activity.

People throughout history have been aware of homosexual practices. Many famous names from the past in all fields of human endeavour have been homosexuals. Alexander The Great, Leonardo da Vinci, Francis Bacon Chancellor of England, several English Kings, Michelangelo, Tchaikovsky, Marlowe, Virginia Woolf, Gertrude Stein, Nureyev are some of the many examples. Indeed, to the extent that people masturbate, we are all homosexuals. Male and female anatomy, physiology and psyche share much in common. Even those who appear to be violently against homosexual practices have fantasies about people of the same sex. What offends the common sense majority is the flaunting, promiscuity, and degradation of sexuality whether heterosexual or homosexual. Over the past few years, homosexuality has received much publicity and, hence, celebrity status. Thus, homosexuality has become a fashion item as well as a public activity that once was more private and is now almost a pop culture imperative. David Bowie, a pop icon and 'gender-bender' has this to say:

> You don't know how difficult it has been being a closet heterosexual.

Another aspect of popular culture that gets more corrupt and sleazier as it becomes increasingly 'modernised' by experts, is sport. For example, the Olympic Games and soccer are awash with greed, bribery and immoral acts of all kinds. The 1992 book by V. Simon and A. Jennings entitled *The Lords Of The Rings* catalogues the vast corruption in the Olympic Games. It is about greed, power and drugs 'where money is spent on creating a fabulous life style' for a tiny minority of experts and where funding 'destined for sport has been siphoned away to offshore bank accounts'. D. Yallop's 1999 book, *How They Stole The Game* highlights the great tide of immorality in soccer. The book illustrates how power-seekers continue to alienate the common sense feelings of the layman for the game by the use of corrupt, expert theories. All this sleaze is rationalised under the name of modernis-ation, progress and justice. Soccer has taken on the image and values of the pop music industry. In the 1960s, George Best was called The Fifth Beatle. In the 1990s, there were players referred to as the Spice Boys.

Whenever soccer players generate any good behaviours or skills, they want to take credit for them. They put acceptable successes down to personal effort, determination, commitment, loyalty and the like. Any sleazy, violent behaviours that do not pay off, they blame on their sad lives or now, more frequently, their genes. They can rationalise their gross behaviour by claiming they are genetically programmed sleaze, violence or sex machines, which reflects expert theories. They are unable to help what they do and say things like, 'That's who I am. That's me and I cannot change. It is an essential part of my success on the field.' Such egocentric nonsense has become the norm in pop soccer culture. Great players in the past like Pele, Matthews, Finney and Charlton were gentleman on the field as were many others compared with our present day pampered spoil-sports. What is getting increasingly overlooked is the obvious fact that:

> **If you reward sleazy or violent behaviours, you will get sleazy and violent behaviours.**

Young fans and older ones are walking around with the names of these sleazy anti-heroes printed in large letters on replica soccer club shirts. To pay the exorbitant wages of these pop icons, professional soccer clubs change their strip regularly so that loyal fans will keep extra money rolling into the bottomless pit. This is in addition to the much over-priced match tickets. Players rationalise their demands for huge wages by saying that unlike ordinary jobs, they could be injured and unable to play at a very young age. They go on to argue that since this is the case, they must aim to have financial security for the rest of their lives by getting massive wages in a short space of time. Common sense people respond to this by thinking, 'Well get another job like the rest of us would have to in a similar situation.' Indeed, if they had another part-time job, they might be better players. Because of the greed of players, almost all professional soccer clubs are in debt. If some players were paid what they were worth, in a fairer society, some would be lucky to get a packet of crisps and a bottle of pop. Perhaps I should use the phrase 'a bottle of lemonade' rather than 'a bottle of pop' as too many soccer stars are already overly 'popped'. From clubs that are struggling financially, we are often told that they are seeking to 'put a package together'. This is a politically correct description for getting some rich person to pay for the exorbitant demands of players.

If expert coaching worked, there would be more Peles, Finneys and Bests running around. Great players from the past explored and developed their natural skills in all kinds of situations. They played ball or games anywhere, on their own or in small groups which they preferred to large ones as they got more contact with the ball when numbers were less. Their playgrounds were in the streets, the house, the fields, the beaches or any place a ball could be kicked, headed, trapped, caught or thrown. We do not have to teach children to walk, run, kick, throw and catch. They have these natural abilities within them and we just have to allow or help lead them out. Expert coaching does not do this and blinds people with science by flying in the face of the natural instinctive feelings for skill development. This contributes to skill levels going down. Kevin Keegan was appointed as the new English coach and seen as a saviour or messiah for the national team. He was unlikely to do any better than many of his predecessors. Young players' innate natural abilities have been submerged under a morass of expert theories and practices. Keegan over-estimated the skill levels of modern day professional players. Now as I write, Sven Eriksson, the Swede, is the England manager and perhaps qualifies more readily for Graham Taylor's nickname 'Turnip' than ever Graham did. Sven chants the mantra that is a myth which basically states that private lives are totally separate from professional duties. Who is he trying to kid – Nancy – surely not any common sense people?

Before expert coaches told them how to play, players relied more on inner sensing for what to do.

Expert soccer coaching has invaded school with increasing momentum since World War Two. A common practice has been to see seven to eleven-year-olds aping professionals and playing eleven a side games. In these matches, expert tactics and coaching result in some players, like full-backs, getting only two or three kicks a game. Children are desperate to have much contact with the ball and this is the way to allow them to develop natural abilities and skills to a high level. Small, two versus two and three versus three games on small pitches, with low cross-bars on goal-posts, is the way to lead out instinctive potentials. Experts inhibit inborn skills. For example, children usually start kicking the ball with their toe-end. Immediately experts tell them not to do this. Toe-ending is a highly useful skill. It needs less back-lift and is therefore good for getting off a quick shot at goal in a crowded penalty area, a snap pass or quick prod to disposses an opponent:

Expert coaches are the disease for which they pretend to be the cure.

Experts tread a similar path in cricket coaching. Youngsters play eleven a side and imitate professionals. They can be bowled first ball and that can be the total of their skill development in that game. What they want to do by nature is to be batting, bowling, running or catching and throwing the ball as often as they can. To achieve this, cricket games should have one person batting, one bowling, one wicket-keeping, one fielder on the offside and one on the leg-side. Players take it in turns and rotate to do all these activities, often in a short space of time. Experts also reverse the nature of skill development in batting. They start with straight-bat and defensive shots when children instinctively begin with cross-bat attacking strokes. An ancient wisdom in the context of these sports reads:

More expert coaching, less skill development.

Much coaching language contains commands and words like, think, concentrate, focus, aggression, work, effort and so on. These directives do not allow the common body-mind-wisdom to operate properly as much of it is at the subconscious or unconscious level. Like expert scientists, expert coaches ignore or cannot deal with the subconscious or unconscious. Expert coaches focus the conscious at the expense of its opposite – the unconscious and by so doing they hinder skilled performance. A simple example of this is that we can run up and down stairs perfectly well most of the time. If however, we are told to concentrate and consciously think about running up stairs, we are very likely to stumble and fall. The same principle applies to skills in sport. Any soccer fan could pick an England team that would do as well or better than those selected by most expert coaches. When high skill is witnessed, spectators say things like, 'It seemed so effortless.' Since such a player is *performing* there is *effort* present, but it is by nature largely subconscious or unconscious. If you asked Pele or other great players to tell you exactly how they do what they do, they could not tell you because most of their performance is guided by skill and effort from the unconscious:

Opposites define high skill as effortless effort or using the unconscious as well as the conscious.

There is a wide variety of other sports, games and physical activities that are popular cultural activities. People participate in walks, swimming, cue sports, keep fit, yoga, cycling, darts, weight lifting, training, golf, jogging, and numerous others. Involvement in golf seems to have increased over the past decades, though some 'wags' still refer to golf as cross-country snooker. Other popular leisure culture activities in addition to watching television include visiting public houses, restaurants, libraries, cinemas, historic buildings, holiday resorts, discos or night clubs, funfairs and friends. We do

DIY, listen to radio, records and tapes and do home crafts such as needlework, cooking and gardening. Many of these activities have been 'modernised'. We even have, 'sexercise' and 'catwalks or fashion parades for children' as pop culture pastimes:

Cool Britannia is no longer a nation of shop-keepers, we are a nation of image and pop-keepers.

It seems that no matter what cultural pursuit a person chooses, it is invaded by pop values such as noise, extreme focus on the self, greed, materialism, crude sexuality and semi-literate, foul language. For example, let us take the popular cultural activity of reading. Though we have one of the richest traditions in literature with icons like Shakespeare, Dickens, Jane Austen and a whole host of others, people are ignoring these classics and have turned more and more to publications with 'pop' values. Some illustrations of these are, *The Sun*, *The News of The World*, *Girl Talk*, *Smash Hits*, *Barbie*, *Big*, *Just Seventeen*, *Gay*, *Attitude*, *Vibe*, *Jockey Slut* and similar 'modern' offerings:

Opposites define culture: there is high culture, but low culture dominates and is growing.

Low culture reflects modern political culture and ideology. Sleazy self-centred values saw the Conservative Government ousted in 1997. Then Tony Blair's government gave more momentum to sleaze by its projection of the fashion image of a modern, youthful, Cool Britannia. In the run up to the 1997 General Election, Tony Blair was not reticent to inform us that he himself was of the rock and roll generation and that he had once been a member of a pop group. After he became Prime Minister he said of stability in the economy that it was 'sexy'. Tony Blair's statement is reflected in Ruud Gullit's comment when he was appointed manager of Newcastle United Football Club. Gullit promised the supporters 'sexy' football. We must give Gullit his due. After seeing Newcastle United in the 1999 FA Cup Final, I feel he delivered his promise in terms of political New Truth. The performance of his team was such that Ruud and his players did spend most of the match in the missionary position, though they did not score. The opposition won by two goals to nil and if this was 'sexy' football, we have to worry about Gullit's personal life. This sexy soccer could promote a celibacy cult on Tyneside and give a whole new meaning to 'Wor Geordie'.

In Britain's realm of anti-wisdom more politicians are leading by example.

As well as alternative relationships and families, we have alternative comedy. Government has told us what alternative families are, but a question arises in respect of comedy, 'Alternative to what?' When we observe alternative comedy to see how it is different, the most notable features are its crude vulgarity and bad language. Great comedians like Tommy Cooper, Phil Silvers and many others did not have to rely on gross sleaze to be funny. Humour is a human imperative and permeates both work and play. It is popular culture, although like too many modern entertainments, the quality of comedy programmes is grossly low. Fame and fortune in 'progressive' comedy is gained by glorifying sleaze. Excess fame and fortune, no matter what field they are in, rarely live up to the expectations of those who seek them. Great penalties in body, mind and spirit have to be paid for fame and fortune. Tony Hancock, John Lennon, Jimmy Hendrix, Janis Joplin and many, many others illustrate this common-place observation. An ancient and common wisdom warns us of the pitfalls:

All fame is dangerous: good, brings envy; bad, shame.

CHAPTER 11

Common Paranormal Sensing

Things are not always as they seem.

Ancient and Common Wisdom

It is difficult to find anyone who has not had strange or unexplained happenings in their lives. As a hard-nosed scientist most of my life I have been very sceptical of claims about paranormal activity. Even now, when I am aware of my own involvement in the great fallacies of science, if someone told me the stories that I can personally relate, I would probably still find it difficult not to rationalise them exactly as scientific experts would. Such an attitude shows the great degree to which I have been socialised or influenced by experts and the Scientific Society. So potently have I been conditioned by rationalism or reasoning and science that I still find it difficult to accept some of my own subjective experiences. On the other hand, quite unwisely, I did not doubt science. There are various wisdoms in almost every culture that apply to putting too much faith in narrow specialised views such as expert theories and knowledge. One Persian proverb is, 'Doubt is the key of knowledge.' Another related common wisdom advises:

Don't put all your eggs in one basket.

When I was about five or six years of age I lived next door to an old couple, Mr and Mrs Rawson, who were about eighty years old. With them lived their daughter Elsie and her husband Charlie and they would be in their middle fifties. Charlie had been wounded in the First World War and was unable to work. He spent much time supervising my various 'building' projects which I enjoyed doing in the garden. One winter afternoon I was in my neighbour's house, as I frequently was, when I witnessed something that made my eyes pop and the hairs on my neck stand on end. A pair of socks, one folded in the other, fell from the top of a chest of drawers to the floor. To my amazement, the socks moved slowly across the floor to a half-open door three or four feet away and began rising slowly up the door. The socks disappeared over the top of the door and then, as if to check I

288

had seen them, they reappeared back over the top of the door, paused for a few seconds and then dropped to the floor. My eyes seemed incapable of blinking in the time this was happening. When I could find the words I asked, 'Did you see the socks creep up the door?' The old lady said, 'I didn't see anything.' Her husband just chuckled. Elsie told me it was time for me to go home whilst Charlie was smiling and quietly commented, 'Socks from Marks and Spencers are always playful.' Over the next four or five years at my neighbour's house, I saw on one occasion a decanter and its stopper move on their own whilst on another visit a vase jiggled around unaided. Thus, according to my young eyes and Methodist Church background:

> God may move in mysterious ways, but so do socks, decanters and vases.

After the incident with the socks, as soon as I got home I told my parents about it. My mother said, 'You must have dozed off and had a funny dream.' When I said that I was wide awake my father suggested it was due to having a fertile imagination. The reaction of my parents is interesting because it reflected precisely what expert rationalists and scientists would have said. My parents, who if asked what they knew about rationalism and science, would tell you they knew little or nothing about them. Like most people, my parents came into contact with science mainly through technology. Nevertheless, here my parents were rationalising my unusual experience in the same way as experts would explain it. Socks climbing up doors is against the laws of science so expert scientists would not accept it. Religious experts would not accept it unless they could attach some Godly purpose to mobile socks. We can be strongly conditioned by experts and be relatively unaware of our conditioning. All our present population was born into the expanding scientific and the declining religious culture. They are a part of it even if only as consumers of technology with the occasional reference to religion when a technology lets them down and then they might say, 'Jesus Christ'. However, even reference to religious figures in this manner is giving way to more modern modes of expressions:

> The paranormal is also known as extra sensory perception, psi or psychic phenomenon.

Much attention has been given to objects which seem to move of their own volition and without scientific or religious explanation or blessing. Such movements have been observed in different cultures for centuries along with the rest of the phenomena mentioned in this chapter. Perhaps the most famous example in Britain over the last few decades concerns Matthew Manning. He has been the subject of television programmes, newspaper, magazine and academic journal articles as well as an object of research by scientists. When he was a schoolboy in the 1960s his presence at times was accompanied by strange self-propelled movements of objects which were witnessed by other schoolboys and members of staff including the headmaster. Even some expert scientists have testified to the phenomena that Matthew Manning precipitates. Most scientists however, seem unable to accept anything which does not fit into their orthodoxy rather like other religious orders:

What has given power is not easily discarded.

The activity linked with Manning in his schooldays is associated with the term 'poltergeist'. A poltergeist is a noisy, mischievous spirit. If the movement of the socks, decanter and vase that I saw at my neighbour's house was due to a poltergeist, it was a gentle one compared with many reports. Some poltergeist activity is extensive and chaotic as well as being mocking and tormenting. All manner of objects have been witnessed flying around in an uncontrolled fashion from paving slabs to most types of furniture. Fish have rained from the sky far away from sources of water, whilst in more technological times, havoc has been played with electrical systems and other modern appliances. Activity of poltergeists is unpredictable:

Poltergeist activity is not unlike that of sub-atomic particles;
both mock rationalists and modern scientists.

The activity of a poltergeist is associated with the presence of a particular person like Matthew Manning in his schooldays. Often in the early stages and even later, the person can be unaware that the paranormal activity is associated with him or her. Therefore one might say it is the subconscious or unconscious mind that is influencing the moving objects. Even when a person realises that the poltergeist activity is associated with him or her it can take considerable time and effort to gain control over it. Our minds and thoughts, even in their conscious form, never mind the below conscious levels, are often like poltergeist activity – difficult to control, unpredictable and mischievous or malevolent. Paranormal activity obeys the common sense law of opposites that exists in normal activity.

There are influences of mind over matter and the opposite – matter over mind.

Whereas poltergeist activity seems naughty, contrary and relatively un-predictable, the movement of some objects is far more controlled, being the direct result of people willing them to move. Getting furniture to move just using the power of the mind became almost a pastime for some people from the middle of the nineteenth century. Brian Inglis documents the extensive history of 'table-turners' and points out, 'The enlivening of wood by human contact was not new. It had been reported from communities, in classical literature and by travellers in India and Tibet.' Many people, including famous scientists, testified to the authenticity of tables and other objects moving without physical force or contact. Queen Victoria also witnessed the effects of table turners' efforts. Many establishment figures who did not want to violate the experts' interpretation of the laws of nature, searched for explanations in theories that stayed within the realms of science such as magnetism or electricity:

Science defining the laws of nature is like politics defining the truth.

In his 1986 book entitled, *The Hidden Power*, Brian Inglis presents the most comprehensively researched material on virtually all aspects of paranormal phenomena. This volume, I feel, is the very best compilation of systematically examined cases of psychical activity there is. The rigorously scrutinised and documented evidence demonstrates the existence of psychical energy which is outside the realm of the physical or materialistic explanations of modern science. This book along with his other writings should be required reading especially for science students. The works of Inglis are full of common sense and balanced investigations and analyses. He shows time and time again that:

Many assumptions of modern science are wrong, but experts continue to act as if they are right.

Another paranormal or psi experience happened to me when I was working in London in the 1960s. I shared a flat with an old school friend of mine, Nobby Clarke. We met two young ladies who lived with two old aunts of one of the girls. Sometimes we were invited to Sunday lunch which was always delicious as the ladies were wonderful cooks. Everyone called the two old ladies Auntie Mo and Auntie Fran. I learned from one of the girls that Auntie Fran was a keen spiritualist and attended the Spirit Church on Sunday evenings. Being curious, but sceptical about all things religious never mind with the added draw-back of having the term 'spiritualist' tagged on, we asked Auntie Fran about her beliefs. She spoke of God, Jesus Christ, astral planes, healing and contacting spirits of those who had passed on beyond our physical existence and world. Many Christians shied away from people who spoke of the spirit world in this fashion even when God and Jesus Christ were central to the beliefs of the Spirit Church:

> **Differences between religious denominations have made
> for unholy conflicts throughout history.**

Since we had asked Auntie Fran about her religion she suggested we join her one Sunday at the Spirit Church to have first-hand experience of it. On the Saturday before we were to accompany Auntie Fran to the church, Nobby got injured playing soccer and could not come. On the way to church, I asked Auntie Fran what form the service would take. She told me it was like a normal service with the exception that if I wanted to contact someone in the spirit world I had to hand in some personal object such as a signet ring or watch. Psychometry is concerned with ascertaining facts about someone by touching an inanimate object closely associated with that person. Years later I learned much research had been done in the field of psychometry. Many respected and reliable people including reputable scientists testified to the existence of psychometric ability even though they could not explain it. The person who was conducting the service I was attending that evening was to make connections between the owner of the personal object (like a ring or watch) and someone from the spirit world. This was achieved by feeling the person's spirit or life-force and its associations in the personal object such as ring or watch. All hocus pocus I thought inwardly, but handed in my wrist-watch as we went in secretly fascinated by what some stranger could possibly say that was relevant merely by holding my watch. The leader of the service that evening had a name that sounded something like Budepair. Towards the end of the service he began to pick up the personal objects left by people who wanted a 'reading' and told them such things as, 'You lost someone recently and that person wants you to know . . .' I scoffed under my breath and thought the messages Budepair was giving could apply to almost anyone. However, some people did seem to receive some more specific information with which they identified and seemed highly satisfied. I rationalised this more specific information by thinking, 'All these people know a lot about one another so the information should be pretty common knowledge and hence, accurate.' Being a died-in-the-wool student of a mechanical universe made of real touchable matter, I murmured to myself, 'What a lot of twaddle this spirit nonsense is':

Rationalism and science have produced many closed minds.

Budepair came to the watch I had handed in and held it in his fingers for a few seconds whilst gently savouring its touch and said, 'The spirit watching over you today is a man who died three years ago and he is a man of great wit and humour. He says not long before he passed over you and he were sitting by a river and he teased you by saying your language was getting so expert that he would soon need an interpreter to understand you.' This rather shook me and took a little wind out of my sails. How did he know about a private conversation I had with my father when no one else was there? Had I told Auntie Fran or the two girls who lived with her? I had not and I felt guilty of thinking the old lady would be involved in any kind of deception just to impress me. If there was any lady who was worthy of trust, it was Auntie Fran. Although she was a lady of integrity, I had put her belief in spirits down to her great desire for there to be a life after death. After all, if some people had sufficient faith in something, their actual physical perceptions and sensations could modify themselves to fit the beliefs. I felt really expert that I could rationalise Auntie Fran's behaviour in such a plausible way. However, a common wisdom warns us:

Self-praise is not the best recommendation.

However, my explanation of Auntie Fran's non-scientific beliefs did not account for how this man I and Auntie Fran had never met before (he was a visiting speaker) could repeat word for word a statement my father had made to me in private. How did he know my father and I were by a river? It was not a place we had been before. How did he know my father was so popular with everyone? Budepair told me this also. Even children used to come knocking on our door when my father was over forty years old asking my mother if my father was coming out to 'play'. Budepair also told me I would be moving north to take up a particular new job by Easter. It was now February and on the way home I took great delight in telling Auntie Fran that his prediction about having a new job by Easter could not possibly be true and I listed several reasons why. Auntie Fran merely said, 'Well no one is right all the time, but we'll have to wait and see.' To cut a long story short, my mother became ill and so I moved closer to where she lived. I got the job at Easter as predicted in spite of 200 highly qualified people applying. Even with this experience, I still took the line that although I could not explain things scientifically, I was missing some piece of information somewhere and once I identified that all things would fall into their rational and scientific place. Amongst other things, this was a case of:

> You can lead a horse to water, but you can't make him drink.

Like any true scientist worth his salt, I suspected some kind of trickery on the part of Budepair. Even his name sounded like a show business one. He was merely an entertainer with church people as a relatively captive audience. Perhaps the most famous spiritualist in England was Harry Edwards who performed religious healing through the Spirit Church. He died in 1976 over eighty years old with a high reputation for having been instrumental in healing all kinds of illness including cancer. The scientific and medical communities used all kinds of rationalisations to avoid giving credit to Harry Edwards and spirit healing. The expert explanations included denying the patients had cancer in the first place to saying it was the medical treatment that the patients had received much earlier that was having a delayed action effect. Basically scientists would accept any kind of materialistic explanation but rejected anything concerned with spirit. The common sense law of opposites says that:

> Spirit and its opposite material give existence and meaning to one another.

The next personal brush I had with the paranormal was in my house in the north of England. It had four bedrooms with two of them in an attic that had beams and sloping ceilings. I enjoyed a change of bedroom occasionally and chose to sleep in one of the attic rooms on this particular evening. It was warm and quite light as I had decided to go to bed early. I climbed into bed under the covers and lay on my back. No sooner had I got into bed than I began to rise slowly in this prone position up toward the ceiling. I could not believe it and was terrified and said out loud, 'This is no dream.' One side of the covers was trapped between the bed and the wall as well as being tucked under the mattress on that side so as I moved skyward in this horizontal body mode the sheet was sliding off me on the non-wall side. My terror increased to screaming pitch but I remained silent except for the pounding of my heart and I wondered, 'Am I dying?' Is this the way people die by floating upward? Would I actually go through the ceiling and up into the sky? How could I possibly die here and now? I was young and fit:

> Man may know better where and when he is born, than where and when he shall die.

My body did not feel ethereal or light as you would imagine a spirit-like form should be if it were bound for another world. I was solid, physical and alive; I was sure I was not dead yet. My body felt as if I was going to take some ceiling and roof tiles with me on my journey to the sky. As I rose steadily and relentlessly upwards the sheet was slipping off my body altogether. I gripped the sheet and prayed that it would stay tightly jammed between the bed mattress and the wall so I could use it as an anchor to halt my progress to the ceiling. I felt that if the sheet pulled out from its wedged position, my connection with this world could be over. Here I was suspended in the lying posture two feet or more above my own bed clinging on to a sheet to prevent me rising higher. Fortunately the sheet held and after what seemed an eternity I came to a very gradual halt. My ascent had been stopped, but would it begin again I wondered. With great anxiety, I used the sheet to pull on ever-so-gently in the hope that it would not break free and I could tug my way back on to the bed. Whilst doing this it crossed my mind that this could be an out-of-body experience so I looked down on to the bed. There was no me on the bed. This was my twelve-stone body rising. This was levitation:

Levitation has a long history in ancient and modern cultures.

Very carefully and holding my breath, I continued to pull on the anchored part of the sheet a fraction of an inch at a time. Whenever I felt the sheet come a little loose from its attachment to the bed, I would pause and plead it would not come free altogether. After numerous stops and starts with the tuggings my body was eventually back down on the bed. As soon as it was I could not get out of the bed or room fast enough and shot downstairs two floors below. Here I sat on the edge of an armchair and said, over and over again 'I cannot believe it.' Levitation, of course, has both an ancient and modern history in all kinds of civilisations. Though levitation has been witnessed down the ages by paupers, princes and popes as well as scientists, sceptics and scoundrels, it had not been witnessed by me, never mind me as the one levitating. This act of levitation, if that is what it was, certainly was not consciously willed by me. Rising into the air like that should not happen to a scientist or anyone else; it defies the law of gravity:

Levitation is the opposite of gravitation.

Paradoxically, though I was a rationalist at the time, I did not reason as rationalists would that my levitation was in my dreams and that I must have fallen asleep for a while. I was convinced that it was not a dream and that I was wide awake on my ascent toward the ceiling. Dreaming is another type of consciousness where the laws of physics can be defied or suspended. In dreams we can levitate, travel back and forth in time and space, fly and meet and talk with people long since dead in our scientific reality or world. I stress it is the laws of physics and science that are suspended in dreams, not the laws of nature, because dreaming is a part of nature. Everybody does it:

Dreaming is a common sensing of a non-scientific reality.

Various aspects of dreaming are dealt with by Lyall Watson in his fascinating book *Lifetide*. This volume together with some of his other works such as *Supernature* and *Gifts Of Things Unknown* cover a whole host of paranormal happenings and is compulsive and wonderful reading. This multi-talented man writes with great skill and authority on philosophy, mysticism, science – including biology and anthropology – as well as many other subjects. Indeed, he is a holistic investigator and thinker who readily re-integrates what experts such as scientists have unwisely split asunder. Some of Lyall Watson's personal experiences of the paranormal are staggering. In the opening pages of *Lifetide* he tells of a small girl he saw turn a tennis-ball inside out by stroking it. The ball retained air pressure and would still bounce. Lyall Watson says of this paranormal event, 'It still disturbs me. I know enough of physics to appreciate that you cannot turn an unbroken sphere inside out like a glove. Not in this reality.' This is an example of a common saying which is true if you accept there are numerous kinds of reality. One form of the common statement is:

Few things are impossible.

One of the realities that has been around since time immemorial is having glimpses into the future. Ancient writings and traditional folk tales in all cultures bear testimony to this ability. Perhaps one of the best known figures to have visions of what would come to pass is Joan of Arc. A more up-to-date example of seeing ahead in time would be people who refuse to board aircraft because they foresee a crash. Though I have heard many stories of similar premonitions, my personal experience is highly limited. However, about two years ago I had a very vague feeling that our car was going to be involved in an accident but no one was going to be hurt. The only way I can describe it is to say I had a brief flash of a picture in my mind of our blue car with a crumpled off-side front wing. There were no people in the short image I experienced. I told my wife about it. About a week later I was alone in the car and driving towards Bexhill to visit my sister and it was dark and raining. My sister who is over sixty complains that Bexhill has too many old people for her liking. She says very old people come to the seaside town to die and then forget what they came for. At some traffic lights I braked a little too late and only avoided hitting the car in front by a whisker. On returning home, I recounted the incident to my wife who suggested this was the potential accident I had referred to earlier and it had been averted. Two nights later in a dream I saw our car with a dented wing. The next morning, which was Thursday, I told my wife of the dream. On Friday my wife returned home from work in the car with a squashed offside front wing as I had described. A friend of my wife said, 'You and your damn premonitions and dreams!' Actually, I hardly ever have a premonition or recognisable predictive dream. However, as I had envisioned, no one was hurt and my wife said how kind the man whose car she had bumped had been to her:

Truth can be stranger than fiction.

A rather long-lasting involvement in the paranormal concerns having my mind or thoughts read by pet cats. What might be labelled a telepathic sense is demonstrated by our cat Willow. Like many cats she enjoys sleeping on beds. When she is asleep I may go into that bedroom several times a day for different purposes. I may enter the room to get a book, an article of clothing, a pair of shoes or to open or close a window and perhaps just to stroke Willow. Since she likes being in the house and on the bed so much, I sometimes shoo her out of the bedroom to go into the garden to get some fresh air. On these occasions when I go upstairs with the express intention of chasing her out of the house, she knows and is coming out of the bedroom at speed almost before I get to the bedroom door and scoots downstairs and into the garden. In other words:

Cats can sometimes read people's minds.

Bodie is my wife's all-time favourite cat and she seems to be his all-time favourite person. Though my wife's office is miles away from our house, the cat knows when she is setting out from work to come home. It is at this very moment that Bodie goes to sit in the bay window to wait for her. My wife has worked at several different offices which have been at different distances and journey times from our house. Also, because of the nature of her work, she sometimes leaves the office at variable times. In spite of these variations he seems to know when my wife sets out from work to come home. Even if my wife stays at a party in the office until ten o'clock at night, Bodie still senses the time she leaves to come home. One evening he went to the window at 5.40 p.m. and since it took my wife 20 minutes to get home from this particular office, I expected her at 6.00 p.m. She did not arrive until 6.40 p.m. so I remarked to my wife that Bodie was 40 minutes out that night. This turned out not to be the case as she had indeed started out from work at 5.40 p.m. when Bodie had gone to the window, but she got held up in the car park for 40 minutes. A member of staff had a problem and mentioned it to my wife as she was getting into her car and they spent 40 minutes discussing it before my wife continued on her way home:

Cat sensings reflect the laws of nature, not the laws of modern science.

Since ancient times cats have been worshipped as demi-gods and subjects of fear and witchcraft. My wife has elevated Bodie to full-god status though a vulnerable one; he has had bad hips since he was an unwanted kitten. If the weak are to inherit the earth, Bodie will have vast territories. My wife can sleep through the cries and howlings of all kinds of cats outside at night, but if Bodie as much as squeaks she hears it and awakes immediately:

Things can be out of sight and conscious mind, but present and extremely influential in the unconscious.

Though we love our cats dearly, they do not have special talents compared with other cats. Indeed, there has always been a constant flow of amazing tales about cats and other animals even in modern times. Thought-reading by animals is often claimed by pet owners when they make statements such as, 'My cat frequently knows just what I'm thinking.' So widespread are the tales of the paranormal behaviours of animals, that a few scientists are no longer dismissing the stories as nonsense. Reports of cats and other animals making long journeys to find someone in places they have never been before are matters of record. These and other feats defy rational or scientific explanation. Some cats and dogs predict that a particular person is about to telephone by going to the instrument only when that specific person is about to call. Others demonstrate they know when a loved one is coming home even after years of absence. It is not unusual for animals to sense events in advance of their occurrence. Down the centuries there have always been some people who have used behaviour of animals to predict happenings such as earthquakes, weather conditions, land fertility, illness, death and other life events. Fortunately, animals' psychic abilities are unencumbered by expert theories. Animals are more in touch with their natural common sensings or wisdoms than are we humans whose reality and behaviour are conditioned or defined in large part by our modern scientific and materialistic culture:

Animals have not read expert theories and do things that expert theories say are impossible.

To the small but growing band of scientists who take psychical or paranormal activity seriously belongs Rupert Sheldrake. He is a famous biologist and author who in 1999 published a volume entitled, *Dogs That Know When Their Owners Are Coming Home*. This title is self-explanatory but the book contains all kinds of examples of paranormal animal behaviour reported by over 1000 randomly chosen pet owners. Sheldrake suggests that influence across time and space without the transmission of any energy known to science might be accounted for by 'morphic resonance'. Basically this theory of morphic resonance proposes that species tune in to appropriate connective vibrations that guide their various structural forms, functions and behaviours. When Sheldrake first put forward his speculative theory or hypothesis in his 1981 book, *A New Science Of Life*, it was not in keeping with traditional science. That part of his work that enters the realm of the paranormal is still regarded suspiciously by the scientific establishment because it still tends to view psychical activity as so much nonsense:

> Sheldrake's theory of morphic resonance is a modern name
> for ancient and common sensings.

Sheldrake, like a few other scientists, is rediscovering ancient abilities in animals that humans have replaced with materialism, rationalism, science and technology. In other words, visionaries like Sheldrake are reinforcing the notion that we have to return to ancient and universal sensings to get a better view of the realities that modern science has denied or hidden from our view. Extra sensory perception, psychical force, spiritual energy, morphic resonance, call it what you will, there are powers that experts reject because they mock the laws of modern science. Dogs howl and become distressed when owners are injured or die even though they may be thousands of miles away. Of course humans can sense death and disaster also. There are numerous cases where some people have woken up suddenly in the night to announce that a relative has been in an accident or died even in a distant country. Their time of awakening has coincided with the moment of accident or death of the relative:

> Such extra sensory perception is extra to the normal senses
> or perceptions of sight, smell, taste, hearing and touch.

There have been many reports over the years of pets finding owners who have been injured or dead even in places the pets have never been previously. The opposite is also common where owners find injured or dead pets in unusual locations or circumstances. In my own case one instance is still referred to by my wife as 'uncanny'. Some years ago one of our female cats did not return after two days. This was very unusual and we were very worried. We searched her usual haunts and pathways calling her name to no avail. My daily routine was to walk into town to work which was about a mile away. On my next journey into town, I was drawn to a spot in an expanse of high grass by the road-side. After only a few seconds in this long grass I found the dead body of our precious cat. In essence, I had walked directly to where the cat's body was in rather a large expanse of uncut grass. Blood was congealed around her mouth. It looked as though she had been clipped by a vehicle but had managed to get to the side of the road and into the grass verge. This location was not one of her usual territories. I do not know what made me look in that particular area. It was not a part of the systematic search nor a reasoned logical choice to go to that spot:

There is more to this world than meets the eye.

A more systematic but paranormal activity to locate things that are not visible is called dowsing. People accept dowsing or water divining perhaps more than any other paranormal activity. Maybe this is because it has been highly visible in the media; it is easily demonstrated and with a little practise almost anyone can enjoy some success. Traditionally, a forked hazel twig moved in the dowsers' hands when they walked over an underground source of water. Now many things have been sought by dowsing or divining as it is sometimes known. As well as water; oil, metals, lost objects, archaeological artifacts, places of special significance with extra energies or spiritual connections such as places of worship and ritual have been dowsed. Ley lines are also of importance to dowsers as they link pathways to places revered by the ancients. With the passage of time dowsing sticks have become more varied in their material make-up. Technology has caught up with this ancient art as some use plastic divining sticks:

Dowsing has been tested empirically by some scientists and they have testified that dowsing does work.

Still some scientists do not believe in dowsing in spite of the evidence. It seems to be a case of psychic will and scientific won't. At this point I would ask your indulgence for a small diversion. It was at Christmas 2000 that I left this page and book to be finished later. It would only take a short time as I had nearly finished it. Now it is May 2003. Thus, one could say that it has taken me over three years to write this page – talk about the relativity of time and writing matter! I am prone to obeying new sense pop law such as, 'Never do today what you can put off until tomorrow'. Finding all my notes, books and files needed to complete the job has been a frustrating and unenviable task. For example, I had loaned some books and I know not to whom. I now regret, as I usually do, that I had not stuck to common sense laws the virtues of which this book is extolling such as, 'Do not put off until tomorrow what should be done today' or:

A stitch in time saves nine.

Meanwhile back to dowsing and the paranormal. I met a long lost friend a few days ago. Brian was a former schoolmaster and lately a businessman who conducts historical tours. He asked what I was up to at the present time. I told him I was writing a small section on dowsing. 'Oh, I do some dowsing and teach it a bit,' he said. The bit turned out to be a lot. Several hundreds had been trained by him over a number of years. When I asked him how he got involved in teaching dowsing, he said, 'I used to think all this ESP lark was a load of nonsense, but a while ago some of us were fooling around and I had a go for a bit of fun. It worked; I couldn't believe some piece of stick was turning in my hand and seemed to have a mind of its own.' I asked Brian, as a teacher of dowsing, what insights he had to tell me. 'Well,' he said, 'nothing special; most people can do it. Children seem especially sensitive to it perhaps because they are more open to things with less conditioning against it. I had a few clerics who were determined to show it was to fail for them. Maybe it was because divining is pre-Christian and associated with Paganism. Nevertheless they could not deny that they experienced movement of the dowsing stick just like the others and ended up being enthusiastic converts to dowsing. People have their own style of divining just as cricketers have their own batting style. 'What is the most productive type of dowsing stick?' I asked. 'None in particular, individual experimentation and choice seem to work best. I've actually used a blade of grass and it functioned OK for me.' I didn't ask him if he terminated his classes on dowsing with the comment, 'May the force be with you', for I believe, though it may be dormant:

The force is with everyone and everything.

It would be interesting to see how the female TV weather forecaster Charlie Neil would fare as a dowser. According to today's paper Charlie announced, 'I've got a feelin' in me water we're going to have a dry week.' Shortly afterwards, there were torrential downpours. Perhaps Charlie is a reverse psychic. Never mind the Midlands, think of what she could do for the Sahara. My return to this chapter on the paranormal and to dowsing, at a time of meeting a long lost friend who is a teacher of dowsing is an interesting coincidence. Some would say it is an example of synchronicity, a term favoured by experts such as Jung. Synchronicity is the coincidence of events that are not causal but are connected and share meaning. Astrology is an example of synchronicity. It signifies the connectedness of the individual to the whole and the reflection of the whole cosmos in the individual and the opposite – the individual's reflection in the cosmos. Experts regard people who believe that the moon is linked to human behaviour as lunatics. Astrologers believe not just that people are connected to the moon but to all the planets. Why on earth should not people believe they are connected to the planets? Such a belief is consistent with the ancient and common sense laws that:

The whole is reflected in the part.

Much evidence exists to show planets affect us, like the sun. Astrology has been a potent aspect of all cultures throughout history. It is about meaning, of feeling connected, of belonging to a greater whole or unity. Astrology and astronomy used to be together, then when some experts developed sophisticated measurements they regarded astrology as psuedo-science. On the dimension of association of planetary movements with people's characteristics or behaviour, astrologers can do as well or better than behavioural scientists with their personality inventories. Expert personality theorists can bear witness to this. Not that you are allowed to choose, (experts are forced upon us) but who would you prefer to believe concerning what is good for you and your lifestyle – politicians, social engineers, lawyers or astrologers?

The history of astrology exhibits far more wisdom and meaning than expert politicians, lawyers and scientists.

When a child is born it makes an imprint or impression on the cosmos just as the cosmos makes an imprint or impression on the child, but together they make the whole. The hand does not cause the rest of the body, but they are intrinsically connected. Scientists are discovering a drop of a person's blood is telling more and more about the person, which common sense law predicts. Wisdom or common sense law says the drop of blood contains everything about the whole person:

The part reflects the whole.

Similarly a drop of time contains everything about the cosmos including the child and its character. The birth moment or drop of time is of special significance as is the death moment. Some people seem to think astrology was designed to predict the personality of individuals from planetary movement. It was not. It was and is about meaning, association, identification, the wisdom of nature and unification of all things. People interested in astrology keep in regular touch with their feelings of relationship with the nature of the world, other planets and the universe as a whole:

Astrology recognises the unity of all things.

Another reason astrology is ridiculed is due to experts' view of matter. We were led to believe that matter was made up of long-lasting balls. This is true in respect of long-lasting for we have within us some atomic materials of Jesus not to mention Stalin, Hitler and Uncle Tom Cobbley and all. Experts told us that matter was solid, inanimate and tough. This is in spite of the fact that in all recorded history including present day there have been and are an inestimable number of reports to the contrary. We all have seen relatively delicate plants crack solid rocks and concrete. Sometimes so called inanimate matter acts in animate ways. To be fair some experts have questioned the criteria that define what is animate and what is inanimate. Over a hundred years ago J.C. Bose, a professor of physics, showed, as Brian Inglis points out, the similarity between so-called inanimate matter and animal tissue. We are all familiar with the term 'metal fatigue' and, according to Bose in respect of metal and animal tissue, 'fatigue could be removed by gentle massage or exposure to a bath of warm water'. Where does the inanimate end and the animate begin? Ancient wisdom and common sense law indicates that:

Life-force is to be found in every aspects of nature.

We, with our consciousness, mind or psyche, came from matter according to modern science. If this is so, then one could argue that consciousness, mind or psyches are embedded or inherent in the matter. We all know that matter of all types and sizes influences us from Stonehenge to houses, tables, chairs, cars, computers, watches, diamonds and so on. Also, we invest so-called inanimate matter with feelings, consciousness and intellect, by talking to, stroking, kissing and even thumping our cars, computers, tennis racquets and other love-objects that are given human names. We also have animate names like head of the valley and foot of the hill. One social scientist called my home town by a rude name for the human anus. Obviously, he had just passed through. The ancients believed that the spirit in matter, under certain conditions, could express itself in a variety of animated ways. All types of materials can be used for storing information and memories that can be communicated like music discs so why not stone, wood and other matter? In the grand scheme of things, it is only in relatively recent history that experts, especially modern scientist, have ridiculed the idea of matter being invested with mind, spirit or psyche:

To our ancestors modern experts might be seen as aliens.

It is not just a few people who believe that matter contains mind, life-force, spirit, psyche – call it what you will. Feeling at odds with expert scientific views in our modern society can make people embarrassed to admit it. However, even young people perhaps unconsciously, point to mind in matter. Today I went into an optician to have a screw replaced in my spectacles as an arm had come off. The young lady who mended my spectacles said, 'Those screws have a mind of their own.' Since I was writing about mind in matter this very day, was this another example of synchronicity? Lyall Watson in his 1990 book, *The Nature Of Things: The Secret Life of Inanimate Objects*, relates by his wonderful stories a whole host of objects that seem to have a will of their own. The book jacket tells us, 'Stones sing, statues move, valued possessions return to their owners, computers have bad dreams.' Lyall Watson says of computers, 'that these odd instruments have "periods" tending to misbehave more often when the moon is full or the sun unusually active'. His books are a mesmeric reading experience and Lyall Watson's independence of thought reminds me of what Aristophanes said:

> Wise men, though all laws were abolished, would lead
> the same lives.

Since science sees the universe as a great machine and mind coming from matter, God could be a machine. Lyall Watson hints at such a possibility. What we do know is that machines which were meant to serve us are now our masters. We are increasingly becoming slaves to the demands of machines. A growing number of people no longer see much of nature let alone appreciate it as we make gods and high priests of high tech. modern machines. Tony Blair's mantra is, 'Modernise, modernise, modernise'. Since wisdom and common sense laws can't be bettered by being modernised, one assumes he means technology. As he has already indicated, he would like to see every pupil in school computered. All this leads me to believe that God is The Divine Machine for Tony worships computers but obviously not common sense laws associated with a wise god. Some would say as he is so keen to have computers for every child in school, when youngsters already spend a dangerous amount of time in front of screens, that Tony is a nincomputer. I gleaned the term nincomputer from a Lyall Watson Book:

> Imitation is a good form of praise.

The paranormal used to belong to religions and ancient gods. In Christianity miracles such as the feeding of the five thousand on five loaves and three fishes, changing water into wine, parting the Red Sea to allow people to cross and Jesus rising from the dead are examples. Priests of religions defined a lot of what reality was supposed to be. They still do, along with new priests of materialism and pop gods whether they be of a scientific bent, a musical bent, a political bent or just bent. Even Christians extol the virtues of materialism over spirituality. Is it because science, especially some of its celebrity vendors, pooh pooh its paranormality? Tony Blair, a church-goer and one assumes a believer in God, stresses a god of materialism over the God associated with spirituality, morality and goodness. One typical example is in 2000 when he said, 'What's important is that we get back to fundamental issues – an economy that's stronger than for decades and investment in public services.' The fundamental issue for society is not strengthening a separated matter or materialism from mind, morality and spirituality. Just the opposite is required.

Following the lead of science of splitting things up, politicians separate private lives from their public duties. They have changed a former pop law, 'It's alright to be immoral so long as you don't get caught' into a stronger new sense pop law:

Being immoral and boasting of it or denying it publicly, both bring celebrity status and success.

Some of the recent work in physics has rediscovered more of ancient wisdom and common sense law which says that mind and matter are one. Private and public life cannot be separated. Science has changed its mind about matter. Matter used to mean material, chunks of hard bumpables and ball-like atoms. Now matter is clouds of probability – puffs of mathematics more nebulous than some images of spirit or ghosts. Dr Roger Jones in his 1983 book, *Physics As Metaphor*, does a wonderful job in illustrating the foolhardiness of the modern science of separating mind and matter. Jones says, 'Mind and matter are not separate and distinct, but form an organic whole, in my view.' This is a reiteration of an ancient wisdom as Jones appreciates. To the modern scientised minds this is paranormal. Reading Roger Jones' book on physics seems, to our over-rationalised minds like science fiction, which of course is paranormal to modern scientists but which anticipates many of the so-called discoveries of science. One ancient wisdom and common sense law which again predicts what science is slowly learning about matter or material is:

All things are relative and that includes matter.

One joke, that not only illustrates the relativity of matter or materialism but also the relativity of time, is as follows:

Man praying:	God, what's a billion billion years to you?
God:	A second.
Man:	What is a billion billion Euros to you?
God:	We don't do Euros in heaven.
Man:	Oh, what is a billion billion pounds to you?

God:	A penny.
Man:	Dear God could you give me a penny?
God:	Just a second.

The scientific theory of evolution for a time became as paranormal to religion as religion became paranormal to evolution scientists. Some aspects of science like gravity had enough gravity not to upset religion. To the ordinary person the scientific theory of evolution that we came from gas, rocky matter and slime was more paranormal than a divine spirit, like God, creating everything. The notion that evolution was down to chance or randomness neglects the influence played by the psyche and also runs counter to common sense law of opposites:

Chaos gives existence and meaning to order, just as order gives existence and meaning to chaos.

A consequence of this common sense law, which modern science has largely ignored, is that ordinary people's experience of chance can be the opposite of expert theories. Whereas physicists and mathematicians believe that shuffling a pack of cards increases chance, workers at gambling establishments say the reverse. That is, shuffling the cards decreases chance. Arnold in his most fascinating book of 1992 entitled, *The Corrupted Sciences: Challenging The Myths Of Modern Science*, highlights the issue. This brings to mind another common sense law:

There is no substitute for experience.

Einstein said 'God does not play dice.' This is against the common sense laws of opposites. Cause and order are the basis of science so the notion of chance or randomness does not sit well with its experts. The Christian God had to use opposites to show his existence and purpose. Good and evil, God and Satan, heaven and hell, chaos and order and light and darkness are illustrative of such opposites. My own concern is about some popular notions of the nature of God who might be described as the ultimate paranormal phenomenon. What kind of God is it who creates man in his own image and then demands to be worshipped everyday and for all time by the beings he created? There is a huge element of reality in this even though I do not like it. Pop stars, be they musical, political or any kind, want to be worshipped just like God. As more and more people desire to be famous and worshipped in our obsessive celebrity culture, God has certainly created man in this aspect of his own image. Though I say 'man' we must include Madonna (not just because she has a significant religious name like Madge) and any other female wannabe celebrities. Science has found a selfish gene. Do we have a wannabe or celebrity gene? It seems for God, pop stars, poltergeists, children, youths and their grandmas:

Fame is the spur.

Fame used to be associated with honour, bravery and goodness generally. Jesus was all of these and could be the most famous person of all time notwithstanding John Lennon's comment. Jesus practised what he preached, especially the Ten Commandments passed down to man from a supernatural God of miracles – his father. Incidentally, the Ten Commandments are common sense laws that seemed to be around before the Christian story was told. New sense pop laws, which the Church of England appears to be adopting, state the reverse of the Ten Commandments. Stealing is rationalised to a new sense or meaning. It's OK; your drug addiction was responsible, not you – or stealing is an alternative mode of shopping and there are worse things than thieving. John Lennon was better known for breaking religious commandments and practising new sense pop laws. He was more associated with infamy, unlike Jesus. The line uttered by the funnyman, Kenneth Williams is becoming more prophetic for celebrities like John Lennon. Williams said in *Carry on Cleo*, 'Infamy, infamy, They've all got it in for me,' which is another example of a common sense law:

Many a true word spoken in jest.

It can be argued that science and religion see humans as programmable machines and therefore not really responsible for their actions. The increasing acceptance of new sense pop laws by the Church of England and the judicial system is prompting some to seek spirituality elsewhere. John Lennon did this. He went to India with the rest of the Beatles. More and more people in the Western World are turning to Eastern religions because of the decadence of the West and Christianity. Islam, Hinduism and

Buddhism are spreading because, to some people, these religions hold to an important common sense law far more rigorously than does Christianity of the Western World. That law is:

Practise what you preach.

Another thing that perturbs me about Christianity is the portrayal of Jesus. Though he is a wonderful example of goodness and I would love such a being to be my personal saviour, a central belief-pillar of Christianity is very shaky. Jesus, according to Christians, made the ultimate sacrifice to save us all by being crucified and dying on the cross. Thus, he and his father are worthy of worship and of faith in their existence. We all know of a lot of people throughout history who have made greater sacrifices than Jesus. Some people have sacrificed their life in an even more horrific death than crucifixion. Of these, some were non-believers and so did not have their terrible sacrifice cushioned by the thought of eternal life and treasures in heaven. These poor mortals did not expect to sit on the right hand of the king of all creation as did Jesus. Such acts of sacrifice are praised by all religions and gods. We all know that man is capable of acts of supreme goodness and evil. It was the degree to which Jesus overcame temptation and exhibited so much goodness that make him supernatural and deservedly God-like and worthy of worship. All of us do acts of goodness including sacrifice, but not to the same degree as Jesus and other supernatural God figures:

An individual's act of goodness such as sacrifice, adds to the collective spirituality.

My own beliefs about God are, like those of many other people, constantly pricking my consciousness – but ragged. I want some aspect of Christianity to be true and my admiration of the figure of Jesus Christ is huge. The thought of eternal life, even if it were in an eternal bloom of youth, is not my cup of tea. It reminds me of a medical doctor friend of mine who tried time and time again without success to persuade a 97-year-old lady to have a hearing aid. Finally in desperation he asked her why the hell she was so against a hearing aid. She replied, 'Look young man, I'm 97 and I reckon I've heard enough.' For me being eternally happy sounds like a new sense slogan and political sound-bite that goes against the common sense law of opposites. How could you know what happiness was without knowing sadness? Death to some is a relief from politicians and lawyers:

God had to invent death so we'd know what life was.

Good is a synonym for God and I admire or worship goodness. Consequently, I believe in choosing kindness over cruelty, peace over violence, cleanliness over pollution, good manners over bad and so on and so forth. Basically, common sense laws are what I aim for, especially 'Do unto others'. Aiming is one thing, scoring enough is another. I pray too for people who suffer infirmity, illness, violence and any kind of trouble or being at odds with the world. I say things like:

Please help her god.
In the name of goodness let him get well.
Mother earth, please make him whole.
Let the positive energies of the universe be with her.
Good spirits of the cosmos enter their being.

These saying are not very awe-inspiring or supernatural, though they may be paranormal or weird to some scientists. However, it appears the vast majority of people use similar prayers or incantations. Our psychic, moral or spiritual life is far more important than our scientific life even to those who do not claim to be religious and extol science. Yes, and like most of the rest of you, as well as talking to animals and plants I talk to matter. I sometimes wash and clean my razor whilst stroking and talking to it by praising its performance. In this way the razor can retain its good cutting power longer. I subscribe to the ancient wisdom that in reality:

Mind and matter are two sides of the same coin.

Actually, a few physicists, particularly those at the 'cutting edge', would no longer find it so peculiar or paranormal for someone to talk to a razor. Indeed, I have suggested many scientists who ridicule such talk do it themselves. Stranger things are happening in the new physics. As indicated earlier, ancients used to pray and talk to objects as well as to animals and other people. Connection to everything is deep within the psyche and the opposite has essence: the psyche is deep within connectivity. Evolution is a web of connections. Thus:

Psyche or psi influenced evolution.

Religious people were amongst the early scientists. Newton is one example. Some present day scientists believe in God and some don't. Francis Collins of the human genome project says, 'I'm a geneticist, yet I believe in God.' Richard Dawkins on the other hand thinks those who believe in religion and a creator, God are 'scientifically illiterate' and views religion as a virus. Science and religion fulfil the prediction of various common sense laws such as:

All aspects of life have their ups and downs.

Religion and science were together when science first came on the scene. Then, with the advance of science and its materialism, spiritual life tended to be suppressed, especially Christianity, as science predominated in the West. Next, religion accommodated evolution as God's plan. Since this uneasy tolerance, Christianity has generally lost much spiritual ground to the materialism of science and commercialism which are more fashionable Gods. Now there seems to be a greater search for spirituality by some people. Also, perhaps because of the excessive use of technology, science and religion are being discussed more fervently as new technological creation takes us closer to its opposite – destruction. Professor Paul Davies, a theoretical physicist wrote a book in 1983 with a very interesting title, namely, *God And The New Physics*. He believes the only way to understand the world is through a holistic or multi-disciplinary approach including a consideration of good and evil. Paul Davies claims 'that science offers a surer path than religion in the search of God'. Paradoxically, his book contains much common sense but he believes that quantum physics 'turns common sense on its head'. The reality is quantum physics has rediscovered some common sense laws. It is the earlier thinking in modern science that has been turned on its head, not common sense. Quite the reverse is the case:

Science is rediscovering common sense laws.

The paranormal is a term used by experts particularly scientists to describe something they cannot explain. Another way of naming the paranormal is extra sensory perception (ESP). Again it is experts who have defined what are normal senses and what are extra to the normal ones. The five senses acceptable to expert scientists are, seeing, hearing, smelling, tasting and touching. Of course seeing is a very important sense in science as observation is central to its purpose. Scientist have far too narrow a view of seeing. Science does not readily appreciate that when a man sees a pretty girl every part of his body, mind and spirit are involved. This includes his conscious and unconscious, the collective conscious, collective unconscious, the environment and the cosmos – everything. Science is only starting to acknowledge the ancient and common sense law that:

Everything is connected to everything else.

Perhaps ESP should be more accurately called extra scientific sensing. Until experts ruled out a sixth sense or any other additional senses other than the scientifically acceptable five, people regarded them as normal. Some people still do and these ancient sensings are widespread. They are common sensings. However, they have been hidden or in decline because of lack of use. People also have been afraid to admit to such beliefs because we have been conditioned to think only oddballs are involved with such psychic sensing. In addition, there has been less need to communicate telepathically in modern cultures as technologies like the telephone have diminished the necessity for ancient connective sensing, though not the need to express it:

**Psychic sensings such as telepathy are common sensings
that have been suppressed by politics, science and religion.**

Paranormal is often defined as phenomena beyond the scope of normal scientific understanding. Normal dreams can suspend the laws of physics and science's interpretation of its central concepts – space, time, matter and measurement. It is another universe. Tony Blair and New Labour have suspended the laws of common sense. Blairland is also another universe. New sense pop laws define our modern reality. What words and meanings come to mind when we think of what Tony Blair is doing to democracy, justice and public services? Normal, paranormal, abnormal patho-normal, psycho-crony; your meanings will be as good or better than mine. One term that we are hearing more and more about New Labour and politicians at large is, 'Unbelievable' and they are not talking about ESP or paranormal here:

Much of what expert scientists, politicians and lawyers call
paranormal or extra sensory perception is common sensing.

In conclusion then, there is and has been for many years overwhelming evidence for the existence of psi. No right-minded, nor indeed left-minded person would disagree with that. What better testimony than from science whose laws the paranormal break? Well, yes, your own experience, that of relatives, friends, strangers, pets, your plants, house and Uncle Tom, cobbles and all. However, some world-renowned scientists are happy to confirm the existence of psi. Many other scientists, when pressed, will acknowledge its presence though they are reticent to admit it because science cannot explain it. It defies the laws of science. We have cars, computers and other 'inanimate' objects and machines about which we all insist at times; 'are kissable', 'have a mind of their own', 'play up', 'are bloody minded or evil' and such like. Are these types of statement an unconscious admission that all of us deep down know mind is in matter and everywhere? Mind, no matter what, I cannot see how the paranormal can be outside of common sense laws such as:

There are advantages and disadvantages to everything
including psi or the paranormal as well as mind or machines.

CHAPTER 12

Summary and Conclusion

There is no substitute for common sense
Ancient and Common Wisdom

The accelerated moral decline of the Western World since the 1950s concerns laws and is most observable in Britain and America where I have lived. Laws shape society and society shapes laws. The purpose of this essay was to compare ancient and common sense laws with expert and modern laws. That a college lecturer should claim, and get, tens of thousands of pounds for being called an 'Irish prat' whilst war veterans or their widows are often made to live in abject poverty is illustrative. This single example not only shows the lecturer was indeed a right or rights' prat, but also highlights the dire state of politics, the law, family, education, work, tax, pensions, the military, culture, race relations and so forth, including health. If you are not stressed and sickened, like the war veterans and their families, by the unfairness of the compensation culture, you are an exception. Our society is out of balance. It is one of excesses and is getting more and more out of control. The college lecturer-war veteran comparison demonstrates that institutions and people are connected. You may not like being linked to Hitler, but you are. One important ancient wisdom or common sense law is:

All things are related.

The compensation culture is only one of the many monsters modern political law-makers and their allies have created. British confidence is low. One strategy that Osama Bin Laden and Al Qaeda could use to lower the morale of Britain even further would be to help keep a government like that of, say, Tony Blair, in power. Such a government saps the essence of its people on a daily basis. It sometimes seems that Hitler, for all his efforts, did not depress the bodies, minds and spirits of the British people as much as modern politics. It could be any major political party in power. They all subscribe to political correctness and the abolition of wisdom and common sense. In November 2004, when the USA said it would not accept the

315

'rigged' elections in the Ukraine, Mahood the cartoonist has a worried-looking Tony Blair lying in bed with his wife saying, 'I hate to admit it, Cherie, but I slept better when John Major was PM.' Another common wisdom or common sense law is:

Many a true word is spoken in jest.

Tony Blair boasts he has no reverse gear which does nothing to dispel the growing belief that he is unwise and dangerous. It is understandable, to a degree, why the Prime Minister claims to have no reverse gear. With Peter Mandelson behind his every move, Blair may be more careful than we give him credit for and might explain his surprise fatherhood. Isn't Blair's state of being married to a woman rather than to both a man and a woman an act of discrimination – both sexual and against single parents – not to mention possible offence given to minority races, religions and other alternate families or lifestyles? Is it inclusive and does it celebrate diversity enough like one of his party's mantras advises? Because the negative aspects of the concept of discrimination receive all the publicity, we must not forget its positive side. Discrimination is involved in almost all we do such as learning, choosing and valuing. Racial hatred is often initiated or sustained by expert theories, laws and race-relations bodies that are busy:

**The idea that some races are superior is an experts' myth;
It is refuted by history, experience and common sense laws.**

Tony Blair's promise of a 'whiter than white' New Labour Government (seems to be some racial undertone here) is delivered. Have the British people ever been subject to such sustained whitewash? I was going to say Campbell, Hutton, and Butler spring to mind, but this would be unfair; there are so many spin-stars in this whitewash machine. Blair's government has not 'reduced crime and the causes of crime'; it has increased them. Our freedoms are being persistently eroded. All our worthwhile institutions and traditions are being destroyed or threatened as are the natural and built habitat. Political planners and architects have created too much ugliness. Expert planning laws are not usually quotable but this one might be, 'There shall be no unauthorised erections on The Village Common.' Blair's government is guilty of numerous grave offences. An ex-peace marcher, trust-me-Tone has taken us to war five times in seven years and we are still counting. The Prime Minister is making the nightmares portrayed in George Orwell's novel *Nineteen Eighty-Four* come true:

> **Big Brother, The Thought Police, New Speak and Double Think are with us in Blair's Britain and are New Labour's main legacy.**

Prime Ministers, along with politicians in general, lawyers and other so-called experts in human behaviour professions, have abandoned wisdom or common sense. They do not want to be common. Common is as common as muck or dirt. Experts want to be different, special, uncommon or unique. They do not accept ancient and common wisdoms. Experts think they can produce better laws than common sense laws. The constant generation of great wads of expert legal laws shows this is the case. The motto of political law-makers seems to be, 'Never mind the quality or the consequences of laws, look at the infinite quantity.' The common sense law that follows has never been in such need of being paid attention to as it does today:

> **More laws less justice.**

Common sense laws are regarded by many experts to be mere platitudes chanted by the ill-informed masses. There is nothing trite about them. Common sense laws are more reliable, objective, valid and useful than expert laws. And so they should be, because common sense laws are the results of millions of years of observation, experience and experimentation by millions and millions of people. Not only do they contain knowledge and scientific laws, but also aesthetic and moral laws which give guidance to behaviours that are necessary ingredients to a meaningful life and a worthwhile, qualitative society. A few scientists are beginning to admit that the most advanced theories and laws, like relativity and quantum physics, are embedded in everyday language or common sense and have been for thousands of years. Indeed, there is more and more evidence to indicate that discoveries in science are really rediscoveries of ancient wisdoms or common sense laws. Everyone knows relativity theory even though experts have conditioned us to believe only they are party to this so-called esoteric knowledge. Hence, members of the general public may not realise they know relativity theory or its laws, one of which nearly everyone states regularly:

All things are relative.

Incidentally, scientists in their aim to explain and predict things have been less successful in their predictions than science fiction writers and children's comics. Scientists abandoned wisdom and common sense long ago. modern scientists claim science is unable to deal with value-judgements concerning what is good or bad or right or wrong. Thus, the argument goes, science cannot have anything to say about wisdom or common sense – which is most certainly about value-judgements or morality. Actually, scientists' insistence that science is devoid of value-judgements is an illusion. The life-history of the scientist affects his observations. What the scientist chooses to observe, where he chooses to observe it from as well as why, when, with whom, how and with which instruments, are all personal selections and are value-judgements. It is interesting to note that the instruments of science reflect or exemplify the actual laws they are designed to investigate. Technology is science in action or is it vice-versa or both? How many technologies are used to destructive excess such as; cars to gridlock; TVs to couch potatoes and rubbish; computers to obsession-depression; mobile phones to verbal mugging and so on? One ancient and common wisdom with which great scientists such as Newton would no doubt agree is as follows:

**Knowledge, science and technology without wisdom
are dangerous.**

Scientists, along with other minority groups, wield too much power for the good of democracy. True democracy is about common agreement and all the people sharing power and these characterise common wisdoms and common sense laws but not the laws of so-called experts in an elite minority. Too often governments are voted in by a small section of the whole population and, hence, do not represent the vast majority of the people. For politicians to seek such a great amount of power for such a long period of time shows they are psychologically unbalanced. If you think this is an exaggeration, select some political leaders at random and identify those who do not exhibit some kind of psychopathology. Even those who set off with good intentions become contaminated after a time:

Power corrupts and the corrupt seek power.

My suggestion for a true democracy is for local people (not central party political offices) to select their representative, perhaps at random, who will be in office for six months only. Then another representative will be elected and so on. Representatives would be expected to use common sense laws. In this way many people would get to be a political representative whereby a true democracy evolves by people being more directly involved and meaningfully sharing power. Most important to a true democracy is the participation of all the people in the justice system. My proposal is to have groups selected at random as in juries, who would not only decide upon innocence or guilt but on any punishment also. Again they would use common sense laws that are known to almost everyone. Judges and professional lawyers would be dispensed with along with their galaxy of 'expert' laws and the group selected at random from the citizenry would do all the questioning in the courts. Justice is about morality or wisdom and there is no evidence of any kind now or throughout history to suggest that judges or other lawyers are any more moral or wise than other members of the population selected at random. We must take the law back into our own hands. The universal expansion of lawyers and laws is proportional to their greed, fees and pensions. Expert legal processes are interminable, obscenely expensive and unjust. One expert suggests that no matter where we are, there is a rat within ten yards. I reckon with lawyers, it is five yards:

Political law-makers and lawyers separate the legal and the moral, common sense laws have a holistic history.

It is difficult to find much that governments do that is not against the will and common sense quotient of the vast majority of people. Vandalising industries such as the railways, fishing and agriculture is an example. Taking the police off the streets to make them bureaucratic paper-chasers rather than criminal-chasers is another. Because of expert laws and theories, police cannot catch criminals as in the past. An unspoken but much-practised strategy is, 'If you can't catch criminals, criminalise those you can catch'. Formerly, before we surrendered our justice system and sovereignty to political correctness and the corrupt incompetents in Brussels, we recognised a hero. It was someone who would defend person and property with vigour against criminals and the criminals would go to gaol. We have reversed this such that too often the person who tackles the criminal ends up in gaol. Swaggering foul-mouthed louts, some less than five years old, laugh at expert laws and terrorise people everywhere, even in their homes. Now let us focus briefly the NHS. What about the replacement of matrons, nurses, doctors, dentists, basic cleanliness and beds with managers, other superbugs, targets, waiting lists, queues, dirty instruments, dirtier lawsuits and even dirtier lawyers and statisticians. Government NHS targets have caused creative counting, patient pain and death. In other contexts I could mention foot and mouth, the Dome, school playing fields as scrumptious building sites, but experts balance plummeting standards in our institutions with a rising self-aggrandisement:

Self praise is no good recommendation.

I am sure the readers have their own special horror stories of things done against their will. For me, the most important is the ban on common sense for it is the main cause of any other acts of folly. Are not the powers that be planning to outlaw common sense on the grounds that it can upset minority groups because it is not diverse enough? Such is the inclusivism and equality of modern governments. Innumerable things done against our will are concerned with punishment not fitting the crimes and rewards not fitting the deeds. Common sense is not the false image of illusory achievement too often spun by experts. It is the most meaningful substance in life. Its suppression or ban is substance abuse of the worst kind:

Our problem is not civil disobedience, it is civil obedience for we accept far too much expert folly.

A growing number of people from all walks of life describe us as a sick (I nearly wrote sucker) society. Sick here can mean loutish behaviour, not just self-selected, but boasted about and also medical illness such as measles. Britain is a leader in the infliction of disease and wounds on the psychological and physical health of self and others. Scientists have split things into smaller and smaller parts and this is evidenced by the selfish gene and the number of specialisms in medicine, other disciplines, professions and most jobs. Yobs love the selfish gene. They can say, 'I can't help it mate, it's in me genes; it's science innit?' This is how toffs speak as it is, like, the 'now', 'must-have' fashion to do so, know what I mean? They are known as toffers or some such name. Like most technology, genetic engineering will be flogged to death or to eternal life. This is not something to look forward to as politicians will come first – as in most things like pensions. Imagine one immortal Tony Blair let alone clones of Tone as well. Unlike the obsession of science with separating things, common sense deals with the whole as well as the parts. One well known common wisdom is:

The whole is greater than the sum of the parts.

According to common sense laws, opposites give existence and meaning to much of our reality. Examples are love-hate, modest-boastful, division-multiplication and so on including in medical science – health and disease. In a society where the acceptance of individual responsibility has been modernised by experts to being a foregone illusion, the selfish gene is a godsend if you believe in the god – science. Richard Dawkins is most famously associated with the selfish gene. He is a wonderful writer (I wish I was a fraction as good) and talks much common sense. However, according to the common sense law of opposites, if there is a selfish gene, there is also an unselfish gene. We should not blame genes too readily for our actions for, in evolution, it is the environment that shapes our genes. In keeping with common sense law, the opposite is also true, our genes help shape our environment. Just as some health problems are of our own making, much of our healing is down to us because the very nature of our bodies, minds and spirits is geared to self-healing. Doctors can aid or hinder this natural healing process. We can, by will-power, overcome the potential of some genes. Even experts can agree with this, including Desmond Morris. For example, experience tells us that many fat people can lose weight by the will-power to eat less. Doctors, dedicated though they may be, cannot always live up to the superman image their own profession helped history bestow upon them. When we are told it's a virus it can mean the doctor doesn't know what it is. Doctors are trained to treat symptoms rather than causes and prescribe substances which can do more harm than good. Speaking of doing more harm than good, psychiatrists and other assorted counsellors like social workers are often in greater need of help then their clients. People you meet at the bus stop will talk more common sense about your problems than some psychobabblers. Therapy works to the degree it uses common sense:

Physician or psychobabbler, heal thyself.

Much ill-health and violence is due to overcrowding and we have too many people in Britain. Nature tends to balance itself and is doing so in thinning down the citizenry. AIDS, sexual diseases causing infertility, superbugs, the human form of mad cow disease, war, murder, pollution, the regeneration of TB and malaria, as well as technology (including biological agents whereby one person can wipe out increasingly huge swathes of population – not unlike missionaries of old) are some examples of nature's remedies to overcrowding. Upset the balance of nature and you have to live with the consequences:

You can have too much of a bad or good thing.

Gradually some practices from ancient wisdoms and common sensings are entering the medical arena. Rather than treating parts of a patient, the whole person is being focused more. We have holistic, alternative, complementary associations and practitioners embracing such areas as yoga, homeopathy, osteopathy, acupuncture, chiropractic and numerous other healing systems. Integrating practices from ancient wisdoms with biomedical science is a common sense thing to do. Because holistic practitioners' skills are based on ancient wisdoms does not mean that all of them are of high integrity or morality. Charlatans can appear to wear the cloak of wisdom. All of us can point to many who can talk a far better game than they play. Biomedical doctors ignore a potent common sense law when prescribing anything be it drugs, antibiotics, or surgery and holistic practitioners will disregard this law at their peril. What modern scientific law has more universality than the ancient and common sense law that follows? It is:

There are advantages and disadvantages to everything.

Modern expert theories and laws have crumbled the main building blocks of a good society. Traditional families with women married to men to raise children in a time-honoured, moral and commonsensical way are penalised psychologically and materialistically. Tax and punish them is the experts' motto. The experts view (surely they can't believe what they say) is that different value systems, types of families and life-styles are equally acceptable. This is dispensing with wisdom and morality and it has become the law of the land. Terms such as marriage, father and mother are frowned upon in case they offend unmarried single parents and children who have no idea who their mother and father are. Here is a little modern fairy story. A twenty-year-old girl with six children went to the social welfare benefit office. In taking information, the customer service officer asked the names of the children and the mother said they were all called Darren. She said it was useful because when it was meal times all she had to do was call the name Darren and they all came running. The customer service officer asked what the mother did when she only wanted one of the children and the mother replied, 'Oh, I just use their surname.' The customer service lady said, 'That's brilliant – I mean, knowing the names of all the fathers like that. I have four children and I haven't a clue who the fathers are although one could be from West India because my youngest just loves Bob Marley':

Without shame, there can be no pride.

One school helped a girl to have an abortion without informing her mother. This girl, who is pregnant again at 15, says she is going to keep her new baby. If only – it will be the tax payers who "keep" it.' Another young girl has six children by three different men and is expecting twins by a new man. Does she expect strangers (tax payers) to look after her family irrespective of numbers of fathers and children? In terms of relativity theory, at a time of world under-population this lady would be a heroine. She does however, defy Dave Barry's theory that 'children are nature's own form of birth control'. The excesses of the welfare system have become a way of life for far too many people. It is counter to common wisdoms, creates dependency and harms society, especially the recipients. A growing burden for the tax payer is sexual promiscuity of younger and younger children. It is not surprising because wherever we turn our eyes we see images of sex and its exploitation. School sex education would qualify as pornography in earlier days as would the issue of the morning after contraceptive pill to eleven-year-olds without their parents' knowledge. There can be little left in society that has not been made 'sexy'. Cocoa has, coffee has, shaving cream has, cars have, in fact let's not beat about the bush, almost everything has. Even infant school children dress and act like the worst kind of fashion model, pop star or designer tart. The term paedophile may fade away as children's rights to have sex with whom they please is made law by experts. Sex has become a sport for school children and at a younger and younger age. Competitions already exist concerning who can have sex at the youngest age and with the most partners in the shortest time. Of some particular girl, Frank Sinatra might have said, 'She is a classy broad.' For example, one girl said of the eleven-year-old father of her expected child, 'He'll make a good father.' Class, like everything else, is relative. Experts reward promiscuity – free food, accommodation, no tax, no-cost everything, and notoriety which is a plus in modern times.

Using expert theories and laws, the state is preventing parents bringing up children using common sense laws and practices. Not only have politicians taken over the state parenting of children, some parliamentarians sire children directly and adulterously, sometimes to recently married girls. Nearly always in such cases, they bring up the old chestnut that private life is separate from public life. John Kennedy, John Lennon, Bill Clinton, David Kelly (arms expert on Iraq) and everyone else and his dog know full well from personal experience that private life affects work and work affects private life. What happens in outer-space, in America, Iraq or anywhere affects our work never mind something as close to home as our private life. A common sense law that experts ignore, including scientists is:

All things are interconnected.

Trying to separate private life from public (I wrote pubic and had to put in the 'l') life is against various other common sense sayings such as private life and public life are two sides of the same coin. We all want to embrace or at least be able to acknowledge the existence of some, even a few politicians, that were not corruptible. Greater folly hath no man than he should lay down his integrity for a lay and a lie. But with regards to those in high office, we cannot avoid the common sense law which tells us if you have it long enough:

Power corrupts.

Since power corrupts, all we have to do is to identify those who have the power to know who is corrupt. Quite right – it is experts, particularly politicians, lawyers, scientists, money-men and other assorted celebrities. Politicians and lawyers so loved science that they aped scientists and dispensed with morality. This is true especially when it suits them such as when they commit immoral acts. Placing their own children in schools that they are trying to close on ideological grounds is an example. Obviously, in a moral society, this would be hypocrisy; in the immoral ethos political lawmakers have created, it makes inclusivity and exclusivity equal and New Labour and other political parties want equality for everyone except for an elite who call the shots – not only in wars either. Politicians put education only after the economy in order of importance because it can be a vote-winner with the majority, namely, parents. To justify their existence, experts alter the education system regularly. This is achieved by expressing high concern for education and promising to solve problems with 'new initiatives' together with additional legislative powers to deal with the dire consequences of their last set of initiatives and laws. New Labour, perhaps more than any other government, is politicising the monarchy, the civil service, and education also. Trying to orient any or all school subjects and lessons with celebrating racial diversity is one example. P.J. O'Rourke gives an additional perspective, 'Liberals have invented whole college majors – psychology, sociology, women's studies – to prove nothing is anybody's fault.' Lord Salisbury's conviction too, is more relevant today than when he said it:

No lesson seems to be so deeply inculcated by the experience of life as that you should never trust experts.

One of the major characteristics of present day politicians is their arrogance and ignorance in their assumption they can dispense with common wisdom and replace it with their own 'superior' modern wisdom. Charles Clarke, the Secretary of State for Education confirms this arrogance and ignorance when he expresses his views on education. Amongst the more printable things he has said about those who believe in traditional values or common wisdoms in education, is they are old-fashioned or 'out of time'. Truth is old-fashioned and the government has clearly put it 'out of time'. Modern education flies in the face of nature's common sense laws or wisdoms. Mind, Charles Clarke is the man for the job for he looks and sounds like someone who has flown in the face of nature for too long. Nature tends to balance itself in periods of time and areas of space. In education the natural balance between freedom and discipline, routine and variety, imitation and creativity, big and small school size and so on and so forth is being systematically destroyed by many experts:

Vanity, thy name is expert.

Too many schools are far bigger than is suitable for children to feel secure, develop their skills, knowledge and wisdoms in meaningful communion with others. Schools are so big that children do not know the names of most of the teachers or other pupils. With secondary schools of 500 or less all the teachers and pupils know everyone in the school and are also aware of where individuals are and what they are doing most of the day. This makes for a good school community. Indeed, one common wisdom that refers to effective community size is, 'Small is beautiful.' There are some groups that develop a whole philosophy and way of life around this wisdom. Individual responsibility can be lost in big schools as large crowds are not conducive to a good educational environment including the appropriate discipline and freedom needed for learning. Giving students too much freedom is harmful. There are various common sense laws that deal with freedom. One is that one person's freedom is another person's bondage. Bullying is one of an almost infinite number of examples. Another, which like other common sense laws is relevant in society at large and not just in education, is:

There can be no true freedom without discipline.

It is interesting to note that experts ban physical punishment. This leaves only psychological punishment in our psycho-physical world. However, experts agree that psychological punishment is more harmful than physical punishment, so experts have a problem. Now experts are trying to dispense with punishment altogether. The common sense law of opposites makes this impossible because if we did not know what punishment was we would not know what reward was either. Apart from it being impossible, the attempt to get rid of punishment is extremely harmful and it shows in schools. We know that a five-year-old cannot just disrupt the functioning of one class, but can also close the entire school. It is not that teachers cannot deal with disruptive pupils; they used to do so effectively until experts stuck in their destructive theories and laws. It is not a mere matter of spare the rod and spoil the child, the issue is very much wider:

Spare common sense and spoil the education system.

The expert idea that children do not know the difference between right and wrong until they are – how old – is it until they are able to have children or grandchildren? Since experts have dispensed with morality, what do right and wrong mean anymore? Children do know what is right and wrong before they can walk and possibly earlier. It is probably grounded in their genes. The most effective measure as to what is right and wrong is, if you wouldn't like to have something done to you, don't do it. Even tiny tots don't like having their toys yanked from them and both the yanker and yankee know it is wrong. This is concerned with the ancient and common sense law that could replace, to excellent effect, all expert legal laws. No, it is not, 'Don't disturb the peace', though that would do. It is:

> Do unto others as you would hope they would do unto you.

Man is curious and the result of curiosity is learning. Indeed, it could be argued that the curiosity or exploratory drive embraces all other drives such as sex, drive for affiliation and so forth. Since man was man (and before), he has been a learner and a teacher. Animals are learners and teachers too. What person does not like to show others how to do things, teach them knowledges and skills? We seek novelty which again results in learning and teaching. So everyone is a learner and teacher including very young children who can be excellent as can granny, the butcher the baker and candle-stick maker. Teaching like learning is in our genes. Much teacher training (that which uses expert theories and not common sense laws) can do more harm than good. Non-professionals may be better teachers than trained teachers, because they are less contaminated by expert theories. Some trained teachers do ignore experts and use common sense, but if discovered by official education spies, they get 'down-sized' (sacked) or harassed and prosecuted in courts of expert law. Readers will have seen friends and relatives who are by nature, good teachers. I knew a carpenter who became a wonderful and well-known teacher – no not that teacher for Christ's sake. We are not short of teachers. We are all teachers and parents are highly significant in education. The whole community and culture are educators:

> Man is by nature both a learner and a teacher.

Since man was man learning and teaching were central to survival and evolution. Thus, all elements of education like aims, methods of teaching, learning and modes of assessment have been tried and tested over aeons of time and by almost all the people who ever lived. What the successful processes of education boil down to is applying common sense laws. Governments produce uncommon nonsense, but regularly. Shutting village schools, trying to get 50 per cent of students into university, suggesting cutting degree courses to two years and forcing closure of indispensable university courses like chemistry are examples. Imposing targets and curricula and thrusting counter-productive health and safety measures together with 'expert' education inspectors upon teachers longing for common sense to prevail are more examples. Perhaps worst of all is the avoidance of criticising or being judgemental of pupils' behaviour or work. Everything is 'brilliant' even for the most trivial attainment. Excess praise leads pupils to have unrealistic expectations and makes everything worthless:

> Common sense education uses a balance of reward and punishment.

Lowering standards while raising grades along with experts' demands for mountains of paper work (90 per cent of which is doing harm) are further illustrations of practices against common sense laws. Teachers' planning of lessons goes on morning, noon and night; ideas are constantly bubbling in their minds as well as in their subconscious. To have to write plans down to satisfy the demands of 'experts' is a counter-productive, stressful waste of time:

> Quality planning is in the mind, not in the quantity of paperwork.

True education is the leading out of wisdom which is an integration of knowledge and morality. Anyone who has been in education for long enough, as well as most ordinary citizens, knows that education has been dumbed down. By the way things are going it will not be long before all students are A-grade. Many modern teachers have been through our expertly dumbed down system and can be relatively illiterate and uneducated. Some wits claim that in future you will get a degree if you can write your name and an honours degree if you spell it correctly. Who was it who said that education was marvellous because if you could not sign your name you would have to pay cash? Common sense laws reflect nature's balance. Politicians balance incompetence with acts of self-preservation:

> **Government balances the fall in attainment with a rise in grades.**

Employers are well aware of the poor state of education because they have to bear the consequences of it. Politicians have done to work what they have done to education – abandoned common sense. With the technological revolution, experts told us we were moving to a leisure society. Some, using predictions based on common sense laws, said technology would not free us, excess use of it would enslave us. This is how such a prediction was made. If you do something to great excess, it turns out to achieve the opposite of what you intended. For example, if you like exercise such as running and you keep running without stopping for long enough, the like of running will turn to dislike and will eventually kill you. Since the twentieth century has been marked by excess, including technology, the prediction of technological enslavement was almost certain to come true. People often accuse me of being anti-technology. I tell them that I am not against technology for it is a crucial part of evolution. What I am against is the excessive use of technology that can be counter-productive. Some people believe that technology can save us from all ills including the excessive use of technology that can destroy us.

Cars, trucks and buses have made the streets like exhaust pipes down which we have to travel daily. This is not to mention the weapons, biological or otherwise that your mother-in-law can buy on the internet. At least experts have made some shopping easier. While technology is being used to excess, common sense law of opposites predict it will harm us rather than save us. Now let us write in bold one of the most important and obvious ancient or common sense laws that goes unnoticed by almost everyone, including many expert scientists:

> **Excess in one thing leads to its opposite.**

Even if it were attainable, a leisure society is against the nature of man. It is in the context of men working together sharing intelligence (the idea of individual intelligence is like talking of the temperature of a single subatomic particle), skills, values and knowledges, including humour, that common sensing or wisdom came into being. The desire to work is in our nature. It is the very stuff of evolution and yet year upon year the number of people trying to get out of the work force increases. Expert laws created the rat race and speeded it up further with an endless stream of laws until more people are saying 'enough is enough'. What do politicians know about real work? They have spent most of their lives trying to avoid it by getting into parliament and staying there which is contrary to wisdom and common sense laws. Parliament is a talking shop and as the old saying has it, 'Talk is cheap'. Politicians are always 'trying to find the right words' to rationalise their wrong deeds. Professional politicians are unnatural, flawed beings beyond the norm and their behaviour demonstrates this. As John Quintan points out:

> Politicians are people who, when they see the light at the end of the tunnel, order more tunnel.

Small businesses that reflect our nature as opposed to the dominant, corrupt big business empires, are being hounded to destruction by experts. How many new laws, rules and regulations has the New Labour Government foisted upon small businesses – it was over 2,000 at the last count I made? These are grinding small businesses into the ground. Businesses cannot even advertise for a hard worker as it is not inclusive of non-hard workers (obviously politicians preparing themselves for the modern labour market when their incompetence and corruption leads them to higher things). Big business bosses are protected by immoral contractual law because, when they bring down an organisation to its knees or bankruptcy and leave, they have huge golden handshakes for their failures and massive pensions, whereas the ordinary workers lose their jobs and their small pensions:

> There is one law for power brokers and one for ordinary workers.

Common wisdoms or common sense laws indicate that we should live, work and play in small communities and be relatively self-supporting. Closing village schools, post offices, police-stations and other important amenities is systematically destroying communities which give quality and meaning to life. That some local farmers are letting fruit, vegetables and other commodities rot when we are importing stuff from all around the world shows that money or the profit motive is the main concern. Exporting work or importing workers to get cheap labour is immoral with great costs to all. Experts have even got their economic greed wrong. If it appears that you save money by destroying community and jobs, the financial costs created by the destruction of the social dynamics of the community are greater than the initial financial profit. What experts have chosen to ignore are laws of common wisdom such as, 'Money is the root of evil' and that moral problems, which are the dominant ones in our society, cannot be solved by material answers. Indeed, one potent wisdom tells us:

> Get the moral values right and the economic ones take care of themselves.

Inevitably science entered the world of work. Science's self-inflicted amorality or immorality, its over-emphasis on specialisation and treating men like machines did not tap into the birthplace of wisdoms – men working together. Many changes were thrust upon workers by experts who complained when some of their changes were resisted. The workers' resistance to change was justified for many of the changes were for the worse. It is only experts who would believe ordinary common sense people would resist changes for the better. One of the vast number of changes for the worse was getting rid of matrons from hospitals. Now some experts are suggesting bringing matrons back. This would not work as modern matrons would still be saddled with all the expert laws that are grinding nearly all workers into the ground. The hallmark of matrons of yesteryear was their use of common sense which expert law has banned and even reversed. Never-ending expert laws are always accompanied by endless displays of information. Notices are on walls, notice boards, doors, corridors, windows and roads – they are everywhere. If you want a long read, do not go to a library, which may have been modernised out of existence when you get there, go to a hospital and peruse its notices. If you read them all you will be in hospital longer than any patient having treatment. Forget, 'Cleanliness is next to godliness', the expert modern rule is:

> Bureaucracy is next to godliness – probably above it.

The greater the bureaucracy and number of laws, the more the government diminishes our freedom. Tony Blair's claim that his government was to be the servant of the people, not its master, turns out to be merely paying lip-service to what a real democratic government should be. At least he knows what to pay lip-service to. A democratic government should administrate the will of the people. The people know what is required and how to achieve it. For example, in respect of law and order, everyone knows, apart from experts that is, police should be on the streets, live in the community they police, use common sense laws and dispense with unjust expert laws and all the destructive paperwork or bureaucracy that engulf them. Politicians do not have to make policies or laws; common sense laws, and hence policies, are already there and known to almost everyone. The political mantra that policies and not personalities are important is a long standing confidence trick of politicians. New Labour played up Tony Blair's personality for all it was worth to get elected. If personalities were not important, then the type of scheme I recommended with local people selecting their own political representative every six months would have been put in place long ago. Continuity of policy would be achieved as never before in modern times by using time-honoured common sense laws that all know and understand. Politicians seek personal fame and fortune under the guise of selfless public service. Ambrose Bierce is correct when he observes:

> Politics is the conduct of public affairs for
> private advantage.

Joining Europe decreases our freedom, personal and national. It was against true democracy and immoral on the part of successive political parties. European union is against the diversity politicians extol. One European official was forced to admit there was great incompetence and corruption and that Brussels could not sink much lower. This expert's rationalisation would have had the comedian Eric Morecambe saying, 'There's no answer to that'. Indeed, the official's pronouncement could form the basis of a modern oath or law for politicians. The Eurocrat stated:

> The greater the incompetence and corruption, the greater
> the room for improvement and reform.

The Chancellor of the Exchequer, Gordon Brown, apart from many stealth taxes and raiding pension funds, some to extinction, has sold the British family gold reserve. He is an economic alchemist who has turned gold into paper. Promissory notes are as reliable as political integrity. Brown's speeches on the economy are long and full of modern terminology which blinds people with science, economic jargon and impenetrable money schemes. The Chancellor disobeys the common sense law, 'Keep things simple'. His speeches are punctuated with the term prudence (often used as a synonym for wisdom) which acknowledges, at the lip-service level, that wisdom has not been banished totally yet by the thought police. Brown and other members of government are always telling us how well the economy is doing. Even if this were true, what is the point of a booming economy when our institutions, infrastructure like roads and the natural habitat are getting worse by the day? The way the governments get money from us and the projects on which they spend our money is immoral and undemocratic – against the will of the majority. Since this is so, it is understandable that more and more citizens try to avoid paying governmental demands for money. Adam Smith was well aware of politicians' attitude to what is often legalised robbery:

> There is no art which one government sooner learns of another than that of draining money from the pockets of the people.

The Prime Minister exhorts us to celebrate diversity while demanding the opposite, unity, in his own party and from the public in support of his policies and laws. History, observation and experience, not to mention the common sense laws of nature, show that there are limits to diversity and unity just as there are to growth, expansion and the number of chemical elements:

> Nature's law is to achieve balance between unity and diversity.

Sometimes politicians do talk common sense and can get ostracised for it. Such was the case when Frank Field, a member of the New Labour Government, stated, 'Like many of my constituents, I have decided there is no point in calling the police.' Experts have made our streets unsafe and thugs have created no-go areas. Zero tolerance, which has enjoyed much success, where practised, is spoken of as if it were a new modern strategy. It is not. It is a rediscovery or restatement of ancient and common sense laws such as, 'A stitch in time saves nine', or 'Deal with small problems so they do not grow into large ones' and:

Nip bad behaviour in the bud.

It is not only in important areas like law and order where the government shows its ignorance and incompetence. It is interesting to note, even in modern times, members of the royal family are still judged by the majority on the extent to which they behave in accordance with common sense laws. One modern mantra used so often by all kinds of political parties is a continuous – 'We must give people more choice.' Too much choice can be confusing, stressful, against quality of life and often proffered by exploiters. J.K. Galbraith points out, 'Under capitalism man exploits man. Under communism it's just the opposite.' We can't choose to have or not to have local amenities like work, village shops, police stations, post offices, hospitals or railway stations. We have great choice of things, whether we like it or not, that benefit power-brokers such as ways of borrowing money or types of bank account whose institutions have to be big, elsewhere and destroy communities. A common wisdom tells us:

We can be spoiled by too much choice.

Because politicians have lost control of law and order and violence is rising faster than they can spend the tax payers' money, our leaders rationalise their awful failure and patronise the electorate by saying that violence has always been around. What people are devastated by is the increasing degree of violence since around the end of the Second World War. Politicians now speak of terrorist attacks and our leaders are prime targets. Because of what the New Labour Government has done, it would be unsurprising if some of its members and their families were not subjected to the type of violence and other sufferings their policies and laws have sanctioned. It need not be some religious or political fanatic. It is just as likely to be an ordinary Yorkshire man with an ancestry in that county going back hundreds of years. Put in the Yorkshire vernacular:

Them as live by t'sword, mun die by t'sword

Tony Blair is, indeed, a man for all seasons, and a religious man. Not surprisingly all religions have the same core values and their command-ments or laws are common sense laws or wisdoms that pre-date all types of institutionalised religion. In that religion is not immune to the law that power corrupts, religious leaders should change regularly as I suggested for political representatives. Incidentally Bin Laden was regarded as a good guy by the West when it suited USA and Britain. Bin Laden's view of the West that it is decadent and has dispensed with morality is difficult to deny. In fact Tony Blair has confirmed Bin Laden's view. The Prime Minister, in the winter of 2004, declared that, 'moral issues should not determine whether a politician is fit for office'. Sadly other politicians, including the leader of the opposition, Michael Howard, basically agree with Blair's stunning dismissal of morality. One will expect Blair, then, to restore the politician Saddam Hussein to office as leader of Iraq. The Prime Minister's statement releases politicians from morality unlike religions and his many holier-than-thou stances on self-proclaimed moral high ground. Blair's statement about moral issues should not shock us, though it did. The Prime Minister has long been associated with immorality and courted some of its stars. He boasted that he was of the rock and roll generation and belonged to a rock band. Everyone knows that rock and roll is associated with drugs, promiscuous sex and violence. Indeed, was his aim not to be a 'pop' Prime Minister? A permeating present-day wisdom is:

> The modern holy trinity is celebrity, money and promiscuous sex.

Pop is an abbreviation for popular culture and is associated with the entertainment industry, particularly with rock and roll music and its descendants. The history of the stars of popular culture is, in a nutshell, as follows. Idols broke taboos, but hid immoral acts to avoid censure, loss of fame or prosecution. Next, stars allowed some of their minor misdeeds to become public as expert laws turned a blind eye to what was previously disallowed, for this made them appear different as attractive rebels. This process of exploring degeneracy increased or as one pop expert put it 'to continually push back the barriers of taste and decency'. Now in 2004 pop stars boast about and glorify their immorality and viciousness. Wisdom's aesthetic values are being reversed. One new sense pop laws is:

The more violent you can be the more publicity and success.

Apart from pop music other forms of entertainment especially soccer (the new rock and roll), fashion, and spectacles like the Olympic Games are increasingly associated with corruption, greed, drugs, violence including group sex along with gangster, and paedophile chic. These 'stars' or celebrities are role models for tiny tots as well as teenagers and adults. If this is not an indictment of our society, what is? I have asked lots of youngsters what they wanted to do as a job. Pop star, fashion model, footballer or to be famous and rich were the dominant selections – hardly any wished to be plumbers, builders or train drivers. Heart-breaking is how I would describe one little seven-year-old waif when he said he looked forward to the day when he would receive his giro (welfare payment):

We reap as we sow.

It is quite pathetic when schools teach sex education which resolves itself to stressing safe sex, experimenting with same sex partners, oral and anal sex and giving some children around ten years old contraceptive devices sometimes without parental knowledge. Children are confronted with sex everywhere and can know more than teachers. Magazines such as *Bliss* contain explicit and what would, not so long ago, have been classified as pornographic images. Pop culture has gone beyond reversing common sense laws such as, 'Be modest' to 'Be boastful'. Now increasing violence has been added and we have to do things violently in excess. Isn't there a pop group called INXS? We have to be aggressively, 'In yer face an up close an personal, know wha ah mean?' The new beauty is ugliness. Another adopted new sense pop law reverses the common sense law of, 'Moderation in all things' to:

Nothing succeeds like violent excess.

People feel helpless in the face of increasing verbal and physical violence of the pop culture. Because of expert incompetence, corruption and, more importantly, the banning of common sense, there seems to be a resigned acceptance of bad behaviour now at the end of 2004. Too many say of foul violent behaviour, 'Well that's what modern youngsters do nowadays.' Soccer managers who were held in high esteem for their integrity may be now wringing their hands in despair, but rationalise their support of violent players by such statements as, 'Well, it happens in modern football, doesn't it? You've got to expect it from millionaire players haven't you?' We have been conditioned to accept decadence and too many of us have been willing saplings or suckers. To carry this vegetative analogy further:

> Money is the root of evil, politics the trunk, big business and pop the main branches and expert law the fertiliser.

The continuous indulgence in material excesses can get to even the most depraved pop star. Having money past a certain amount does not make for happiness. It can ruin your life as many can testify. Numerous winners of huge amounts of cash as in the National Lottery (and becoming a pop star overnight is like winning the lottery) find the money can spoil their existence. Of course pop stars have to use common sense sometimes and can even put it into songs. They know that, 'Money can't buy me love.' It is noticeable that numerous pop stars get fed up with materialism, begin to help charities and seek some form of balance to the excesses of materialism – spirituality. Even pop stars cannot be immoral and vicious all the time. Carol Doda illustrates the level of pop star moral philosophy when she says, 'I'm a topless dancer, but I see myself as a humanitarian, whatever that means.' Madonna, too, reflects the modern philosophy of our political leaders when she quips, 'Listen, everybody is entitled to my opinion.' Our instincts, developed over millions of years, do not resonate well with persistent excesses and we can all feel guilty at over-indulgence – even pop stars:

> Though your god, family and friends may forgive you your sins, your psycho-physiological systems including genes will not.

Often people say, politicians prove that aliens exist on earth as their decisions are paranormal or not of this planet. British Trade Secretary, Patricia Hewitt, today announced that nuclear waste from five foreign countries is to be buried in Britain. Hewitt rationalises this decision by telling us, 'The benefits are both environmental and economic.' Money gained from this will be 'used for nuclear clean-up'. The Trade Secretary is obviously reading out Tony Blair's living will, but could not radiate confidence with such nuclear news. Such is the tragic state of Britain that Tony Blair has to be constantly on his toes – rather like a midget in a urinal. We must be fair to Blair though Blair has been unfair to us. Relativity theory tells us that there are greater and smaller political midgets than our Tone. To be politically correct, Britain as a nuclear dustbin does appear to be – well – er, a paranormal decision shall we say? I do not want the new sense police at my door. Old sense says – well – I'll let you decide; you may be braver than me. I brought paranormal into this essay because most people, including me, have been involved in super-natural experiences. It is, therefore, a common experience. Paranormal often means weird; it is defined by experts as events or phenomena that are claimed to be beyond the scope of normal scientific understanding. It is about such concepts as dowsing, clairvoyance, telepathy, astrology and all things to do with extra sensory perception:

> **Historically most people have experienced extra sensory perception; therefore, it is a common sensing with evolutionary resonance.**

A word here about normal science, for it is not always as it seems. At one time, I, together with many other people, believed that The Scientific Method was something invented by elite scientists and, when applied by the chosen few, determined what was fact and what was fiction. I became familiar with the scientific method which is as follows. First a problem is identified and clarified. Next guesses or speculations (scientists call these hypotheses) are made about how to solve the problem. Then, related information and data are gathered to test these guesses or speculations. Certain instruments are used to measure or assess things (the most important being the human sense-organs like the eye) mentioned in the guesses. Finally, calculations (quantitative and qualitative though the latter is incorrectly denied) and conclusions are made indicating the degree to which the guesses or hypotheses are confirmed or not. As you will realise, this is a basic mode of learning and discovery used by you and everyone else scores of times a day. It was there before human history began. This so-called scientific method is also used by other animals like cats, insects, old Uncle Tom Cobbly and all:

> **The scientific method is part of nature; sometimes what science does with it is not.**

Religions are based on paranormal happenings. Most scientists dismiss both. Of late, a few more scientists have turned their attention to extra sensory perception. Perhaps this is because quantum theory and the behaviour of sub-atomic particles are more paranormal than the paranormal. Black matter too is weird. Scientists know very little about it except it seems able to pass unnoticed through material bodies including our own. Had scientists taken the common sense law of opposites to heart, they would have become aware of the possibility of dark matter earlier. They focused on bright or light matter long enough without considering an opposite – black matter. I'll quote another well-known ancient wisdom here:

There are more things in heaven and earth than we know.

Though science is held in high esteem; we are known as The Scientific Society amongst other names, there are those who view science and technology sceptically. Ashley Cooper says, 'The more modern and streamlined aircraft become, the more they resemble those paper arrows we made at school.' Young children, their grandmothers as well as everyone else, have known for thousands of years that cats had reflexes and could also think, solve problems, dream and know what their humans were thinking. Until quite recently, scientists insisted cats behaved purely on reflex and were incapable of abstract thought. Not long ago, scientists discovered cats could dream so they have changed their minds a little. How cats know what we are thinking could be associated with a shared evolution with common sensings that are the basis of a collective conscious and unconscious where the parts can echo or resonate in a greater whole. Now a small but growing number of scientists have made discoveries that show some of the claims about extra sensory perception are accurate. It was the ancient wisdoms of yoga demonstrated by its practitioners that made scientists change their belief that the 'involuntary actions' could not be controlled by the mind. Eastern yogis showed they could control heart rate and other functions that scientists pronounced as automatic or autonomic. Therefore, although scientists have rediscovered some ancient and common wisdoms, they still have a long way to go to catch up with the common sensings of grandmothers, babes in arms and cats. Scientists cannot mind-read as well as cats. They don't even believe in it. Modern science's universe is mechanical, not psychical:

Seeing is believing and believing is seeing.

We are now nearly at the end of this essay that has compared ancient and common sense laws with expert legal or modern new sense laws as well as scientific orientations. I have tried to make it readable by anybody and everybody. Common sense laws transcend time, place and people. There can be no democracy when common sense and its users are outlawed. Common sense laws are genetically based. These laws are the pillars of wisdom and true democracy. Common sense laws contain truth, morality, knowledge, beauty, and justice – that is, all the things that make life meaningful and worth living. The New Labour Government has diminished common sense and hence democracy as never before in living memory according to some grandparents, parents and even experts. There is no hiding place from violence, noise and degradation at large – fewer places to find peace of mind at work, rest or play. Generally, we are still far too lethargic about experts acting in opposition to common sense laws and, to a large degree, we deserve our lot. I believe that the mass of ordinary people will, however, sooner or later activate a return to the reliable and objective common sense laws. Triggers for change are growing:

When the pendulum is swung too far in one direction, it will try to right itself again.

The purpose and meaning of life are concerned with the satisfactory fulfilment of motives such as curiosity and need for affiliation. Using common sense and its laws determines the degree of satisfaction of motives; expert theories and laws make for dissatisfaction. Motivations contain opposites; although there is a search for novelty or difference, there is a need for the familiar also. Similarly, freedom only has real existence and meaning in relation to responsibility. Hopefully, significant motivations, behaviours and consequences are highlighted in this essay. Basically, life is the examination of the values we choose to live by and their relations with the rest of creation. I have tried to cover the main psycho–physical systems, personal, social and institutional, through which we live out our lives. Illustrated also are the wisdoms or common sense laws that give guidance to achieving qualitative thoughts, words and deeds in making life worthwhile for individuals, groups and communities. Wisdom or common sense not only reflects knowledge and morality, it is the yardstick of truth, beauty, justice and real democracy This essay was not to make you wiser, but to remind you how wise you are. I shall finish where I started:

There is no substitute for common sense.